The Superbureaucrats

The Superbureaucrats: Structure and Behaviour in Central Agencies

COLIN CAMPBELL AND
GEORGE J. SZABLOWSKI

Macmillan of Canada

Canadian Cataloguing in Publication Data

Campbell, Edwin Colin, 1943-
   The Superbureaucrats

Includes index.
ISBN 0-7705-1767-6 pa.

1. Government executives — Canada.   2. Canada —
Executive departments. I. Szablowski, George J.,
1928-   II. Title.

JL111.E9C35   354'.71'04   C79-094070-1

Printed in Canada for
The Macmillan Company of Canada Limited
70 Bond Street
Toronto, Ontario
M5B 1X3

To
Elizabeth Campbell Nagel
and
Julie, Tania, and David Szablowski

Contents

Acknowledgments

Our first word of thanks goes to the ninety-two senior officials in the Prime Minister's Office, the Privy Council Office, the Federal-Provincial Relations Office, the Department of Finance, and the Treasury Board Secretariat, who generously gave us their time for interviews. Senators Keith Davey and J. J. Connolly helped us greatly by writing letters to the principals of all five agencies.

We want to thank our research assistants. Pradip Shastri served as our appointments secretary in Ottawa. Robert Nigol, Glen Robertson, Carolyn Baxter, Robin Esco, and Gary McKenna all participated in the arduous task of coding and analysing interview data. Alan Meisner and Gary McKenna ferreted out much of the legal documentation on the origin and authority of central agencies in Canada.

We believe that we have profited greatly from the critiques of several scholars and practitioners who have gone over earlier drafts of this book. These include Harold Clarke, M. A. Cohen, David Good, Peter Hogg, Michel Rochon, Richard Rose, Gordon Smith, and two referees approached by Macmillan of Canada.

Marilyn Landau, a free-lance editor in Berkeley, California, did a painstaking stylistic critique of the first draft. The staff at Macmillan of Canada, especially Margaret Woollard, Else Jones, and Wendy Jacobs, made further editorial suggestions. Julie Szablowski compiled the index for this book.

The Canada Council provided seed money for our project by way of a research grant, and a leave fellowship to Szablowski during 1977–78. Later, it came to our rescue with a supplementary grant. In addition, York University supplied two smaller grants, a considerable amount of computer time, and a sabbatical leave to Szablowski during 1977–78.

We are grateful, too, for the help and support of many colleagues at York University, especially Anne Beer, Robert

Drummond, Fred and Martha Fletcher, Robert Presthus, David
Shugarman, and Harvey Simmons. Liliana Perciballi and Lilian
Polsinelli, secretaries in the Department of Political Science,
helped us through more than one pinch by typing letters and
interview schedules. Leleith Smith and Sonia Davis of the
Faculty of Arts, Secretarial Services, typed the various drafts of
the manuscript which were proofread under the sharp eyes of
Eileen Comba and Marjorie Fryer of the same unit.

Campbell thanks his Jesuit colleagues for their support, especially Jacques Monet, S. J., who stood by helplessly as his
Ottawa apartment was turned into the "project switchboard"
during the summer of 1976.

Colin Campbell
George J. Szablowski

The Superbureaucrats

Introduction:
Why Study Central Agencies?

The average Canadian knows too little about his or her government. Although ignorance may be bliss to some, more and more Canadians are realizing that knowledge of governmental structure, processes, and behaviour is a basic prerequisite to full, active citizenship. We subscribe to the view that what happens in Ottawa should be open and accessible to all.

Governments tend to take advantage of those who are poorly informed, who do not understand how and by whom decisions are made, who fail to appreciate the limits of public authority and the obligation of public responsibility. Inevitably, modern governments evolve intricate bureaucratic structures which function in complex ways. One consequence of this complexity is that, as much in the interest of "efficiency" as anything else, the actual process of government is a mystery to the ordinary citizen. The burden is, therefore, on us to get beyond the official rhetoric and to discover what really takes place. What is needed is to get inside the apparently closed circle of politicians and officials who wield power and to examine their activities.

This book represents such an effort. In it we look at five central agencies of the federal government: the Prime Minister's Office (PMO), the Privy Council Office (PCO), the Federal-Provincial Relations Office (FPRO), the Finance department, and the Treasury Board Secretariat (TBS). The senior officials who work in them are among the most powerful public servants in government. In performing their duties they often cross the line between bureaucrat and policy maker, a line which in recent years has become increasingly blurred. Through the investigation of the structure and operation of the selected agencies and by interviewing their personnel, we sought to accomplish two things. First, we have tried to show how these agencies differ from traditional bureaucracies; second, we have pursued a better knowledge of how government works.

Central Agencies in Advanced Liberal Democracies

What exactly are central agencies? They perform functions which directly affect all other government departments. First, they often co-ordinate the interdepartmental development of policy. Second, they frequently develop policies which other departments must follow, in fields such as expenditure control and personnel management. Third, they often monitor the performance of other departments. These functions usually stem from the authority of an agency to perform certain tasks within government. An agency might carry out a mission from a committee of the Cabinet (as does the Treasury Board Secretariat in Canada); from a chief executive of a government (as does the Office of Management and the Budget in the United States); from a prime minister and a cabinet (as does the Central Policy Review Staff in Great Britain); or from a prestigious portfolio (as does Her Majesty's Treasury in Great Britain). Whatever the source of its authority for the tasks it performs, a central agency stands above other departments in that it performs functions which are thought to be crucial to the *common* interests of government departments, and which relate to matters of major importance.

It is hardly necessary to cite facts and figures to show the pervading and ever-growing impact of government on society. The traditional line of demarcation between the private and public spheres in social, economic, and cultural life is disappearing rapidly. Few individual or collective activities escape governmental control, regulation, or funding, in whole or in part. We believe that the permeation of the private, societal sector by government is here to stay and that new types of institutions are emerging in response to the changing role of government in society.[1] The five central agencies we have chosen for our study are examples of such institutions.

Classical, hierarchic, and highly disciplined bureaucracies are not suited to these new roles. They are devoted to the service of particular, program-oriented interests closely tied to clientele groups, which depend upon the expected distribution of social and economic benefits. Their statutory mandates and organizational structures discourage violations of jurisdictional boundaries and demand respect for their clientele groups' definition of the public interest. They see merit strictly in terms of the task performed and resent intrusions from outsiders. They claim political neutrality, and ascribe policy decisions to the politicians. The idea of public accountability is rejected as inconsistent with the purely professional, advisory functions they say they perform. They find support for these assertions in a constitutional and administrative theory which distinguishes between politics and administration.

In advanced liberal democracies, however, bureaucracy has increasingly engaged the interest of students of politics as well as students of administration. Two developments have encouraged political scientists to view central agencies as distinct from other, more traditional, bureaucratic departments. One concerns changes in the perspective of public administration as a sub-field of political science; the other relates to refinement of the mandates of central agencies.

With respect to public administration, a gradual broadening of the sub-field's horizons has allowed for treatment of such questions as the co-ordination of political and administrative objectives in government. This trend contrasts with the initial stance of public administration. For instance, Woodrow Wilson, one of the fathers of the discipline, held that there must be a sharp dichotomy between politics and administration:

The field of administration is a field of business. It is removed from the hurry and strife of politics. . . . It is part of political life only as the methods of the countinghouse are a part of the life of society; only as machinery is part of the manufactured product. . . .[2]

Wilson, of course, went on to be President of Princeton University and, eventually, of the United States. Undaunted by the master's defection to politics, students of public administration continued to study the government administrator purely in terms of his role as an "organization chief who, knowing his goals clearly, desires only additional knowledge of how to manipulate his subordinates and 'customers' more effectively."[3]

But by the 1960s, the validity of such a dichotomy was increasingly questioned by political scientists concerned with the interrelation of politics and administration. Scholars began to emphasize the ways in which administrators are policy makers.[4] Some even wondered whether bureaucrats seek personal goals which are contrary to the public interest,[5] or, consciously or unconsciously, stand in the way of change.[6] In Canada, at least one academic-cum-bureaucrat went so far as to argue that politicians cannot take voters' demands as given, and must rely on public servants' analyses of the political consequences of alternative policies, including how various alternatives might affect the chances of re-election.[7]

Hugh Heclo and Aaron Wildavsky have employed the term "political administrator" to indicate that senior career civil servants share a collegial bond with cabinet ministers and/or top political appointees as they serve Cabinets and departments.[8] At the core of this bond, Heclo and Wildavsky have found that political administrators — elected politicians, political appointees, and career bureaucrats — all give primacy to two tasks: integration of political and administrative goals; and maintenance of both formal and informal mechanisms whereby the integration might be achieved.

As the distinction between politics and administration has blurred and new nomenclature such as "political administrator" has emerged, so has the authority of many central agencies been reshaped. By the 1960s, governments in several advanced liberal democracies had broadened their view of administration to include such functions as program budgeting, management by objectives, and efficiency evaluation. Governments began to see the need for "effective choice", that is, "giving guidance through choosing goals and objectives, and showing sufficient management skill and stamina to make the department move toward them."[9] Thus, a number of studies examined political administration in big government. Recommendations from these studies led to clearer mandates for central agencies to carry out political-administrative objectives. As early as the mid-1960s, in response to Canada's Glassco Report (prepared by the Royal Commission on Government Organization), the Treasury Board Secretariat was separated from the Finance department as a means of increasing Cabinet's control of expenditures.[10] In the United States, a presidential task force proposed a sweeping reorganization of executive agencies which would strengthen co-ordination of policy choice and implementation, especially through new means to resolve conflicts between departments.[11] Richard M. Nixon responded to this proposal by creating the Domestic Council and by reorganizing the Bureau of the Budget as the Office of Management and the Budget. In Great Britain, the Conservative party, while in Opposition, began in the late 1960s to ask certain people in the private sector how they thought management might be improved in government. When the party came to power in 1970, it established both Program Analysis and Review (PAR), under the Treasury, and the Central Policy Review Staff (CPRS), a cabinet agency, to improve Cabinet's capacity to evaluate individual programs and their results, and to establish priorities between proposed policies and programs.[12]

Notwithstanding the importance of these adjustments in institutional machinery, several factors which underlie modern government suggest the continued development of central agencies. These are: the growth of the interventionist state, the concentration of control in the bureaucratic sector through central agencies, the increased collegiality between politicians and bureaucrats, and the general decline of legislatures as effective institutions for political control and accountability.

With respect to the interventionist role of the state, as the gap widens between the number and difficulty of political problems and governments' problem-solving capacities, the need for active rather than reactive policy making becomes more evident.[13] One author has recently suggested that the main instrument of this intervention shall be the expenditure budget;[14] presumably, public spending may be used to control a nation's economy and social life. Yet, anyone familiar with attempts to employ PPB (Planning-Programming-Budgeting, a system of decision making intended to co-ordinate government objectives and expenditures with efficiency and effectiveness of its operations) would be satisfied just to attain an adequate control of bureaucratic appetites.[15] The efforts of advanced liberal democracies to introduce greater rationality into public decision making have not always produced tangible success. Indeed, the adoption of such techniques has often fulfilled the gloomy prophecies of incrementalists who maintain that significant departures from the burden of existing commitments are not possible.[16] Yet incrementalists also argue that, the limits of such techniques not-withstanding, even the very marginal benefits they yield justify their use.[17] In addition, some countries, such as West Germany, appear to have consistently more success in economic management than others.[18] Thus, in light of increased intervention by governments in advanced liberal democracies, and their spotty, often marginal, success, an important question emerges for any study of central agencies: how might central agencies be designed to fulfil more effectively the requirements of control in big government?

The concentration of control in the bureaucratic sector poses real problems of overload for central agencies. Politicians have given a great number of control functions to public servants.[19] The size and complexity of bureaucracy has reached the point where often only insiders can master its operation. Indeed, the insiders often must divide labour. For instance, in 1977, within Canada's Treasury Board Secretariat six branches performed control and review functions which ten years ago were housed in one branch. The six were: the Program Branch, the Planning Branch, the Administrative Policy Branch, the Financial Management Branch, the Personnel Policy Branch, and the Efficiency Evaluation Branch. Thus, on the one hand, bureaucratic power was centralized because politicians ceded to central agencies responsibilities which became too onerous for them. On the other hand, even the central agencies have found it difficult to divide the functions into manageable chunks. Thus, two questions remain unanswered with the rise of central agencies: Who is in control, the politician or the bureaucrat? And are there sufficient mechanisms within and between central agencies to co-ordinate the work of political administrators?

Collegiality among top elected politicians, political appointees, and career senior officials, although not new to liberal democracies, seems to have intensified with the growth of central agencies. In Canada, senior officials from central agencies participate practically as peers of political leaders in cabinet committee meetings. Indeed, officials from the Finance department and the Treasury Board Secretariat often substitute for their minister in cabinet committees. In France, the President, the Prime Minister, and the Minister of Finance recruit almost exclusively from the ranks of civil servants for their political staffs.[20] In turn, service in such "cabinets" greatly improves one's chances of being selected for senior departmental positions.[21] These practices indicate the degree to which the bureaucratic vocation has merged with the political-administrative function. We hope to explore in more detail both how this trend has revealed itself in Canada's central agencies and what dysfunctions, if any, have arisen as a result of such collegiality.

Last but not least, the rise of central agencies is closely related to the decline of legislatures as effective institutions for political control and accountability. Legislatures have lost immense portions of their policy-initiation, rule-making, and surveillance functions. Cabinet ministers have taken up the slack, but only with the help of senior officials in central agencies. A recent episode in Canada reflects the willingness of legislators to relinquish control to central agencies. Dissatisfied with the time difference between the federal government's actual expenditure of funds and review by Parliament's Auditor General and the Public Accounts Committee, MPs campaigned for better financial administration. Rather than pressing for improved parliamentary review mechanisms, however, the legislators accepted the government's proposal to establish an Office of Comptroller General reporting directly to the President of the Treasury Board and eventually to the Cabinet. Clearly, this solution was to the advantage of officials eager to preserve the "integrity" of financial administration as their exclusive domain. We ask, regarding the decline of legislatures: have legislators in advanced liberal democracies surrendered too much to bureaucrats, particularly central agents? If bureaucrats maintain accountability within a substantive field, how do they reconcile the dictates of expertise and the commitments of their particular community of officials to the goals of political leaders and the general public?

The Canadian Variant

When Pierre Elliott Trudeau won the leadership of the Liberal party in 1968, two crucial elements coalesced in an extraordinary way. First, at the institutional level, the existing structure of government became visibly inadequate to meet the rapidly multiplying demands made on government by various segments of Canadian society, so that things were ripe in Ottawa for a major change. Second, the philosophical approach of the new leader, which combined an intense commitment to rationality with the pursuit of functional, pragmatic politics, suited the needs of the moment.[22] During the four years of Trudeau's first mandate, the machinery of the federal government underwent unprecedented surgery.[23] The Cabinet was remodelled into a system of interlocking, functionally defined committees. New bureaucratic organizations were created to break down the monopolies of older departments. Task forces and interdepartmental committees sprang up bridging the traditional gap between executive and bureaucratic decision making. Central agencies greatly consolidated their roles, first as co-ordinating institutions of the growing array of intra-governmental processes, and then as the hub of bureaucratic involvement with key issues of national policy. All these organizational innovations received an added strength from the influx into the public service of a large number of new recruits, many of whom came from the professions (such as law and accounting), the universities, and even from the business world, and who were quickly promoted to positions of responsibility and influence.

Our decision to embark upon the study of federal-government central agencies arose from our conviction that the institutional changes in Ottawa were of major significance and were likely to lead to lasting consequences for the entire country. A comment by Alan Cairns in his 1977 Presidential address to the Canadian Political Science Association highlights the problem:

The impact of society on government is a common theme in the study of democratic polities. Less common is an approach which stresses the impact of government on the political functioning of society. . . . Although I do not doubt that government rides such a tiger of social change that the sweet smile of victory is often on the face of the tiger, . . . I am convinced that our approach to the study of Canadian politics pays inadequate attention to the weight of the rider, and to his possession of reins to steer, whips to beat, and various inducements to make the tiger responsive to his demands.[24]

Recent studies by several Canadian political scientists have opened the way to a new understanding of governmental functions and processes, and have laid the groundwork for further exploration. Our study is in the same category as this type of institutional/behavioural research, and focuses on the executive and bureaucratic sectors of government.

We interviewed individually practically all senior officials in the five central agencies. After analysis of the data thus obtained, we concluded that the activities of the agencies may be conveniently grouped into broad functions which reflect their authority structure:

1. Development of strategic planning and formulation of substantive policy;
2. Development of integrated economic and fiscal policy;
3. Allocation of budgets and management of governmental resources;
4. Management of senior personnel;
5. Conduct of federal-provincial relations.

These functions are discussed in detail in Chapter 2.

Central agencies possess, with differing degrees of intensity, certain characteristics which make them institutionally and politically distinct from traditional, program bureaucracies. The following chapters examine in detail the distinct characteristics of central agencies. Here we provide an overview of our observations and suggest the direction of the on-going institutional change. We acknowledge that in recent years many operational departments such as Consumer and Corporate Affairs, Communications, or Regional Economic Expansion have departed from the classical bureaucratic model and assumed explicit policy-making and co-ordinating roles. Indeed, the ministries of state first introduced in 1971 (Urban Affairs, Science and Technology, and more recent varieties) had been originally designed as policy think tanks free from the burden of program administration. All these developments indicate a continuous process of transition and institutional innovation. In our view, central agencies are the best and most striking examples of this on-going departure from the traditional bureaucratic structure; they show most clearly the trends of future government organization. In order that the reader may fully appreciate the direction of the institutional change taking place in Ottawa, we have built two sets of contrasting generalizations outlining the key characteristics of traditional, classical bureaucracies, on the one hand, and central agencies on the other. These generalizations depict the archetypal rather than the actual characteristics of governmental structure. They are meant to be a guide to the rest of the book, and to provide the reader with a conceptual framework within which to examine our findings.[25]

This book examines the characteristics of central agencies under the following headings corresponding to the key issues around which the book is organized:

1. The structure of authority and organizational roles (Chapters 2 and 3);
2. The personnel — the socio-economic backgrounds which play a significant role in recruitment and promotion, career paths, and perceptions of personal efficacy and satisfaction (Chapters 4 and 5);

3. The work world — the routine interactions permitting the exertion of individual and organizational power and influence (Chapter 6);
4. Accountability and the links with outsiders (Chapter 7).

The Structure of Authority and Organizational Roles

According to the classic model of bureaucracy, departments possessed exclusive jurisdictions and specialized mandates granted to them by statutory law open and available to the public. They enjoyed a minimum of overlap and protected their exclusivity from any undue interference or penetration by competing organizations. They developed expertise in particular fields and expected others in government to depend on them. Their roles were tailored to their formal mandates in a strictly hierarchic fashion. They maintained a necessary separation between their structure and the structure of the political executive, and firmly relied on existing constitutional theory supporting this basic distinction.

The characteristics of central agencies in this regard differ markedly. Their jurisdictions are broad, flexible, and ill defined; their mandates are often difficult to determine with clarity and precision, and in many respects are kept from the eyes of legislators and the public. There is a considerable overlap among their activities; and they usually do not have exclusive control over their territories. Their organizational structures and operations, though on the hierarchic-collegial continuum, tend towards the collegial. Finally, they promote the ultimate integration of the appointed-bureaucratic sector of government with the elected-executive sector, and seek the required adjustments in existing constitutional theory for that purpose.

The Personnel

Traditional bureaucracies depended upon personnel recruited in accordance with the criteria of merit. These criteria were normally defined in terms of the particular duties and tasks to be performed. High academic qualifications and specialized degrees were not preferred, except when dictated by clear need.

On-the-job training, in-house experience, and seniority, as well as departmental loyalty, were given the highest value. Promotion was a reward for dependability and long service, and direct appointments to senior positions of those outside government were seen as violations of the principle of merit. Such considerations as ethnicity, sex, geographic origin, language and cultural background, and regional representativeness were either irrelevant or downright detrimental to the development of a neutral and objective officialdom.

Central agencies exhibit quite different personnel preferences. Here the concept of merit involves consideration of language, ethnicity, sex, and of geographic and cultural representativeness. PhD degrees and other specialized academic attributes are highly valued. In-house experience and seniority are replaced by intellectual originality and collegial competitiveness. Professional talent developed outside of the public service (in industry, the professions, or academic institutions) is drawn upon as a matter of course. Promotions are offered to those who excel, even if young and inexperienced, and loyalty to particular departmental interests is discouraged and replaced by loyalty to the system as a whole.

The Work World

Traditional bureaucracies insisted upon political neutrality and shied away from political considerations in favour of pure administration. They maintained a clear distance from the political executive, whom they viewed as their master. Administration involved looking after, in orderly fashion, the physical and budgetary resources allocated to particular programs. It did not extend beyond the principles of probity and prudence, and clearly excluded questions of political feasibility and policy preferences, which belonged to the elected-executive sector. The daily routine work centred on interactions with bureaucratic peers largely within the confines of one department. Work relations with politicians were unprecedented; ministerial committees and committees of officials did not mix, and only the deputy minister was permitted regular contact with the political executive; but even he was expected to do business with his departmental minister and to refrain from direct interaction with other ministers. Traditional bureaucracies made demands for greater allocations based on past experience, and measured administrative success by the proportion of the budgetary pie allotted and used, rather than by performance; that is, they were what is known as "typical incremental budget maximizers".

The work world of central agencies presents a different picture. Officials there experience regular and intense involvement with policy issues and recognize that political factors and preferences cannot be excluded from their concern. They maintain close and often collegial links with ministers. They interact routinely with senior officials from other departments and agencies of the government. Mixed task forces and interdepartmental committees constitute the lifeblood of their activities. The typical central agent may participate regularly in the deliberations of ministerial committees and may, on occasion, be asked to perform on behalf of ministers. Central agents are optimal budget maximizers: they demand that future budget allocations be increased only for those programs which show a high level of performance, and they tend to include political considerations in the measurement of bureaucratic performance.

Accountability and Links with Outsiders

Officials in traditional bureaucracies did not see the need for public accountability. Viewing political objectives and preferences as given to them by their political masters, they considered individual ministerial responsibility and the collective responsibility of the Cabinet to Parliament as sufficient and adequate. Internal accountability meant to them simply the faithful discharge of their administrative duties in accordance with the directives of their hierarchic superiors. In addition, they drew upon a sense of professional integrity as public servants, but did not substitute their notion of public good for that of their masters. As servants, they insisted that they be exempt from open scrutiny and criticism, and protected from publicity which would only interfere with the orderly conduct of the business carried on by them on behalf of and for others. If the public became dissatisfied with the policies and programs these bureaucrats administered, it could exert pressure on the government through MPs and Senators and ultimately vote its masters out of office. They professed to be willing and ready to serve any political executive which commanded the confidence of the House of Commons. Mindful of their particular organizational self-interests and expertise, they maintained close contact with established interest groups in society, whom they saw as primary clients and recipients of the benefits they distributed on behalf of their political masters and in the name of the public good. For example, officials in the Department of Industry, Trade, and Commerce have traditionally maintained very strong links with the Canadian Manufacturers Association and other business groups. Such relationships made the accommodation of business demands easier, reinforced the department's own organizational status, and guaranteed its continued survival and growth.

Central agencies, all of which, except for the PMO, are staffed by career officials, exhibit somewhat different characteristics with respect to bureaucratic accountability and links with outside groups. As promoters of the interventionist role of government in contemporary society, they recognize the need for public accountability of senior officials who participate in the decision-making processes almost to the same extent as the members of the Cabinet. At the same time, they are aware of the difficulties inherent in such a change. Mindful of their own interests and protective of the secrecy which is so deeply associated with executive policy making, they are, as we shall show, cautious and ambivalent about advocating basic reforms in bureaucratic practice and in constitutional theory. They distinguish sharply between their own activities and those performed by traditional bureaucracies, and prefer to see different forms and standards of accountability adopted accordingly. With respect to internal accountability, they strongly promote quantitative measurement of bureaucratic performance and the adoption of generally applicable criteria of measurement as a rigorous and much more reliable method of control than that supposedly exercised by Parliament and parliamentary committees. They voice some dissatisfaction with a constitutional theory which requires that the government renew its mandate every four or five years, as this makes consistent and comprehensive planning very difficult. They maintain that they are unencumbered and free from the influence of established interest groups linked to the traditional bureaucracies, and insist that their "clients" are those who, at every level of government, are routinely engaged in policy formation and implementation.

For us, this study of Canadian central agencies has proved to be highly rewarding and instructive. The reader is invited to share our findings, observations, and conclusions. We hope that in the end he or she will feel — as we do — that government and its processes must never escape attention; that the ultimate measure of good government rests in the capacity of ordinary citizens to scrutinize and evaluate its activities continuously — and not just at the time of general elections.

2   What Central Agencies May and Ought to Do: Structure of Authority

Some eminent social scientists argue that governmental organizations emerge and develop like physical organisms.[1] A felicitous arrangement of inducing factors and conditions can produce a new department, agency, board, or commission. Decision makers, the argument goes, recognize that the gestation period is complete and give a formal "birth certificate" to the new organizational offspring, either by passing a statute, by issuing an order-in-council, or by invoking some other instrument of authority. However, we might claim that this process of creation and growth is the product not of an inevitable bureaucratic evolution, but of conscious human design. Indeed, "machinery of government" specialists who design and assemble new organizational structures would clearly reject the view that political man is at the mercy of his own institutions. Our aim in this chapter is not to defend either view, but to describe the sources of central agencies' authority, the birth of each, the content and limits of their mandates, and, finally, their organizational structures. At the conclusion of this chapter, the reader can reconsider the two views of how central agencies come into being and decide for him- or herself which is closer to the truth.

F. G. Bailey wrote:

Only after we understand the rules can we start evaluating the behaviour and so in the end come to a judgment on the men, if we wish to do so.[2]

Our superbureaucrats operate strictly in organizational settings which are bound, first and foremost, by rules. The most fundamental set of rules defines the central agency's authority — it provides what the agency *may* and *ought to* do; that is, the realm of authority is both permissive and normative. We agree with Bailey that the study of rules must not be separated from the study of behaviour and we propose to follow this approach throughout the book.

Sources of Executive and Bureaucratic Authority: Convention and Statutory Law

There are two sources of authority which prescribe what central agencies may and ought to do: statutory (written) rules and conventional (unwritten) rules; both define the boundaries within which political institutions operate. Conventional rules hold particular sway over Canadian executive behaviour. Central agents operate at the boundary which separates the top political executive — the Prime Minister and his Cabinet — from the programmatic, line bureaucracies. Central agencies also provide the link and create the integrative forces which render this traditional boundary line much less distinct and sometimes downright illusory. Strict statutory rules often make little sense for central agents as they face modern political and institutional realities.

According to British constitutional and administrative theory, which Canada continues to follow, full executive authority belongs to the Crown or, as the British North America (BNA) Act states, "is vested in the Queen". In 1947, the monarch formally delegated this authority to the Governor General,[3] and under the recently unveiled Constitutional Amendment Bill, 1978 (if passed), the Governor General would actually replace the Queen as the ultimate source of executive authority. However, it is politically most significant that, whatever the source may be, executive authority is firmly under the control of the Prime Minister and his Cabinet. We propose to adopt a convenient description of executive authority: *it is the constitutional capacity to make policy decisions intended to be followed by all those to whom they are directed or whom they may affect.*

Policy is a difficult term and few political scientists are in

agreement about its meaning. We borrow a definition from the
Treasury Board Secretariat which emphasizes the distinction
between executive acts (policy) and bureaucratic acts (programs), and permits us to demonstrate potential shortcomings of
traditional constitutional theory and to question the authority
enjoyed by some central agencies.

Policy
— A policy is the Government's statement of a principle or set of
  principles it wishes to see followed, in pursuit of particular
  objectives, which may be stated in such a way as to suggest possible
  courses of action (programs) and as to indicate how success of the
  policy may be measured (criteria).

Program
— A program is a course of action or instrument to implement a
  Government policy (or policies), sometimes involving legislative
  mandates and, usually, public expenditures. (A program also has
  objectives, which will in general be more operational than those of a
  policy, and be suggestive of possible criteria against which
  accomplishments of the objectives may be measured.)[4]

  In general, policy decisions are not based on statutory authority; rather the Cabinet has a full constitutional mandate to
act as it deems fit, on its own. Jennings's observation that
"Cabinet has a life and authority of its own" applies equally to
Canada as it does to the United Kingdom. Its acts (decisions)
cannot change the existing law, nor produce direct legal consequences, but they may initiate the legislative process and
thereby eventually modify statutory authority. In principle,
program decisions should always be based on statutory authority.
Invariably, programs involve the expenditure of public funds and
the accountability for it to Parliament. In constitutional theory,
all is well as long as Cabinet makes policy, Parliament passes
laws, and the bureaucracy faithfully implements programs. How
and where do the central agencies and their authority fit into this
tidy picture?

According to constitutional and administrative theory, bureaucratic authority should be express, specific, and delegated by
Parliament to a department or agency created by it. The
department's accountability to Parliament — through the inter-
mediacy of a responsible cabinet minister — should cover all
administrative acts and budgetary expenditures. On the other
hand, executive authority exercised collectively by the Prime
Minister and the Cabinet should be implied, general, and arising
from the very obligation and commitment to govern. Policy
decisions are the real political results of the use of executive
authority; and there is no accountability to Parliament for policy
making, except in the broadest sense — the Ministry must always
have the confidence of the House in order to govern./If this
confidence is lost, dissolution follows and the people are permitted to decide the fortunes of the party in power, unless another
party can form a government and capture the confidence of the
House.

Do central agencies exercise executive or bureaucratic authority? They administer virtually no programs, and their activities are most intimately related to the formulation, analysis,
and implementation of policy decisions. If they are institutional
extensions of the Cabinet and the Prime Minister, how much may
they be permitted to grow without violating the principle of
bureaucratic accountability? Should this new breed of executive-bureaucratic institutions, placed in a privileged and protected milieu, and operating largely under Cabinet's authority,
continue to escape public scrutiny except for budgetary appropriations? Later chapters will deal with these issues in some
detail. We do not question the political and practical necessity of
meeting the continually increasing policy- and decision-making
demands, nor the obvious benefits which accrue to the Ministry
and to the government in general from the work performed in
the central agencies. We simply claim that these developments,
no matter how useful and necessary, should raise some doubt
about the soundness of traditional constitutional theory.

Statutory law, as we have already stated, is the usual source of
bureaucratic authority. It spells out, often with some precision,

TABLE 2:1
CENTRAL AGENCIES' SOURCES OF AUTHORITY

	STATUTORY AUTHORITY	CONVENTIONAL AUTHORITY
PCO	Statutory law British North America Act Inquiries Act Governor General's Act Ministries and Ministers of State Act Statutory Instruments Act	Directives from Cabinet and PM Strategic Planning, Emergency Planning, Machinery of Government, Senior Personnel (Plans Division) Substantive Policy in Discrete Sectors (Operations Division)
FINANCE	Statutory law Financial Administration Act (Direction of financial affairs of Canada)	Directives from Cabinet Macro-economic Policy National Budget
PMO	None	Directives from PM Domestic Policy Advice Communications and Media Relations Legislative Advice Nominations and Appointments Correspondence

the exact content of what a department or agency may and ought to do. It nearly always contains an enabling provision for a more detailed description by regulations which must fall strictly within the scope and the letter of the existing statute. Our statement that, pursuant to constitutional convention, Cabinet itself is the source of executive authority, requires some explanation. Originally, the monarch derived very extensive prerogative (meaning: natural and subject to no restriction) authority from English common law. In the course of history, statutory provisions either replaced or modified many of these prerogatives; in addition, political practice and constitutional convention harnessed and modernized them. Today the Prime Minister and his

	STATUTORY AUTHORITY	CONVENTIONAL AUTHORITY
TBS	Statutory law Financial Administration Act (Administrative policy; Organization of the public service; Financial management; Expenditure plans and programs; Personnel management) Official Languages Act Public Service Staff Relations Act	Directives from Cabinet Priorities for Annual Expenditures Evaluation of Programs Management of the Public Service
FPRO	None	Directives from Cabinet and PM Political and Constitutional Strategies for Unity — Quebec (Co-ordination Secretariat) Conduct of Intergovern- mental Relations and Co- ordination of Federal and Provincial Policies and Actions (Federal Provincial-Relations Secretariat)

Cabinet have all authority necessary and sufficient for effective governing, whether of prerogative origin or not. Nevertheless, they still use it officially under a variety of labels, such as the Crown, the Governor General, or the Governor-in-Council. Because all remaining royal prerogative is now exercised only in accordance with constitutional convention and practice, it seems superfluous and merely legalistic to make more than token reference to it.[5] We will thus use exclusively the term *conventional authority* and include under it everything that the Prime Minister and the Cabinet may and ought to do in the course of policy making as well as those directives and duties which they delegate to central agencies.

The "Birth" of Each Central Agency

THE PRIVY COUNCIL OFFICE

One might expect this to be a straightforward task of simple description. This may be true for some central agencies, but certainly not for others. Let us consider first the Privy Council Office (PCO). The standard, most frequently quoted statement about its origin refers to sections 11 and 130 of the BNA Act, 1867, and to the swearing in of the Clerk of the Executive Council of the United Province of Canada as Clerk of the Privy Council of the Dominion of Canada on the date of Confederation, July 1, 1867.[6] However, even a close reading of these two sections of the BNA Act does not yield a full understanding of how the PCO came to be and what the sources of its present authority are. For instance, section 11, which established the "Queen's Privy Council for Canada", does not even mention the Prime Minister or the Cabinet. In fact, the authority of Prime Minister and Cabinet has no statutory basis, and their functions rest on convention and customs created in the evolution of the British parliamentary system. Paradoxically, however, it is the Prime Minister and Cabinet, not the Privy Council, that exercise effective authority as the political executive of Canada. We can, therefore, apply what Sir Ivor Jennings said of the U.K. Cabinet to our own:

Cabinet has a life and an authority of its own. It is not concerned with prerogative powers alone; it acts whether there are already legal powers or not.[7]

We will return to this important principle of cabinet government later in this chapter. Its political implications are significant.

We see then that the question "When was PCO established, and what are the present sources of its authority?" is more complex than it appears. Sections 11 and 130 of the BNA Act allow for only that part of the activities of PCO which deal with the preparation and registration of orders-in-council, that is, regulations and appointments made by the Cabinet acting under the name of Governor-in-Council. The great bulk of PCO's activities, however, including cabinet-committee secretariats and the Machinery of Government and Security and Intelligence secretariats, are carried on pursuant to the unwritten, conventional authority of the Prime Minister and the Cabinet. It was not until March 1940, indeed, that the cabinet secretariat obtained an organizational identity of its own. This occurred when the Clerk of the Privy Council took on as well the title "Secretary to the Cabinet". It was not until December 1974, moreover, that the Secretary's title received legal sanction from Parliament.[8]

FINANCE

Unlike PCO, the Department of Finance operates under authority granted by statute. The department originally functioned under United Province of Canada statutes concerning financial administration, which were enacted before Confederation and administered by the Inspector General of Public Provincial Accounts. Two years after Confederation, the first federal Department of Finance Act, assented to in June 1869, gave the department "supervision, control and direction of all matters relating to financial affairs and public accounts, revenue and expenditure of the Dominion, insofar as they are not by law or order of the Governor-in-Council assigned to any other Department."[9] This provision directly relates to the authority under which the department operates today; that is, section 9 of the Financial Administration Act. Thus, the authority structure of the Privy Council Office stems mainly from convention, and that of the Department of Finance derives mainly from statute. Nevertheless, each may trace its roots directly to the period of Confederation. Either PCO or Finance spawned all three of the remaining central agencies in our study: the Treasury Board Secretariat, the Prime Minister's Office, and the Federal-Provincial Relations Office. TBS is the first of these itself to give birth to yet another central agency, that is, the Office of the Comptroller General.

THE TREASURY BOARD SECRETARIAT

Treasury Board Secretariat (TBS) was created by the Government Organization Act, 1966. The Act represented a modification of the celebrated Glassco Commission's recommendation (1962) that the secretariat of the Treasury Board — the cabinet committee responsible for expenditure control and management of the public service — be separated from the Department of Finance and housed in the PCO. The officials who sought a way to implement separation recommended that TBS be made an agency unto itself, reporting only to the president of the Treasury Board. This reform proposal sought essentially to institutionalize the division of financial affairs into two distinct categories: 1) intra-governmental control over the allocation of expenditure budgets and management of all in-house resources (TBS), and 2) national, intergovernmental, and international strategy to regulate and influence the economy (Finance). Also in 1966, Parliament delegated authority to the Treasury Board and to the Department of Finance, by means of the Financial Administration Act. Section 5 of the Act authorizes the Treasury Board to act on the Cabinet's behalf in relation to a number of specific matters falling under the umbrella of expenditure control and management policy. Today, the TBS is the organizational and operational arm of the Board. Its history, however, begins much earlier. An order-in-council originally established the Treasury Board in July 1867. Parliament subsequently gave it legislative sanction in 1869, again in 1878, and then again in 1951 when the first Financial Administration Act was placed on the statute books. During these years, however, the Board's secretariat, as part of the Department of Finance, operated under the authority of the Minister of Finance.

On February 1, 1965, the first Secretary of the Treasury Board, George Davidson, announced the separate agency in an internal memo:

We have discussed and agreed upon a plan of organization for the Treasury Board in conformity with the recommendations of the Glassco

Commission, and with the duties and responsibilities which, now and in the foreseeable future, are likely to be assigned to it.[10]

In October 1966, the Treasury Board Secretariat officially became a legitimate issue of Finance. Along with the authority derived from the Financial Administration Act, it now also exercises additional statutory authority under the Public Service Staff Relations Act and the Official Languages Act. With respect to size, the Treasury Board Secretariat has caught up with, and surpassed, the Finance department itself in just eleven years of organizational independence.

THE PRIME MINISTER'S OFFICE

From the formal, legal point of view, the Prime Minister's Office (PMO) is an institutional enigma. Unlike the other four central agencies, it has not even been proclaimed by Governor-in-Council a distinct department under the Financial Administration Act. Thus, PMO's budget is hidden in PCO's estimates. No statutory or any other legal provisions, furthermore, indicate its origin or a mandate. Its chief executive officer, the principal secretary, lacks a legal title and his authority remains unspecified. Its history is further obscured because no one can say just when the shared orientations and responsibilities of the Prime Minister's staff turned the office into a full-fledged central agency. Thomas d'Aquino claims that "PMO did not assume a clear identity of its own until Trudeau became Prime Minister in 1968."[11] He is probably right; and yet ever since W. L. Mackenzie King regained office in 1935, every Prime Minister has had his own staff. No one doubts the institutionally distinct status of Finance or TBS, even though they share adjoining floors in one office building and a number of housekeeping services, as well as a common institutional history. PMO also shares quarters with PCO and the Federal-Provincial Relations Office, but FPRO's institutional beginning was blessed with a statutory enactment, while PMO seems doomed to continue its enigmatic existence.

There are, of course, very good reasons for this state of affairs. If no authority is formally specified, discretion and flexibility are

increased. The conventional authority of the Prime Minister —
which he is free to delegate to his principal secretary and PMO —
is potentially enormous. He may change at will how much
authority he delegates, to whom, and with respect to which
issues or problems. All such delegation is informal and much of it
is also implied, so that authority may be simply assumed by an
officer in the PMO on his own and exercised in the name of the
Prime Minister. As long as the Prime Minister is pleased with the
results, he is not likely to interfere. With the complexity and size
of government today, he does not have time to become personally involved with every issue. Although the authority of PMO
defies one permanently valid definition, we shall attempt to
describe its present-day content, though our findings will necessarily be subject to change and re-examination.

THE FEDERAL-PROVINCIAL RELATIONS OFFICE

The youngest central agency is the Federal-Provincial Relations
Office (FPRO), established in December 1974 by the Act
Respecting the Office of the Secretary of the Cabinet for
Federal-Provincial Relations and Respecting the Clerk of the
Privy Council. FPRO was designated, by order-in-council, a
separate department under the Prime Minister in February
1975.[12] In spite of its apparent statutory origin, the authority
exercised by the office is essentially conventional and unwritten.
This means that the Prime Minister and the Cabinet may
delegate to it any functions they deem expedient provided such
functions fall within their responsibility for the federal government's relations with the provinces. Prior to 1975, the Cabinet's
secretariat for federal-provincial relations was housed in the
Privy Council Office. FPRO exhibits still an affinity to PCO similar
to that of TBS to Finance back in the late 1960s. Newly created
central agencies tend to solidify their independence over time
and consolidate organizational objectives separate and distinct
from those which they have once shared with their ascendants.
There is reason to believe that FPRO will develop in a similar
fashion to TBS.

Content of Authority and Organizational Structure

We have seen already that central agencies possess authority
which in some cases is tantamount to a monopoly; in other cases,
this authority overlaps and transgresses organizational boundaries; in still other cases, it appears to be diffuse and blurred.
Unwritten, conventional authority increases officials' discretionary power and permits the central agency (PMO, PCO, and FPRO)
to attend to the affairs of the PM and the Cabinet without feeling
bound by specific functions defined by statute. Such a degree of
flexibility makes public accountability very difficult, if not impossible. Indeed, under the present constitutional practice, agencies not created by Parliament and not possessing statutory
authority are not publicly accountable for substantive acts, with
the exception of budgetary expenditures. In this sense, accountability relates to the administration of existing policies and the
management of allocated resources. It does not extend to policy
in the making or allocations to be determined in the course of
governmental decision making. To the extent that central agencies participate most intimately in the on-going decision-making
process, the great bulk of their activities are beyond Parliament's
and the public's reach. Two central agencies, TBS and Finance,
operate largely under explicit written statutory authority. Yet,
the broad and general language of the law often protects them
from effective accountability. Later, in Chapter 7, we will discuss fully this important issue of bureaucratic accountability.

Officials in central agencies are closer to the core of the policy
process than public servants in other bureaucratic organizations
in government. Indeed, they jealously guard access to their inner
world, and are largely successful in this endeavour. Several years
ago, a young, able, and ambitious MP was appointed by the Prime
Minister as the parliamentary secretary to the president of the
Treasury Board. He took this appointment seriously and felt that
first he must learn and understand how TBS works. Being a
methodical and serious man, he decided to arrange a series of
introductory and informational meetings with the secretary of
the Board, with all the deputy secretaries, with the assistant

secretaries and, eventually, with the directors. His aim was
simple and reasonable: to get to know officials in the TBS in order
to understand how they work and what they do. He felt it would
be particularly useful to attend the regular Monday morning
senior-staff meeting chaired by the secretary of the Board. The
secretary and the four deputy secretaries received him in their
spacious and elegantly furnished offices; they listened to him and
noted his serious intentions and willingness to participate. All
agreed that this Member of Parliament was an excellent choice
for parliamentary secretary and that his intellect and curiosity
were most refreshing. They also felt, however, that he misin-
terpreted his role. The secretariat needed neither additional
links with the House nor words of wisdom from an MP. His place
was on the floor of the House or in committee, and to be at the
disposal of his minister, the president of the Treasury Board,
whenever he might want to use him. They informed him politely
that further meetings with TBS officials would not be useful and
that his proposed attendance at the Monday senior-staff meetings was out of the question. Of course, the secretary of the
Board wanted to have lunch with him from time to time "just to
keep in touch". The young MP was, to say the least, disappointed.
He decided to see his minister and seek his support. The minister
listened to his story and did not appear unsympathetic; after all
the man's intentions were pure and motivated by willingness to
serve. However, he decided not to intervene, concluding that
this entire episode was a useful learning process for the MP and
for all those concerned, and that it should be left at that.

The inner world of central agencies which this eager and
promising MP failed to penetrate is largely confined to the five
broad functions mentioned in Chapter 1:

1. Development of strategic planning and formulation of substantive policy;
2. Development of integrated economic and fiscal policy;
3. Allocation of budgets and management of resources;
4. Management of senior personnel;
5. Conduct of federal-provincial relations from the perspective
   of federal and national interests.

In order to carry out these functions, central agencies require appropriate organizational structures. We have already described the origins of central agencies' authority. It remains now to spell out the content of authority reflected in the web of formal organizations. We would, however, like to remind our readers again that the discussion in this chapter is confined to what central agencies may and ought to do and it only incidentally touches upon what they in fact do, or how effective or successful they are in doing it.

STRATEGIC PLANNING AND FORMULATION OF SUBSTANTIVE POLICY (LEAD AGENCY: PCO)

Strategic planning refers to choices open to governmental decision makers about issues to be resolved over a longer term. It is "planning" in that it deals with possible future actions of the government. It is "strategic" because the decisions concern the future and attempt to place a given issue in circumstances which will lead to its most effective resolution. This can only be accomplished if all the critical factors in governmental decision making are considered together. These factors include: the annual expenditure budget; the forecast of revenues; the design of the legislative program; the timing of other policy innovations; the evaluation of the performance of senior governmental personnel; and the adequacy of the machinery of government.[13] In other words, strategic planners look at all vital conditions which will affect the outcome of a policy issue or problem. These conditions include the future availability of money, competent personnel and administrative machinery, and the political feasibility of future legislative action in relation to the other proposals which compete for the time and attention of decision makers. Policy proposals which are thus granted high priority must, however, constantly give way to the day-to-day and week-to-week concerns of the government, and to sudden, unanticipated issues and problems. When it does work, though, strategic planning represents an approach to decision making which challenges the short-term, fire-fighting type of decision making characteristic of pluralistic, liberal-democratic political systems.

TABLE 2.2
STRUCTURE OF AUTHORITY: KEY OFFICIALS AND UNITS (AUGUST 1978)

	STRATEGIC PLANNING AND SUBSTANTIVE POLICY	*INTEGRATED ECONOMIC AND FISCAL POLICY*	*ALLOCATION OF BUDGETS AND MANAGEMENT OF RESOURCES*	*MANAGEMENT OF SENIOR PERSONNEL*	*FEDERAL-PROVINCIAL RELATIONS*
PCO	*Lead agency* Secretary: Pitfield Deputy Secretary: Teschke Deputy Secretary: Marchand Machinery of Government Secretariat Security, Intelligence, and Emergency Planning Secretariat Plans Secretariat Operations Secretariat	*Key inputs* Economic Policy Secretariat Economic Advisor: Stewart	*Key inputs* Priorities and Planning Secretariat	*Co-lead agency* Secretary: Pitfield coso (Committee on Senior Officials) Senior Personnel Secretariat	*Key inputs* Secretary: Pitfield Security, Intelligence, and Emergency Planning Secretariat Priorities and Planning Secretariat
FINANCE	*Key inputs* Deputy Minister: Shoyama Associate Deputy Minister: Hood Fiscal Policy and Economic Analysis Branch	*Lead agency* Deputy Minister: Shoyama Associate Deputy Minister: Hood Tax Policy and Federal-Provincial Relations Branch	*Key inputs* Fiscal Policy and Economic Analysis Branch	*Key inputs* None	*Key inputs* Deputy Minister: Shoyama Tax Policy and Federal-Provincial Relations Branch Fiscal Policy and Economic Analysis Branch

Tax Policy and Federal-Provincial Relations Branch

Economic Programs and Government Finance Branch

Fiscal Policy and Economic Analysis Branch

International Trade and Finance Branch

PMO

Key inputs
Principal Secretary: Coutts
Designated Policy Advisors and Consultants in Domestic Policy Sector

Key inputs
Senior Consultant: Breton
Designated Policy Advisors

Key inputs
Designated Policy Advisors

Key inputs
Principal Secretary: Coutts
Nominations Secretary

Key inputs
Principal Secretary: Coutts
Designated Policy Advisors and Consultants

TABLE 2:2 (cont'd.)
STRUCTURE OF AUTHORITY: KEY OFFICIALS AND UNITS (AUGUST 1978)

	STRATEGIC PLANNING AND SUBSTANTIVE POLICY	INTEGRATED ECONOMIC AND FISCAL POLICY	ALLOCATION OF BUDGETS AND MANAGEMENT OF RESOURCES	MANAGEMENT OF SENIOR PERSONNEL	FEDERAL-PROVINCIAL RELATIONS
TBS	*Key inputs* Secretary: LeClair Program Branch Planning Branch	*Key inputs* Secretary: LeClair Program Branch Planning Branch	*Lead agency* Secretary: LeClair Program Branch Planning Branch Administrative Policy Branch Personnel Policy Branch Efficiency Evaluation Branch Financial Administration Branch	*Co-lead agency* Secretary: LeClair Personnel Policy Branch Official Languages Branch	*Key inputs* None
FPRO	*Key inputs* Secretary: Robertson Deputy Secretary: Tellier Deputy Secretary: Massé Constitutional Advisor: Carter	*Key inputs* Policy and Program Review Secretariat	*Key inputs* Policy and Program Review Secretariat	*Key inputs* Secretary: Robertson	*Lead agency* Secretary: Robertson Deputy Secretary: Tellier Deputy Secretary: Massé Co-ordination Secretariat Federal-Provincial Relations Secretariat

Note: This table does not take into account the changes made to the TBS in 1978 or the establishment of the Office of the Comptroller General under the stewardship of Harry Rogers.

The broad function of strategic planning in central agencies may be broken down into at least five components. These are:

1. priority determination for the longer term and for the annual allocation of expenditure budgets;
2. major reviews of specific policy areas, such as the review of foreign and defence policies in 1969–70 and immigration in 1976–77;
3. security and emergency planning which has been prominent since the 1970 October crisis;
4. changes and innovations in the machinery of government; that is, in the organizational structure of government and in the jurisdictions of key officials and decision makers; and
5. legislative strategy for effective passing of bills and control of the House of Commons.

The PCO has become the lead agency for strategic planning. Its Plans Division houses the key analytic and advisory personnel grouped into small secretariats which focus on all of the components of strategic planning. Thus, the Priorities and Planning Secretariat supports the Cabinet Committee on Priorities and Planning chaired by the Prime Minister, and helps determine and circulate to other departments priorities and broad policy objectives. The Legislation and House Planning Secretariat reviews draft government bills before they are introduced in Parliament and attempts to control the legislative process. The Machinery of Government Secretariat designs new organizational models and controls changes in departmental mandates and jurisdictions. It directly serves the Prime Minister and supports the ad hoc Committee on the Public Service chaired by him.

Substantive policy has been divided into five discrete sectors, each being the responsibility of "subject matter" standing cabinet committees, each supported by its own secretariat of analysts and advisors housed in the Operations Division of PCO. Currently, the standing committees include Economic Policy, Social Policy (health, welfare, social insurance, manpower, and housing), External Policy and Defence, Culture and Native Affairs, and Government Operations. Government Operations embraces policy issues involving both renewable and non-renewable natural resources, as well as items which do not clearly fall within the mandate of any other sector.

An interesting jurisdictional question may arise when a particular minister, supported by his departmental officials, wishes to submit a policy proposal before one sectoral cabinet committee while other ministers want it to come before another committee. For instance, a recent conflict between the domestically oriented policy assigned to the Foreign Investment Review Agency and Canada's traditional international commitments to the Paris-based Organization for Economic Cooperation and Development (OECD) had to be resolved at the cabinet-committee level. OECD exerted pressure, through the Department of External Affairs, in favour of a lenient and liberal foreign-investment policy consistent with Canada's international position. External Affairs would have liked to have had the matter discussed and resolved by the Cabinet Committee on External Policy and Defence. However, Donald MacDonald, the Minister of Finance at that time, chose a very strong line *vis-à-vis* OECD. He forced the referral of the issue to the economic-policy cabinet committee, largely controlled by Finance. There a compromise was finally worked out between the two factions' policy objectives. PCO indeed plays a highly significant role in all difficult jurisdictional disputes, but in the normal course of business a great majority of policy items are placed on the agenda without squabbles.

PCO's authority to serve as the lead agency for strategic planning and the formulation of substantive policy is not based in statute; rather it derives from the constitutional convention which obligates the government to govern. The precise content and scope of this authority is unclear. It has been correctly observed by S. A. de Smith that

Some of the conventions about . . . the working of the Cabinet system are either blurred or experimental. Codification would purchase certainty at the expense of flexibility; informal modifications to keep the constitution in touch with contemporary political thinking or needs would be inhibited . . . in some contexts the rules ought not to be crystal clear. Clarification would tend to stultify one purpose of conventions — keeping the constitution up to date. . . . Nevertheless [he adds], it is unsatisfactory that the content, and indeed the very existence, of some of the most important conventions should be indeterminate.[14]

PCO's authority with respect to this broad function of strategic planning and substantive policy formulation is unquestionably predominant, but it is not absolutely exclusive. The remaining central agencies, within their respective areas of competence, also play a role in it. In particular, PMO's expected yet much-misunderstood contribution must be acknowledged. Its involvement focuses on those consequences and implications of policy decisions which have to do with:

1. how the public and the mass media perceive the Prime Minister's image and leadership;
2. the over-all chances for re-election;
3. the government party's specific national and regional interests;
4. the Prime Minister's individual preferences, objectives, and ideology.

Especially during the past three to four years, this mandate has not been well served, primarily because the PMO lacks highly qualified, seasoned, and influential officials. The many changes in the organizational structure of PMO — which continues to be in a state of flux — reflect the fact that no principal secretary since Marc Lalonde (1968–72) has been able to sustain and staff the office fully in accordance with its mandate. Subsequent chapters will deal with this important matter.

The statute which grants the Department of Finance its authority imparts to it responsibility to forecast government revenues as well as general economic and fiscal conditions. To the extent that these responsibilities become critical factors in strategic planning and substantive policy formulation, Finance possesses a strong potential leverage in this area. The Federal-Provincial Relations Office must evaluate the impact of strategic planning and substantive policy on provincial governments and attempt to predict and deal with their responses. In addition,

FPRO now has a special mandate assigned by the Prime Minister and the Cabinet to monitor events and to prepare scenarios for action *vis-à-vis* the government of Quebec and the issue of independence. Like Finance, the Treasury Board Secretariat has a specific statutory authority which, when exercised, may have a critical effect on strategic planning. TBS may determine priorities limited to programs (as distinct from policies), with respect to annual and longer-term expenditures, including the allocation of public-service personnel. Policies are the ken of the Priorities and Planning cabinet committee and the secretariats supporting it in PCO. Similarly, TBS authority over "personnel management" in the public service excludes order-in-council appointments and other senior-level promotions; these are the domain of PCO's Senior Personnel Secretariat reporting to Gordon Robertson and the Prime Minister's nominations secretary. Thus, PCO maintains unchallenged supremacy in strategic planning and substantive policy formulation, although all central agencies exercise considerable authority which, in some instances, appears to overlap and to conflict.

THE DEVELOPMENT OF INTEGRATED ECONOMIC AND FISCAL POLICIES (LEAD AGENCY: FINANCE)

The development of integrated economic, fiscal, and tax policies is the second broad function of central agencies. The primary authority for this function is statutory and derives from the Financial Administration Act, section 9, which reads as follows:

The Minister [of Finance] has the management and direction of the Department of Finance, . . . and the supervision, control and direction of all matters relating to the financial affairs of Canada not by law assigned to the Treasury Board or to any other Minister.[15]

In 1976 Michael Pitfield, the Clerk of the Privy Council, called Finance a "lead department . . . responsible for stabilization policy and a court of last review for economic policy". He pointed out further that in order to encourage countervaillance (that is, several competing approaches) in financial affairs, the government has created "a number of new economic departments, such as Regional Economic Expansion, Manpower and Immigration, Consumer and Corporate Affairs, Energy, Mines, and Resources, and Environment — each with its own expert skills."[16] How does this development affect the authority of Finance to supervise, control, and direct "all matters relating to the financial affairs of Canada"? Each of the five new departments mentioned by Pitfield enjoys statutory authority, which, at least to some degree, reduces Finance's hegemony in the economic-policy field. At the same time, however, the existence of several economic units, each with its own specialty and orientation, increases the need for an overseeing eye. Regional Economic Expansion, for example, works to stimulate growth in the economically underdeveloped parts of Canada. Its clients are industries situated in those areas which seek federal support, along with labour organizations and other local groups. Manpower and Immigration promotes the development and placement of Canada's manpower. Consumer and Corporate Affairs furthers the ideas associated with controlled competition, stable price structure, and a gentle regulation of business and industry. Energy, Mines, and Resources, on the other hand, works along with business and industry to increase development of natural resources and to further technological expansion in this sector. Environment represents interests which promote ecological protection, conservation, and limits to growth. There are, of course, other economically oriented departments of an older vintage, such as Labour, or Industry, Trade, and Commerce, which promote their own points of view at the decision-making table. The authority of Finance as a central agency is supposed to transcend all these special approaches and interests; for the sake of economic stability it co-ordinates and controls their efforts.

In consequence, during recent years Finance has divested itself of nearly all operational programs and has assumed a clear central-agency posture. Once some 6,000 strong, the staff of the department today numbers approximately 700. These highly skilled public servants develop and analyse policy in four main areas. Together, the four sectors make up the current content of Finance's authority. They are:

Tax Policy. Here, one division of departmental specialists analyses existing tax measures and new proposals from the perspective of the business community. Within the division a personal-income-tax section examines proposals relating to personal taxation, deferred-income plans, trusts, and partnerships, while a commodity-tax division develops policy concerned with all excise taxes and duties. A legislation division develops tax bills and participates directly in the drafting of sections of the budget concerning taxation. Finally, a social development and manpower policy division represents Finance's interest, especially as related to taxation, in the field of social policy.

Economic Development and Government Finance. Here, policy analysts monitor government's attempts to encourage the development of Canada's natural resources; these include energy, oil, gas, and minerals. Another unit oversees other departments' promotion of industrial development in general; this includes secondary industry, transportation, communications, nuclear energy, science policy, and research. A third unit allots government loans and other financial guarantees (primarily to Crown corporations) and plans investments.

Fiscal Policy and Economic Analysis. One unit within this sector provides central economic intelligence on the over-all economic conditions of the country and prepares forecasts used in the development of national budgets. Another unit, responsible for the fiscal policy, draws up the annual fiscal framework, which forms the basis for the expenditure budget, and forecasts the financial requirements of the government. This unit maintains a very close link with the Program Branch in TBS. A long-range analysis unit employs various mathematical models to project national economic performance. Finally, a capital-markets unit develops policy with respect to private financial institutions and management of the public debt.

International Trade and Finance. The tariffs unit investigates and reports on proposals regarding the Canadian customs tariff pursuant to the General Agreement on Tariffs and Trade (GATT) and bilateral trade agreements. Another unit makes recommendations on international trade policy, particularly with regard to imports. Still another group of experts maintains liaison with international financial organizations and promotes export development. Finally, the international-finance division is concerned with the balance of payments and foreign exchange.

It is evident that the statute which delegates general authority to Finance is so vague that the department can interpret its content more or less as it pleases. Only the Prime Minister and his Cabinet can check this important bureaucratic discretion. For example, Finance once served as the lead agency for federal-provincial relations because of the overriding fiscal and economic implications. Since FPRO was established in 1974–75, however, Finance's authority in this area has diminished; we would not be surprised if FPRO took over most of it in the near future. To be sure, Finance will continue to advise the Prime Minister and the Cabinet in federal-provincial financial arrangements, but FPRO will make the strategic decisions, as it does now. This illustrates our point that the conventional authority vested in the Prime Minister and his Cabinet, rather than statutory authority, dominates the role of central agencies. Constitutional conflict is avoided because, conveniently, statutory authority is so general and vague that the agencies can add or take away particular functions at will.

The controlling and co-ordinating role of Finance in financial and economic matters is, of course, crucial to the effective discharge of the four other broad functions (listed in Chapter 1) performed by central agencies. In strategic planning, Finance provides the fiscal limits, at the national level, within which any major policy issue must be resolved. In the allocation and management of physical resources and expenditure budgets, Finance plays a similar role at the intragovernmental level. In the conduct of federal-provincial relations, Finance's advisory role at the intragovernmental level is self-evident. Typically, then, the predominant authority of Finance in economic and financial affairs is complemented by its increased involvement in other broad functions which characterize the role of central agencies. In other words, because of its presence in several fields, its influence is felt much more profoundly by other departments than if it simply handed down financial and economic edicts.

THE ALLOCATION AND MANAGEMENT OF PHYSICAL RESOURCES
AND EXPENDITURE BUDGETS (LEAD AGENCY: TBS)

The allocation and management of human and physical resources and expenditure budgets throughout government is the work of the Treasury Board, a cabinet committee. TBS, the committee's secretariat, bases its activities on the Treasury Board's statutory authority derived from section 5 of the Financial Administration Act.

Specifically, this authority includes:

1. general administrative policy in the public service of Canada;
2. the organization of the public service or any portion thereof, and the determination and control of establishments therein;
3. financial management, including estimates, expenditures, financial commitments, accounts, fees or charges for the provision of services or the use of facilities, rentals, licences, leases, revenues from the disposition of property, and procedures by which departments manage, record, and account for revenues received or receivable from any source whatever;
4. the review of annual and longer-term expenditure plans and programs of the various departments of government, and the determination of priorities with respect thereto;
5. personnel management in the public service, including the determination of terms and conditions of employment of persons employed therein;
6. such other matters as may be referred to it by the Governor-in-Council.[17]

Money and physical resources are in great demand throughout the government apparatus. To make the best use of them consistently is the work of a successful bureaucratic executive. Operational departments and agencies in Ottawa are, in many respects, like business establishments competing for markets, sales, and profits. The bureaucratic "marketplace", however, permits only competition for person-years, budgets, and physical assets, all of which the Treasury Board is supposed to control and manage centrally. This, perhaps, is only one side of the story. If incremental allocations are the order of the day (or rather, the year), and if operational departments and agencies get at least enough to continue essentially as they are, what is the real meaning of central allocation and TBS control?

Let us examine in some detail four aspects of authority delegated to TBS by statute.[18] We will discuss the fifth, personnel management, in a separate section.

General Administrative Policy. A statutory definition of this function does not exist. In consequence, we must rely on a long-accepted bureaucratic definition which refers to rules based on "equity, probity, and prudence". Their purpose is to govern the acquisition, use, and consumption of various kinds of property by departments and agencies for greater "efficiency and effectiveness". TBS develops and enforces these rules, but the degree of enforcement varies. The rules apply to such highly expensive commodities as computers, telecommunication systems, and office buildings, as well as to desks, rugs, and stationery. An entire branch of TBS is engaged in the development and direction of this policy area.

Organization of the Public Service. This authority seems wide enough to encompass nearly everything in government. A formal organization will contain a complex group of offices or bureaus having explicit objectives, clearly stated rules, and a system of specifically defined roles, each with clearly designated rights and duties; but obviously, TBS cannot prescribe all of these for the entire federal public service. But, does TBS have exclusive statutory authority to do so? Once again we find that the general language of the law permits a competing central-agency secretariat, the machinery-of-government unit in PCO, to assume considerable responsibility in this area in accordance with conventional authority derived from the Cabinet and Prime Minister. The PCO unit organizes the governmental apparatus, establishes jurisdictional boundaries between departments and agencies, and designs new organizational units in the public service. In 1971, PCO's machinery-of-government unit was instrumental in creating ministries of state, notwithstanding the strong opposition of some otherwise influential senior TBS officials. More recently, the TBS's organization division conducted special studies on the effectiveness of particular types of organizational structure, on the relationship between policy-making departments (e.g., ministries of state) and policy-implementing units, and on the advantages and disadvantages of bureaucratic decentralization. *Prima facie,* all these subjects fall within the statutory authority of TBS *as well as* within the conventional authority of PCO. Who wins, and who loses? TBS retains strong authority over the classification changes at the lower senior-management levels (SX-1 to SX-3 positions) and the increases to management complements of departments. It chairs the Co-ordinating Committee on Organization (CCO) in which PCO and Public Service Commission officials regularly participate. In all likelihood, PCO and TBS will continue to share authority in this area. Such sharing creates serious problems of public accountability, particularly when one central agency (PCO) claims exemption from Parliament's scrutiny.

Financial Administration. Until recently, financial administration had been combined with administrative policy in the Administrative Policy Branch. With the re-organization of TBS, the new Financial Administration Branch has found itself in the newly created Office of the Comptroller General (OCG). The term "financial administration" is misleading; it appears to mean the same thing as Finance's authority to direct and control the financial affairs of Canada. However, "administration" here refers to internal or in-house control of expenditures to ensure that departments and agencies actually follow the intentions and aims for which money has been allocated. In this context, moreover, "financial" refers to those rules which promote good accounting practices recognized by professional accountants. Under this authority TBS established methods for control of accounts and internal audits which are now under the stewardship of the OCG.

Review of Expenditures and Determination of Program Priorities. This authority is, in our view, the most crucial in the discharge of TBS activities. Two branches, the Program Branch and the Planning Branch, drew on it until 1978, one directly, the other indirectly. The Program Branch is organized according to five functional groupings of government programs: a) Industry and Natural Resources; b) Transportation, Communications, and Science; c) Defence, External Affairs, and Cultural Affairs; d) Social and Manpower Policy; and e) General Government Services. It controls the annual budgetary cycle; this is when the departmental program forecasts are reviewed, an over-all expenditure plan for the coming fiscal year is approved, and the Main Estimates and Supplementary Estimates are prepared, scrutinized, and presented to Parliament. Apart from the cyclical activity, the branch analyses and evaluates new policy proposals from operational departments and agencies. It comments on the implications for the existing resources that such proposals may have, and on the extent to which governmental objectives and priorities are promoted. In this respect, the branch maintains a close relationship with the secretariat in PCO which drafts the policy guidelines for the Priorities and Planning cabinet committee. The committee's guidelines set out expenditure priorities for the forthcoming budgetary exercise. No wonder, then, that the Program Branch has become the springboard from which senior-rank executives rise to higher-level appointments offered by programmatic departments and agencies. For example, of the ten directors in the branch in 1970, seven became assistant deputy ministers by 1976; in addition, its deputy secretary and assistant secretary became deputy ministers. No governmental unit of similar size and expertise can match this extent and rapidity of upward mobility.

The activities of the Planning Branch rested on the proposition that the evaluation of program effectiveness and program efficiency is an essential prerequisite for control of public resources. In the words of Gordon Osbaldeston, a former Secretary of TBS, evaluation of bureaucratic performance completes the Planning-Programming-Budgeting "cycle".[19] Planning Branch came into its own in 1970 under the direction of Douglas Hartle, a University of Toronto economist; three years later he left public service doubting the practical value of the very analytical techniques and methodologies which he helped to introduce.[20] His contribution, however, has significantly influenced the development of policy and program analysis in government. A quantitative-analysis school operated by the branch trained numerous new specialists who subsequently returned to their respective departments and agencies to man policy- and program-evaluation units. Although, as we said earlier, the Financial Administration Act provided the authority under which this branch was established, its main activities concerned strategic planning and the role played in it by the Priorities and Planning cabinet committee. In addition to the statutory authority, consequently, the branch also acted under conventional authority which the Cabinet delegated to it. By late 1978, Planning Branch had undergone metamorphosis. The in-house quantitative-analysis school disbanded in 1976; the efficiency-evaluation division had been transferred and elevated to a branch in the newly created Office of the Comptroller General; and the organization division had moved to the Program Branch. What was left, the effectiveness-evaluation unit designed for in-depth analysis of programs for the secretary of the Treasury Board, finally dissolved.

Clearly, TBS's statutory authority is more specific and better defined than that of Finance. This does not, however, afford TBS any better protection against encroachment by competing central agencies which rely to a greater extent on conventional authority. PCO in particular has built units and expertise in areas of policy development which, to say the least, coincide with those bestowed by statute on TBS. How does one distinguish the TBS's "organization of the public service" from the PCO's "machinery of government"? It is evident that the ultimate control in this area resides in PCO.

Barely six years ago, A. W. Johnson, then secretary of the Treasury Board, put forward an interesting theory about TBS's authority.[21] He described the Treasury Board itself as a dual-purpose cabinet committee responsible for: 1) the management of the public service; and 2) the expenditure budget. In the discharge of these two functions, the Board forms an integral part of the cabinet-committee system and acts on the decisions made in Cabinet or in one of its regular committees. As we have already noted, early in each year the Priorities and Planning cabinet committee formulates a set of decisions, subsequently confirmed by full Cabinet, called "policy guidelines", which contain specific authority for the allocation of expenditure budgets. It is the task of TBS (Program Branch) to carry out these policy guidelines in the course of the budgetary cycle. Thus, in addition to authority derived from statute (Financial Administration Act), TBS relies and acts upon conventional authority granted to it from time to time by Cabinet. The former is public and subject to parliamentary scrutiny, while the latter remains secret and exempt from it. Johnson's theory permits TBS to claim the status of a cabinet secretariat with exclusive authority over the two areas of policy which, accordingly, are outside the competence of PCO. Moreover, the theory places TBS closer to the apex of power, ahead of Finance, and parallel to PMO, PCO, and FPRO.

Does this study accept Johnson's theory? The answer is both yes and no. The Prime Minister and his colleagues are free to create any committees and secretariats they wish, and to endow them with conventional authority, provided it is not contrary to existing statutory authority. The authority contained in the policy guidelines is merely an example of broader statutory authority to "review . . . annual expenditure plans and programs". In this sense, the Board may act as a dual-purpose cabinet committee, and TBS may be a cabinet secretariat like PCO. But one further qualification must be added. Strictly speaking, from the standpoint of law, the Treasury Board is not a cabinet committee but a Parliament-created committee of the Privy Council, and is ultimately responsible to Parliament. Neither the Board nor its secretariat may exercise greater or different authority from that provided in the statute. If TBS acts as well under the authority passed to it secretly by Cabinet or a cabinet committee, who is to tell whether that authority conforms with or exceeds the provisions of the Financial Administration Act?

In our view, Johnson's theory allows TBS too much discretion and reduces the possibility of parliamentary supervision. TBS's officials are given an opportunity to claim exemption from accountability whenever they act according to cabinet authority as distinct from the authority contained in statute. The distinction between authority obtained from Cabinet and that contained in the statute is, in too many instances, either exceedingly difficult to make or plainly illusory. If TBS forms an integral part of the cabinet-committee system which still operates according to the traditional rules of secrecy and solidarity, enjoying a privileged and protected milieu, it should not at the same time be, nor pretend to be, a publicly created department with full accountability to the House of Commons.

MANAGEMENT OF SENIOR PERSONNEL
(JOINT LEAD AGENCIES: PCO AND TBS)

Highly skilled, loyal, and capable men and women constitute the most precious asset of any governmental bureaucracy. Authority to recruit, train, promote, and compensate these individuals is equally precious and crucial. Until 1967, much of this authority was exercised by the Civil Service Commission, a quasi-independent government agency. During the reforms of 1967, the newly created Public Service Commission did not retain the authority of its predecessor, the Civil Service Commission. Its role is now confined to three tasks: staffing, which it shares with programmatic departments and agencies; training and development; and handling appeals on all staffing decisions. The most important aspect of personnel management in general — the classification of positions and employees and the determination of compensation rates and scales — is now in the hands of TBS. J. E. Hodgetts states unequivocally that the present distribution "leaves little room for querying the location of [the] ultimate repository of managerial authority over the public service."[22] He is right, up to a point. The highly trained staff of TBS's Personnel Policy Branch oversees collective bargaining, pensions, and other non-negotiable benefits; the classification and compensation of all ranks of public servants; and other related duties. However, its authority over the highest level of officials, i.e., the SX or senior-executive category and the DM or deputy-minister category, has been diluted by four developments. These are:

1. the creation of an advisory committee of private-sector executives, at the time of our interviews under the chairmanship of Allen Lambert (Toronto Dominion Bank), who became chairman of the Royal Commission on Financial Management and Accountability;
2. the powerful impact of the Committee on Senior Officials (COSO), chaired by Michael Pitfield and composed of Gordon Robertson (Secretary to the Cabinet for Federal-Provincial Relations), Maurice LeClair (Secretary of the Treasury Board), Edgar Gallant (Chairman of the Public Service Commission), and four other deputy ministers;
3. the work of the Senior Personnel Secretariat in PCO under the direction of Ian Dewar; and
4. extensive and effective use by the government of the GC category, or governor-in-council appointments, where, in Michael Pitfield's words, "lies the key to better administration and better policy development".[23]

The SX and DM classifications are the highest a career public servant can earn. Normally, directors and directors-general merit SX-1 to SX-3; assistant deputy ministers and associate deputy ministers range from SX-3 to SX-4; and deputy ministers range from DM-1 to DM-3 — the top of the ladder. Each class is related to a specific salary scale. Promotion to a new managerial position may not always coincide with a higher classification. An individual may become a director and work as such for some time, while his/her SX classification may be held up pending a pay-related performance assessment, or the lifting of a general freeze on the SX category. Statutory authority to develop policy about the SX classification, to approve individual promotions, to assess performance, and to approve compensation scales is held by TBS. However, it must be recognized that the Prime Minister attaches great importance to the selection of top officials. The Priorities and Planning committee which the Prime Minister chairs evaluates annually the performance of senior personnel; the senior-personnel secretariat of PCO which reports to the PM through Gordon Robertson screens candidates for senior SX and DM vacancies and recommends appointments. In addition, this PCO unit, reporting through Michael Pitfield, advises the PM and the Cabinet on senior-personnel policy.

The Prime Minister approves all governor-in-council appointments, which include DM-1, 2, and 3, and SX-4, in addition to members of federal boards, commissions, and task forces, and directors and senior executives of Crown corporations. Although the Prime Minister has ultimate authority to make appointments to these positions, most of which are provided for by statute, the process of selection is governed by rules developed in PCO under the conventional authority of the Prime Minister and Cabinet.

The Committee on Senior Officials (COSO) advises the Prime Minister and the Cabinet on key aspects of personnel policy for senior public servants (i.e., those in SX, DM, and GC categories), and reports through Michael Pitfield. Its broad mandate embraces also such issues as bilingualism policy, conflict of interest in the public service, the relationship between ministers and officials, post-employment regulations (i.e., restrictions on former public servants to engage in competitive or conflicting business activities or employment), and the work of the Royal Commission on Financial Management and Accountability. The advisory committee of private-sector executives, on the other hand, regularly reviews the salaries of senior officials, making its recommendations to PCO and TBS.

All the activities of the PCO and the advisory committees vitally affect the lives and careers of senior officials and determine the quality and composition of the top bureaucratic elite. They are carried out under conventional authority from the Prime Minister and the Cabinet, over and above the statutory authority which Parliament delegates to TBS and to the Public Service Commission.

Policy on bilingualism in the public service must be viewed as an aspect of personnel management. The Official Languages Branch of TBS serves as the co-ordinating secretariat in this sector of activity. The branch monitors throughout government the implementation of the Official Languages Act, and a resolution adopted by Parliament in 1973. The branch also implements modifications to the policy developed by a special committee of officials and sanctioned by Cabinet. Thus, the branch's authority is both statutory and conventional.

CONDUCT OF FEDERAL-PROVINCIAL RELATIONS (LEAD AGENCY: FPRO)

This is the last of the five broad functions which we have ascribed to central agencies; in its breadth and scope it is the most pervasive, for in Canada no policy issue or problem is exempt from intergovernmental concern. Sections 91 and 92 of the BNA Act, which provide a legal framework for the distribution of legislative authority between Ottawa and the provinces, have been truly put aside by political practice. Although the courts once declared the two governmental jurisdictions "watertight compartments" in a sailing ship,[24] today the constitution in no way inhibits the intricate interdependency developed in the federal/provincial political system. Ontario, for example, uses policy-making authority to influence the design of the federal budget; Quebec (even before November 1976) insists on consultations in cultural and educational aspects of foreign policy; Alberta effectively forces reassessments of national energy policy to suit its own interests; and a number of provinces lead the way to major revisions in federal tax policy and federal-provincial fiscal arrangements.

Authority to conduct intergovernmental affairs is simply one aspect of the executive authority to govern. No federal government has paid as much attention to this activity as that of Pierre Trudeau. Indeed, until 1977, Trudeau chaired the cabinet committee on Federal-Provincial Relations. This committee, which fashioned Ottawa's over-all strategy *vis-à-vis* the provinces, now has merged with the Priorities and Planning committee and consists of the same ministers. Since 1975, FPRO has acted as a full-fledged *second* cabinet secretariat developing policy-review capabilities in all substantive issue areas and in all geographic regions of the country. The organization of FPRO remains flexible and responsive to changing political needs. Until just shortly before the time of writing (summer 1978), its staff comprised two deputy secretaries to the Cabinet, one for operations and one for co-ordination *vis-à-vis* national-unity questions. The operations unit directs a section on regional analysis, a studies and research group, and a policy- and program-review section. The review section is divided according to four issue areas: finance and economic matters; resources; social policy; and urban affairs and transportation. The co-ordination secretariat under Paul Tellier confines its activities to thorny political problems brought to the fore by the recent election of the separatist Parti Québécois government in Quebec. D. S. Thorson, a former deputy minister in the Department of Justice, served (until his elevation to the Ontario Court of Appeal in the summer of 1978, when Frank Carter took over from him) in a special capacity as the constitutional advisor to the Prime Minister during the entire period in which Trudeau developed his package of constitutional reforms in response to the constitutional crisis brought on by the separatist threat in Quebec. There can be little doubt that Ottawa has locked a full complement of its bureaucratic horns with the government in Quebec. At stake is not only the unity of the country, but also the future of the federal bureaucratic machinery, of the federal Liberal party, and of the elites associated and identified with it. In a struggle of such importance, the government will muster and employ all the authority it can. FPRO has been the principal organizational beneficiary of the government's resolve to save federalism.

We thus see that, as with the other broad functions of central agencies, federal-provincial relations fall within the domain of one institution designed primarily to control it. Yet, other central institutions are involved as well. For example, without the expertise and the knowledge generated by Finance in the area of economic, fiscal, and tax policy, conduct of federal-provincial relations is impossible. At the decision-making table, whether in cabinet committee, in an intergovernmental committee, or in an interdepartmental committee, Finance presents its case and its particular point of view which is maintenance of the country's economic stability. Such a view may not always mesh with the more delicate and illusory requirements of political stability, nor with the short-term tactics and scenarios which FPRO may want to employ to gain a political advantage over one or more provinces. Similarly, the TBS, conscious of its own mandate to manage physical and manpower resources of the government, may and will advocate a position at odds with that of FPRO. Because PMO, PCO, and FPRO are literally each other's neighbours and consult together frequently and intimately, the attitudes of the three agencies often dovetail nicely; nevertheless, the individual mandates of PMO, PCO, and FPRO may also produce conflicting views of key federal-provincial issues. These positions clash at many decision-making meetings at various levels and stages of policy formulation, until they reach the cabinet committee on Priorities and Planning, the ultimate forum for federal-provincial relations. Thus, the content of authority in the conduct of federal-provincial affairs is truly multifarious; each central agency makes a significant contribution to the process from the perspective of its own policy responsibility, while FPRO maintains the primary authority in the field. We stress that this unique multifariousness and flexibility in the content and exercise of authority is made possible by the absence of statutory authority in this field, and by a total reliance on constitutional convention and usage emanating from Cabinet.

Summary and Conclusions

This chapter first described the sources of executive and bureaucratic authority and identified its two types: *conventional* — originating from the Cabinet and the Prime Minister and their over-all responsibility to govern, including the royal prerogative inherited from English common law and the Crown; and *statutory* — delegated by Parliament. It has shown that conventional authority is by far the most significant for central agencies. PMO, PCO, and FPRO rate highest in conventional authority and rely almost exclusively on it; TBS enjoys a mixture of conventional and statutory authority, while Finance is wedded to the highest amount of statutory authority, albeit of a very mild form due to its very broad and general mandate.

Next, the chapter dissected the content of authority into five broad functions:

1. strategic planning and substantive policy formulation which belongs primarily to PCO, but concerns the remaining agencies as well;
2. development of integrated economic, fiscal, and tax policies and maintenance of economic stability, which is the domain of Finance but subject to the countervailing forces of others;
3. allocation of expenditure budgets, management of physical resources, and financial management, which form the mandates of TBS and OCG but which cannot be separated from the interests and influences of other agencies;
4. management of senior personnel, which is a shared concern of PCO and TBS, although PCO dominates; and
5. conduct of federal-provincial relations — a field clearly assigned to FPRO, yet so wide and pervasive that it cannot be managed without significant assistance from other agencies.

In summary, the authority structure of Canadian central agencies reveals the following characteristics:

— It is extremely broad and general, even when statutory, permitting engagement in all policy areas under a variety of labels, such as "allocation", "management", "co-ordination", and "control".

— Conventional authority clearly transcends statutory authority. Central agencies strive for the former and shy away from too much of the latter. Moreover, it is often difficult to determine in each particular case whether an agency acts according to one or the other.

— Each central agency (with the notable exception of PMO) enjoys supremacy in one broad policy function; yet upon examination, it becomes evident that, in reality, jurisdictional and authority boundaries between the agencies are blurred; there is much overlapping and sharing. There is also some tendency for competition and conflict, which, however, is carefully managed and contained.

— The constitutional principle that Cabinet (subject only to the wishes of the Prime Minister) is the exclusive master of its own structure and the source of its own executive authority gives central agencies great freedom in the design of their organizations and in the functions and responsibilities they assume.

Finally, the chapter described central agencies as extensions of the Cabinet and of the Prime Minister, speaking for and supporting them as well as guiding their decisions and actions. This is why the men and women who operate the agencies deserve to be called superbureaucrats. The next chapter will teach us how these superbureaucrats perceive their functions and responsibilities.

Looking from Inside: Central Agencies through the Eyes of Their Officials

The day-to-day activities of central agencies focus on relations with the Prime Minister, ministers, and/or the Cabinet and its committees. The PMO serves the Prime Minister as the political head of the government party; the PCO and the FPRO centre their activities jointly on work for the Prime Minister and for the Cabinet and its committees; the Department of Finance advises the Minister of Finance; the TBS assists the Treasury Board and its president. In this chapter we will see how the ways in which senior officials describe the roles of their agencies reflect these various relations with the political executive. We will discover as well that the officials' own views of what they do differ from agency to agency. Seeing beyond organization charts to find out how departments and agencies actually work remains as one of the most difficult tasks of political science. Thanks to the senior officials who described their roles and the functions of their agencies, this chapter fleshes out many aspects of the operation of central agencies which were previously shrouded in mystery.

The Roles of Central Agents: Some Generalizations

Before presenting a detailed profile of what each of our five central agencies does as described by the officials who staff it, an overview of these officials' responses is in order. It is clear that each agency fosters a particular role orientation. The outstanding differences we have found are as follows:

1. officials in the PMO stress above all the "switchboard" function; this entails maintenance of the links of vital communication to and from the Prime Minister, although PMO officials do attempt as well to offer a political input into the policy process;
2. officials in the PCO and the FPRO have dual roles — to give

policy advice to the Prime Minister and to facilitate review of policy proposals by the Cabinet and its committees;

3. officials in Finance mainly view themselves as advisors on policy matters in the economics field, although some also perform administrative functions in the financial sector;

4. officials in the TBS are almost all policy advisors, yet some focus on program effectiveness while others monitor administrative and personnel policy.

We derived these generalizations from our respondents' descriptions of their roles and the functions of their agencies. We asked two questions to determine how respondents view their roles and the functions of their agencies:

1. What are your responsibilities here at ____?
2. How does what you do relate to the role of ____ as a central agency?
   a) What, in your view, is the role of ____ in government?
   b) Is this role being adequately performed? How so?
   c) How might the performance of your agency be improved? Please elaborate.

Respondents' descriptions of their roles fall into four categories: policy development (strongest in Finance); efforts to improve the structure and operation of government (the PMO, the PCO, the FPRO and the TBS); administration and/or monitoring policy implementation (mostly Finance and the TBS); and communication co-ordination both within and without government (largely the PMO). (See Appendix II.)

Our respondents also referred to the style in which they perform their work. They mentioned four main types of activity which occupy most of their time as they fulfil their perceived roles: facilitating policy decisions, advising on policy issues, "managing" the policy process (e.g., processing cabinet documents, arranging meetings, etc.), and maintaining liaison with people inside and outside government. About 20 per cent of the officials in all our central agencies described their style at least partially in terms of facilitation. Finance officials report advisory activities the most, although a majority of officials in other agencies advise as well. Officials in the PMO, the PCO, and the

FPRO manage more often in the policy process than the officials in Finance and the TBS. The PMO, the PCO, and the FPRO have relatively lean staffs and are the focal points of an immense amount of paper, visits, and calls from inside and outside government. Even senior officials in these agencies shuffle mounds of memos and arrange a vast number of meetings. This probably explains why they say that they often find themselves managing. Finally, PMO officials were the only central agents who often said part of their style was communicating with people outside of government.

A look at respondents' answers to questions on the roles of their agencies suggests that they project their perceptions of their own roles onto their department. Their descriptions of their agencies' functions fall into six categories: independent analysis of policies, development of policies, monitoring the implementation of policies, facilitating government business, service as a switchboard, and anticipating potential crises. Officials in all of our agencies say their departments are involved only moderately in independent analysis. We note with interest, however, that officers in the PCO and the FPRO state more often than others that their agency performs this function. This finding corresponds to the belief, registered outside the PCO and the FPRO, that officials there often second-guess proposals, that is, reanalyse them from the perspective of the Cabinet. Finance officials, in keeping with their descriptions of what they do, say overwhelmingly that their department develops policy. TBS officials say more often than others that their agency monitors the implementation of policy; PMO officials rarely do. We find some indication that PCO and FPRO officials more than others view their agency as facilitating government business; almost half of our PMO respondents say their agency is a switchboard. Relatively low proportions of officials in all of the agencies said that their departments forecast problems; this perhaps reflects the difficulties of long-term planning.

We also asked our respondents to describe briefly their agencies' roles in government generally. Officials in agencies which report to the Prime Minister (the PMO, the PCO, and the FPRO) sometimes said their agencies provide general services to government, such as helping Cabinet to function smoothly, whereas none of the officials in the other agencies (Finance and the TBS) said this. When we consider the type of work done in several TBS branches, it does not come as a surprise that almost half of its officials believe their agency helps relate administration to the government's priorities. The majority of officials, especially those in Finance, see their agencies as helping relate policies to government priorities.

We noted at the beginning of this chapter that the five agencies carry out their activities in terms of their different relationships to the Prime Minister, ministers, and/or Cabinet and its committees. Are these distinct agency links reflected in officials' descriptions of their roles? Our respondents generally did *not* refer to specific cabinet ministers while explaining their functions. Oddly enough, we often found this to be the case in Finance which in large part bases its activities on the statutory authority of its minister. This finding reflects two characteristics of Finance which we will explore later in depth. Many of its officials, as we will see in Chapter 5, consider their expertise in economics or related disciplines to be their primary contribution to the policy process. They tend more than officials in other agencies to perceive their responsibilities in hierarchical terms, that is, they say that they report to their immediate superior who, in turn, reports to his . . . , and on up the organizational chart of the department. Such perceptions might cloud somewhat their sense of responsibility to their minister. Many respondents in the PMO, the PCO, and the FPRO, however, cite some aspect of their relation to the Prime Minister as part of their authority; this phenomenon is understandable considering that the authority of these offices largely originates with the Prime Minister. Similarly, the relatively large proportion of TBS officials who cite their responsibilities towards "a cabinet committee" no doubt reflects its secretariat relation to the Treasury Board which is a cabinet committee.

Because the TBS has difficulties maintaining the internal accountability of the public service (Chapter 2), we might expect its officials to be the least satisfied with their agency's performance and the most likely to call for changes. This expectation is borne out in their responses. They are also much more dissatisfied than other officials with organizational structure, both in their agency and in government as a whole. We have already seen in Chapter 2 that the government has split the TBS into two agencies. Our findings — which suggest that before this move TBS officials registered concern about malaise in their agency — thus shed new light on why the government chose ultimately to introduce such a sweeping structural change.

In sum, our respondents' views of their roles and the functions of their agencies suggest four profiles of central agencies as seen through the eyes of their officials. Although the PMO still attempts a policy role, it has mainly moved towards switchboard functions. PCO and FPRO officials, while deeply committed to policy development, seem as well to favour functions which keep government moving. For example, they often say their work is keeping the machinery going; they relate their roles to their agencies' responsibilities to provide independent analysis and to facilitate the business of government. Thus, it is not surprising that they frequently describe their roles and functions in terms of the Prime Minister, that is, the person vested with ultimate conventional authority for finding the common ground on issues and expediting decisions. Finance officials, right down to their relative disinclination to describe their roles in terms of the authority of political leaders, appear as analysts who use their expertise to develop policy. Finally, TBS officials show greater concern for administrative policy than do officials in other agencies. In addition, their relative dissatisfaction with the status quo indicates the degree to which they have found their agency's mission difficult to fulfil. The reader should keep these profiles in mind as we examine in detail what these officials' responses reveal about the functioning of these departments.

What Central Agencies Actually Do

THE PRIME MINISTER'S OFFICE

Reading the conventional literature on central agencies, one might suppose that the PMO sits at the apex of power. In the late 1960s and early 1970s, indeed, many observers saw in the PMO the spectre of a partisan cadre with the capacity to out-manoeuvre Parliament and the Cabinet at will. They suggested, at least, that Pierre Elliott Trudeau's strengthening of the PMO increased the ability of the Prime Minister to dominate the policy-making process.[1]

This view is dispelled when one gets to see what actually goes on in offices of the PMO, currently housed in the Langevin Building — right across Wellington Street from the Parliament buildings. In mid-December 1976, we saw secretaries, even in executive offices, frantically typing envelopes for the Prime Minister's Christmas cards. Some high-ranking officials interrupted our interviews to answer requests by Senators or MPs for cards for constituents who absolutely had to have one.

One anecdote points out how much time the PMO spends making decisions which affect the policy process only very peripherally, if at all. During one interview, a senior official received word that TV crews had arrived at the Langevin Building, and were ready to film the Prime Minister's New Year's Day talk to the nation, even though the PMO had changed the date for the filming. The PMO does amend the Prime Minister's schedule several times a week, and the TV crews were following schedule five while the Prime Minister was working from schedule six.

The official whom we were interviewing sent a message to the Prime Minister, then in Cabinet, that the TV crews were waiting. The messenger brought back a note which the Prime Minister had scribbled, asking the official to contact a superior to see if the speech was in good shape. After the most cursory of readings, the superior chimed back through the intercom, "It's great, go ahead!"

With that settled, the official contacted a colleague and asked, "What suit does the Prime Minister have on today?" The other official answered, "The one he had on yesterday." "Oh," said our respondent, "that should be okay for TV." "Yeah," said the colleague, "it's good." Moments later the colleague buzzed in on the intercom about some other matter and our respondent registered second thoughts about the PM's attire. "Is his tie okay?" he asked. The colleague replied, "Not really, at least not for TV . . . and his shirt is no good either." "Well, we'll have to change them then," our respondent decided out loud. He pushed another button and asked an aide to "intercept the PM when he comes out of Cabinet and tell him to change his shirt and tie when he goes home to lunch." Finally, the official sat back, satisfied. The TV "snafu" had taken forty-five minutes to rectify.

After witnessing this concern for practical, even minute, detail, we began to agree when our PMO respondents claimed they were far from the nerve centre of policy making. Most said their agency is primarily a "switchboard" for the Prime Minister in his capacity as leader of the government party. The switchboard accomplishes a number of things. First, it organizes the Prime Minister's extremely scarce time. In the words of one official: "We are the people who try to squeeze forty-eight hours out of the PM's average day; we try to make life easier for him personally." Second, the PMO develops the Prime Minister's public image for the media. Third, it monitors the political situation in various regions of the country to enable the Prime Minister to build and hold a faithful following along with the viable party organization necessary for victory in the next election. Fourth, it digests for the Prime Minister an immense volume of letters, telegrams, and phone calls from the general public, special interests, and politicians. The switchboard must, in addition, prepare an appropriate response to all correspondence. Fifth, it must determine which letters, visits, telegrams, and phone calls are top priority and will receive the PM's personal attention. Sixth, it recommends appointees to such public offices as seats in the Senate. Finally, when time allows, it advises the Prime Minister on when he should intervene in disputes between departments and, occasionally, it actively promotes specific policy proposals. These last two roles are the only ones by which the PMO switchboard engages in policy making.

How well the PMO performs these various functions changes from role to role. And it depends in good part on who the Prime Minister's principal secretary is. At present Jim Coutts holds this post. He is a master political strategist who, with his close friend, Senator Keith Davey, helped deliver Trudeau's 1974 election victory. As PMO manager he performs from time to time all eight functions of the PMO, yet demonstrates little ambivalence about the function which he clearly prefers: to interpret how political events and policies affect the government's public image and, especially as the 1974 mandate runs out, to assure that the party faithful remain in the fold and girded for the next federal election. Coutts's style differs sharply from that of previous principal secretaries. Marc Lalonde, who was principal secretary from 1968 to 1972, was the political administrator par excellence, who worked behind the scenes to assure that the chief executive kept the maximum possible control over the bureaucracy and the politicians, without having formally to invoke his prime-ministerial authority. Lalonde channelled the major portion of his energy towards resolving brush-fire disputes in government without involving the Prime Minister directly. Lalonde's successor, Martin O'Connell, failed at this role mainly because he lacked a sufficiently forceful yet discreet personality. Jack Austin, now a Senator, stepped into the principal-secretary position in 1974. He attempted to equal Lalonde's over-all influence among bureaucrats and politicians. His direction of the elaborate and ambitious priorities-and-planning exercise after the 1974 election illustrates this bent. The exercise mostly failed, as we will see when we look at the role of Michael Kirby, assistant principal secretary for Policy Planning during Austin's tenure.

Jim Coutts embodies a new realism about the role of the principal secretary. Few people can make such an easy transition to the role of the top political administrator as Marc Lalonde in

1968. Coutts knows that he can at least serve effectively as a political secretary to the Prime Minister. With great confidence, Coutts channels his energies towards maintaining, even strengthening, the PM's standing in the public eye. Several PMO officials support Coutts's aim, since most of them concede the policy function to PCO. As one respondent noted:

Given the present Prime Minister, Coutts has chosen correctly by stressing the switchboard role. Five years ago the role would have been inadequate. But now, with the strength of the Prime Minister's relationship with PCO, particularly through his friendship with Michael Pitfield, he gets what he wants from PCO officials. Trudeau had to learn how to run a country from scratch. Lalonde helped him out and he was necessary at the time. Lalonde, O'Connell, and Austin were all interested in policy rather than politics. Coutts adds a new dimension. For example, Jack Austin went along with the tax on gas in 1975 without really thinking through the political consequences. Coutts would have sensed that the tax on gas would be a political error.

Yet, chances are that the principal-secretary post will revert eventually to a policy-oriented individual. The PMO seems to vacillate between mapping out policy goals after elections and gearing up the political machinery when elections are in the offing. For instance, the fact that O'Connell served Trudeau during a minority government which continually faced the possibility of an opposition-precipitated election perhaps explains why, despite his abilities, he never succeeded as a policy-oriented principal secretary. At this writing, the PMO is stressing re-election of the Prime Minister. After the election of 1979, Trudeau, if he wins, might again appoint a policy-oriented principal secretary to direct planning for his government's new mandate.

Some officials in the PMO do, however, devote part of their time to policy analysis. The two most important policy-oriented posts within the PMO were, until recently, senior advisor for International Relations and assistant principal secretary for Plans and Policy. Ivan Head held the former position from 1970 to 1978, when he resigned to become president of the International

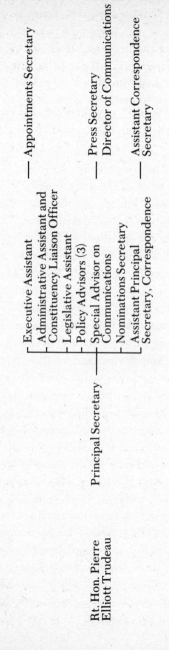

FIGURE 3.1
THE PRIME MINISTER'S OFFICE (PMO), JUNE 1978

Minister

Rt. Hon. Pierre Elliott Trudeau — Principal Secretary

— Executive Assistant
  Administrative Assistant and
  Constituency Liaison Officer
  Legislative Assistant
  Policy Advisors (3)
— Special Advisor on
  Communications
  Nominations Secretary
  Assistant Principal
  Secretary, Correspondence

— Appointments Secretary

— Press Secretary
  Director of Communications

— Assistant Correspondence
  Secretary

Development Research Council. Head, who previously taught at the University of Alberta law school, was to Trudeau what Henry Kissinger was to U.S. President Richard Nixon during his first term. By astutely avoiding publicity and maintaining at least the appearance of detached service to the PM, however, Head escaped the notoriety that Kissinger drew. Trudeau stresses foreign affairs and, as far as is humanly possible, likes to maintain a hands-on relation to the Department of External Affairs. Head monitored the policies of External Affairs for the Prime Minister and acted as troubleshooter. Head's authority derived from Trudeau's strong interest in foreign affairs and an implicit trust in his advisor. It remains to be seen whether Trudeau will choose a successor for Head's former position in the PMO. For the time being, apart from informal consultation with Head, Trudeau will have to rely on the PCO for independent advice on foreign policy.

The other main policy-oriented post in the PMO was that of assistant principal secretary for Plans and Policy. This post was created after the 1974 election victory. Michael Kirby, previously Assistant Dean of Arts and Sciences at Dalhousie University, filled the new position. At that time Trudeau initiated a program for the development of priorities and plans. Kirby and his staff gave the Prime Minister organized and comprehensive advice on major policy issues, based on what the government wanted to achieve during its mandate. The unit worked along with the PCO to help the Prime Minister and the Cabinet establish their four-year objectives and to monitor progress in implementation. The unit gave the Prime Minister political briefing notes to augment, rather than to duplicate, the PCO's analytic briefs. Here we find a bit of a paradox. Since the unit was committed to medium- and long-range policy development, it tended, good intentions notwithstanding, to foster and monitor policies in such a way that the political briefs did duplicate the PCO's analytic ones continually and systematically.

To promote medium- and long-range thinking, the PMO's Policy and Planning unit ensured that its officials kept a close watch on cabinet committees. Second, the unit organized with PCO the annual fall cabinet meeting at Meach Lake, when ministers have a rare opportunity to discuss for an entire day both medium- and long-term plans. Third, once a year, the unit arranged for PMO officials and their PCO counterparts to visit ministers individually and to discuss privately their major pre-occupations.

In 1974, when numerous governments in other advanced liberal democracies had lost their mandates, the Trudeau administration was elated by its overwhelming electoral victory. It was the time, believed the Cabinet, for the Liberal party to leave its mark on the decade. The moment was ripe for such innovative social policies as a guaranteed annual income, and for criminal-code legislation to abolish capital punishment, tighten gun controls, liberalize abortion laws, and legalize or decriminalize cannabis. Most urgent was the need to halt the simultaneous and rapid rise of inflation and unemployment. In January 1975, the ministers produced a general statement of objectives for their mandate, which touched on sixteen programs and involved thirty departments. They expected individual departments to respond to this statement by proposing new policies which would help the Cabinet to achieve its aims. But the departments did no such thing. In bureaucratic fashion, department officials sent mainly self-serving responses which, to quote one of our respondents, merely said, "This is how our existing programs and proposals fit your plan for the next four years." The Cabinet was inundated by memoranda, most of which were useless, in what became known as "the priorities exercise".

By August, public concern over the economic situation had reached the point of agitation. An independent poll taken by Senator Keith Davey confirmed that the public placed much of the blame for high inflation and unemployment squarely on Trudeau's shoulders. The Cabinet, however, remained sceptical of mandatory wage and price controls, particularly since the Minister of Finance, John N. Turner, and most of the officials in his department were just beginning to voice gloomy predictions of the effects of the voluntary program which they had pushed especially hard in the Spring. In the light of the Davey poll, the PMO's Plans and Policy unit made a concerted effort to try to convince Cabinet of the need for firm action. The unit's task became particularly urgent when the resignation of John Turner sparked speculation that he viewed the economic situation as hopeless. Gaining some important allies in the PCO, the unit helped win over Cabinet to the new Finance view that mandatory wage and price controls were essential. It also played a key role in assuring that the eventual Anti-Inflation Program, to be announced by the Prime Minister on October 13, was as fair to various sectors as possible and politically acceptable. While Plans and Policy won the battle, however, it had lost the war. Because it lost so much energy and time during the economic crisis, the unit had to abandon the priorities exercise. In addition, with Coutts now in control, the entire PMO prepared for the immense "switchboard" function that selling the controls to the public called for. By Spring 1976, Coutts had dismantled much of Kirby's unit (which was composed of only four officials) and Kirby was preparing to return to Halifax.

Brian Fleming succeeded Kirby in August 1976. A Halifax lawyer, in 1974 Fleming came within 3,000 votes of beating the Progressive Conservative leader, Robert Stanfield. Although he lacks the title "Assistant Principal Secretary", Fleming directs a group of three policy advisors who double as regional desk men; that is, they not only advise on policy but also shoulder responsibility for political organization in various sections of the country. The new unit keeps a relatively low profile with much less independence from other groups in the PMO than Kirby's staff enjoyed. As one official put it:

We are just a valve at the junction of the bureaucratic and the political. We add a little of the political ingredient when it appears that it has been overlooked. For instance, if I know that an official in PCO is working on a briefing note to the PM on an issue which I'm responsible for, I'll go to him and express the political point of view. I guess we are sort of a Distant Early Warning System for things that are going to cause trouble politically.

Although Fleming's people still cover cabinet-committee meetings, help organize Meach Lake meetings, and follow these up by later visiting individual ministers, they have eschewed anything akin to the priorities exercise of 1974–75. In other words, they function almost entirely as firefighters, concerned with more immediate problems. One PCO official put the shift in the Plans and Policy unit's approach particularly well:

PMO used to play a strong role in long-term planning because Kirby wanted to. Now we have to plead for the PMO guys to do something with us. They have become short-term tacticians. They're mainly concerned about the polls and the next election.

As we have already noted, however, this shift in emphasis might be transitory. PMO interest in medium- and long-term policy planning might re-emerge if the Liberals win another mandate in the next election.

The remaining PMO units relate only indirectly to the policy process. The Prime Minister's executive assistant and his appointments secretary organize his time and screen requests to see him or invitations for him to attend functions. His assistant principal secretary for correspondence manages the communications net which attempts to provide adequate responses to all letters, telegrams, and phone calls to the Prime Minister. Joyce Fairbairn, his legislative assistant, assures that he is adequately briefed in preparation for the question hour each day. Fairbairn, in addition, fulfils the role of PMO liaison in Parliament, at least to some MPs, in that she is the only PMO official who permanently occupies an office in the Centre Block of the Parliament buildings, rather than in the Langevin Building across the street; as a result she is accessible on a drop-in basis. The Prime Minister's administrative assistant, Mary Macdonald — a former aide to Lester B. Pearson — prepares the letters, memoranda, and documents that the Prime Minister must see, and, in "ask Mary . . . " fashion, frequently fields questions on PMO procedure. The sizeable Communications unit assumes all responsibilities which concern the media. Finally, a senior official, Marie Helen Fox, screens and processes nominees for political appointments.

Since approximately seventy people, including secretaries, perform these various functions, we can see that the PMO is a lean operation.

In addition to its difficulties with the policy sector, the PMO has failed in at least three important respects. First, the Correspondence division has at times lacked the personal touch which the public demands from the Prime Minister. Michel Rochon, formerly director of policy under Kirby, took over this unit in 1976 and upgraded its performance. Rochon did such a good job that Coutts entrusted the day-to-day management of the PMO to him from Spring to December 1978 when he left the PMO. Second, the Communications division severely declined in organization and morale after the 1974 elections. There were many reasons for this; as one official said to us, alluding to the Prime Minister's aloofness during this period, "certainly not the least of which was the personality of Mr. Trudeau". In Fall 1975, Jim Coutts coaxed Dick O'Hagan from his communications post with the Canadian Embassy in Washington and gave him carte blanche to straighten out Communications. Since then, the section has operated much more effectively, mainly because of O'Hagan's skill as a public-relations executive. Of course, Trudeau has helped as well by re-engaging himself in politics after the November 15, 1976, PQ victory in Quebec. Third, the PMO faces a considerable problem in that a disproportionate number of its senior officials have served for very long periods in the agency, many of them since 1968. As one official who has been in the PMO since the early days of the first Trudeau mandate noted:

We have lost the old adrenalin. Those in service functions are particularly long in the tooth. They have lost their energy and long for the good old days when Marc Lalonde was in charge. What we need now is more young, dedicated, and imaginative people with enough adaptability to shift from function to function when extra hands are needed.

The three problems with the PMO's performance of service functions seem to be symptomatic of the same malaise — the zeal of the old hands is gone. Long-term staff members tend to rely too heavily upon set routines. Thus, the PMO has lost much of its impact.

THE PRIVY COUNCIL OFFICE

Before our interviews, the authors viewed the PMO and the PCO as partners at the centre of policy making in the federal government. However, the peripheral, sometimes trivial, dramas of practical life at the PMO challenged our expectation.

Interviews in the PCO presented no such surprises. We observed frequent conversations about substantive issues. Let us construct one such exchange that "Mr. Jones", a typical PCO official, might have had with "Mr. Smith", an assistant deputy minister in a programmatic department:

Buzz

MR. JONES: Yes.

SECRETARY: Mr. Jones, Mr. Smith is on the phone and he says it's important.

MR. JONES: Okay, Lillian. Excuse me, Professor Campbell. *(Mr. Jones, picks up receiver.)* Yes Bill, what is it?
(pause)

MR. JONES: Okay. Well, the cabinet committee was fairly happy with the presentation this morning. The view is that you still must settle the difficulty with the Treasury Board. In principle, however, they support what you are trying to do in the proposal.
(pause)

MR. JONES: They were particularly happy that our meetings over the last few weeks ironed out the difficulties with Finance.
(pause)

MR. JONES: No, I don't think they will ask to have you come over again, they simply want to assure that you and the TBS boys see eye to eye on this.
(pause)

MR. JONES: That way of dealing with it sounds close to what the Ministers had in mind. Have you checked it out with

Lefebvre at TBS?
(pause)

MR. JONES: I'd like to see some sort of confirmation of that. Perhaps you could make sure that they get it to me.
(pause)

MR. JONES: If everything is in order next week then I could see about getting it on the cabinet agenda early next month.
(pause)

MR. JONES: I'll write that in my brief to the PM, but they're going to be booked solid for the next few weeks.
(pause)

MR. JONES: Okay, Bill. (Mr. Jones hangs up.)

   This script sums up the role that PCO officials play in the policy process. Mr. Jones, as an assistant secretary to the Cabinet, is in charge of a cabinet-committee secretariat. The caller, Mr. Smith, is concerned about the progress of a proposal sponsored by his department. He headed a briefing team which had made a presentation that morning to Jones's committee. The department had already worked several months in an interdepartmental committee before going to the Cabinet. The proposal was sent to Jones's committee where the Finance department attacked it. Further interdepartmental meetings were held to resolve the difficulties. At the time of our conversation, the proposal had just cleared the cabinet committee, with the rider that further problems concerning the Treasury Board would be worked out before the proposal went to the entire Cabinet.

   Assuming that the department has played the game properly, the caller, Mr. Smith, would have brought the PCO official, Mr. Jones, into the process at a very early stage, even before a proposal was drafted. In fact, Mr. Smith went almost a year ago to Mr. Jones with a preliminary document and discussed plans for an interdepartmental study of the problem. Mr. Jones assigned a member of his secretariat staff to cover these discussions and to give guidance along the way. When the department felt that it had touched bases with all other departments it submitted a formal proposal to the Cabinet, which was first reviewed by Mr.

Jones. Mr. Jones decided that the proposal was ready for his committee only after an additional interdepartmental meeting addressed some questions which he suggested the committee might raise. Upon deciding that the proposal was ready, he arranged for it to appear on the committee's agenda. In this case, he received a request for committee time from a department which still had some serious reservations. The issue, thus, came up in committee more than once. All the while, Mr. Jones watched very carefully to assure that the contesting parties were making real progress. Throughout, he conveyed a sense of the ministers' deliberations to interested parties, and he checked and re-checked that arrangements that the sponsoring department claimed it had made had actually been agreed to by the contesting parties.

When a proposal has cleared the cabinet committee, the official responsible must find time for it in the entire cabinet agenda and brief the Prime Minister, either by memorandum or in person, about its content. If the department has worked closely with the official and responded fully to the committee's objections, the official has probably taken a very custodial approach to the proposal. He is making sure that it receives as full and as fair a treatment as possible. It is his job, after all, to assure that proposals which the Cabinet sees are in top form, that is, that Cabinet's time is not wasted. If the department had not co-operated, the official might have become indifferent, even antagonistic towards the measure. Such an attitude could kill a proposal, particularly if, despite its merits, some departments strongly criticize it. One official gave us a particularly good idea of his role:

If the process goes well, my input is minimal. I simply have to assure that meetings and briefs are properly arranged, that accurate minutes of the cabinet-committee proceedings are kept and that the sense of what happened is adequately conveyed. I also have responsibilities for making sure that cabinet decisions are actually followed. Many times, however, the co-ordination between departments is inadequate or the department decides to shoot the gap without first sounding me out to

see where the committee is on an issue. It really is up to the department. If they are up front with everyone then I simply become a
combination referee-traffic cop. If, however, they play their hand close
to their vest, my role will become somewhat more active. I will have to
decide whether I should join in some effort to pull the proposal out of
the fire or become involved with those who are trying to head it off at
the pass. My decision will be based on my view of what will sell in the
cabinet committee and, ultimately, the entire Cabinet, and, therefore,
is worth spending time on.

Depending upon the nature of a proposal to Cabinet and the
department(s) sponsoring it, PCO officials might simply perform
routine administrative chores related to the Cabinet review, or
serve more significantly as facilitators or gatekeepers.

Michael Pitfield, who holds the title Clerk of the Privy Council
and Secretary to the Cabinet, thus fills the most prestigious and
important bureaucratic post in Canada — head of the Privy
Council Office. Pitfield's interest in a government career began
early. In 1959, almost immediately after graduating from McGill
with a law degree, he went to work for government as administrative assistant to Progressive Conservative Minister of Justice
Davie Fulton. When he joined the Privy Council Office in 1965,
Pitfield already knew Trudeau, who became an MP in 1965 and
whose meteoric rise to the prime ministership had already
begun.

Both men are from Montreal and belonged to its upper class.
Trudeau, while editor of the pro-federalist journal *Cité Libre*,
had, in 1964, written a tract signed as well by Marc Lalonde and
other like-minded Francophone Quebecers. It was a manifesto
which advocated a new rationalist-functionalist view of government in Canada, the principal features of which were what the
authors believed to be a pragmatic rather than emotional approach to political problems, rejection of nationalism, and a call
for a more orderly pursuit of social and economic objectives. The
manifesto's pragmatism would have circumscribed considerably
the type of nationalism which was emerging in Quebec during
the Quiet Revolution of the early sixties. Soon after publication

of the manifesto in *Cité Libre,* an English translation appeared in the *Montreal Star* which left people wondering who the Anglophone among the Francophones was. Michael Pitfield, in fact, had translated the document.

So Pierre Elliott Trudeau and Michael Pitfield "go way back". Trudeau knew Pitfield before he gained the prime ministership. Pitfield's own career, however, was well under way before Trudeau's election. By 1968, Pitfield was already an assistant secretary to the Cabinet. Considering that he was only twenty-nine when he got this position, subsequent promotions up to and including his appointment as secretary and clerk did not come with exceptional speed. Pitfield even left the PCO for almost two years to serve as deputy minister in the Department of Consumer and Corporate Affairs.

We can see, then, that there are important reasons why Trudeau has placed so much trust in Michael Pitfield. For one, Pitfield is a dedicated federalist with ties to the *Cité Libre* manifesto. He has also demonstrated immense organizational skills. In many respects, then, he fills the top political-administrator post left open when Marc Lalonde — also a personal friend of Trudeau's — left the PMO, but he offers the Prime Minister something not even Lalonde did; that is, he came up through the ranks in the federal bureaucracy and knows the ropes in Ottawa as well as anyone.

What exactly does Michael Pitfield do? Above all, he is in constant contact with the Prime Minister. Each morning at 9:30, Pitfield and de Montigny Marchand, his deputy secretary (Operations), Jim Coutts, and Dick O'Hagan meet with the Prime Minister to discuss matters which call for the PM's personal and immediate attention. In other daily settings as well, Pitfield serves as the Prime Minister's touchstone for conducting the affairs of government. Thus, Pitfield performs the same roles as his senior officials, only writ large. He controls the agenda of Cabinet, assuring that it runs as smoothly as possible. He monitors closely the progress of policy proposals through the Cabinet and its committees, intervening from time to time to prod recalcitrants, reconcile antagonists, and pave the way for urgent matters. This task alone involves countless hours of high-level interdepartmental meetings with fellow deputy ministers in committees such as DM-5 which maps out over-all governmental strategy, especially in regard to the state of the economy. He regularly attends meetings of the Priorities and Planning cabinet committee as well as of the entire Cabinet. Pitfield also serves as the final briefer. Not only does he frequently advise the Prime Minister on all important matters, but, from time to time, he freely gives his opinion to members of the Cabinet. In addition to these many functions, Pitfield shoulders ultimate responsibility for advising the Prime Minister on security, intelligence, and emergency planning, the state of the economy, the machinery of government, and policies affecting senior personnel; and he must assure that orders-in-council and legislation are being adequately processed.

Because the PCO head performs so many and such special functions, we can see why Trudeau called upon a political-administrator figure like Pitfield to fill the position; we can see, moreover, why he currently does not select someone in the PMO to monitor the policy process as Marc Lalonde did. We have already noted that PMO officials have conceded the policy role to the PCO, especially since Pitfield has in large part structured the PCO to provide advice to the Prime Minister. Several officials in the PCO pointed out the degree to which this current pre-eminence of the PCO in providing policy advice depends upon the close personal ties between the Prime Minister and Pitfield. Yet Pitfield's own strong and innate "political" orientation is indisputably a key factor. One official contrasted him with Gordon Robertson, the current dean of the Ottawa mandarins who headed the PCO from 1963 to 1975:

Pitfield is ambivalent about the dichotomy between politics and bureaucracy. Certainly, he is less cut and dried than Robertson who stayed out of political matters. Pitfield tends to get involved. If things get screwed up politically, he will say "damn, we should have avoided that!"

The PCO's staff and organization give it a much greater

FIGURE 3.2
THE PRIVY COUNCIL OFFICE (PCO), JUNE 1978

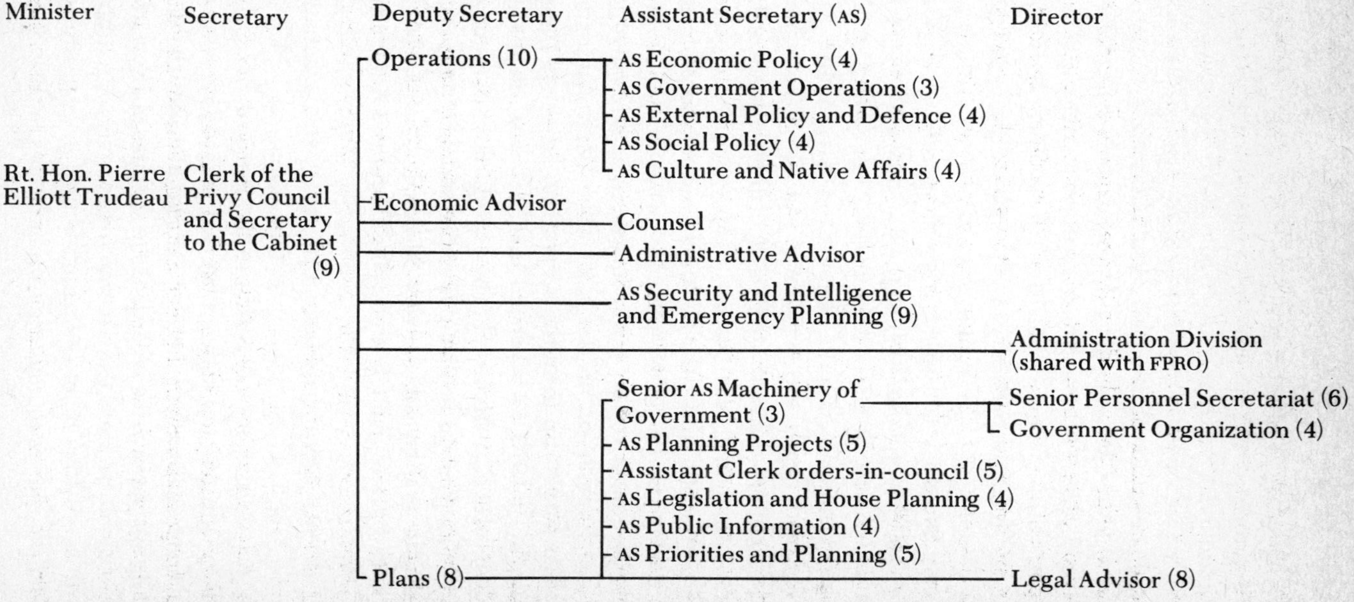

Minister	Secretary	Deputy Secretary	Assistant Secretary (AS)	Director
Rt. Hon. Pierre Elliott Trudeau	Clerk of the Privy Council and Secretary to the Cabinet (9)	Operations (10)	AS Economic Policy (4)	
			AS Government Operations (3)	
			AS External Policy and Defence (4)	
			AS Social Policy (4)	
			AS Culture and Native Affairs (4)	
		Economic Advisor	Counsel	
			Administrative Advisor	
			AS Security and Intelligence and Emergency Planning (9)	
				Administration Division (shared with FPRO)
			Senior AS Machinery of Government (3)	Senior Personnel Secretariat (6)
				Government Organization (4)
			AS Planning Projects (5)	
			Assistant Clerk orders-in-council (5)	
			AS Legislation and House Planning (4)	
			AS Public Information (4)	
		Plans (8)	AS Priorities and Planning (5)	
			Legal Advisor (8)	

(Numbers in parentheses denote number of professional staff members, including personal staff, reporting directly to unit head.)

analytic capability than the PMO has. Its total staff numbers over
350, roughly 80 of whom are professional-level personnel. Four
advisors report directly to Pitfield. First is the economic advisor.
Currently Ian Stewart, who played a key role in development
and implementation of the Anti-Inflation Program, the economic
advisor analyses for cabinet-committee secretariats the economic implications of departmental proposals. He also maintains
close ties with all departments in Ottawa concerned with economic problems, in particular with Finance. Stewart regularly
briefs Pitfield and the Prime Minister on the state of the
economy. Second is an assistant secretary for Security, Intelligence, and Emergency Planning. This assistant secretary processes and assesses reports from various intelligence-gathering
agencies, maintains liaison between the government and the
agencies, and heads the secretariat for ad hoc cabinet and
interdepartmental committees concerned with security and
emergency planning. The secretariat, for example, supported the
interdepartmental and cabinet committees responsible for security during the 1976 Olympics. In Spring 1978, John Starnes,
former director of the RCMP's security division, testified before
the Royal Commission on the RCMP (the "McDonald Commission") that a 1970 tip from the secretariat served as one of the
reasons why, in 1973, he approved an illegal break-in of the Parti
Québécois offices in Montreal. The secretariat had found that a
foreign country might be giving financial support to the PQ. Very
recently, the PCO has added two additional advisors who report
directly to Pitfield, namely the Counsel and the Administrative
Advisor.

Two deputy secretaries head PCO units which manage the
Cabinet's work. These units are Operations and Plans. The
deputy for Operations takes day-to-day care of the Cabinet's
agenda for Pitfield and makes sure that ministers receive sufficient documentation for meetings; he also oversees the work of
five assistant secretaries who direct the staffs of the Cabinet's
operations committees. These committees review program proposals to see if they meet the requirements of a specific policy
field such as the economy. Plans committees — Priorities and

Planning, Legislation and House Planning, Federal-Provincial Relations, and the Treasury Board — review proposals with reference to crucial aspects of the entire governmental strategy. For instance, Priorities and Planning sets goals for the government and evaluates proposals accordingly.

The five operations committees, each served by its own secretariat, are: Economic Policy, Government Operations, External Policy and Defence, Social Policy, and Culture and Native Affairs. The various committees shift their interests according to the trends of the time. Economic Policy works in the sector at present most critical for the government — managing the economy. It reviews all proposals which bear on the government's major economic efforts, such as the post-Anti-Inflation-Program period or revisions of the Bank Act. Government Operations reviews proposals from such fields as agriculture, transportation, northern development, nuclear energy, public works, government procurement of supplies and services, and national revenue. Government Operations thus serves as a catch-all for programs which do not relate directly to the mandates of the other cabinet operations committees. External Policy and Defence handles all questions which normally fall into the external- and defence-policy fields — such as, for example, the decision to purchase the Lockheed maritime patrol aircraft. It also handles international economic questions. Social Policy services the cabinet committee responsible for fields such as justice, social security, labour, and health. Culture and Native Affairs emerged recently from a re-shuffling of operations-committee responsibilities with somewhat narrower terms of reference. The cultural field includes publishing, broadcasting, leisure, and sports. Native rights, of course, currently command considerable attention by virtue of the land claims which the government must settle over the next few years, particularly those required as part of northern pipeline construction. We will examine the cabinet-committee system more thoroughly in Chapter 6.

The deputy secretary for Plans supervises secretariats attached to two cabinet committees — Priorities and Planning, and Legislation and House Planning. He oversees as well six service units which handle orders-in-council, planning projects, machinery of government, senior-personnel policy, legal advice, and public information. The Prime Minister chairs the cabinet committee on Priorities and Planning. Thus, both the deputy secretary for Plans and the assistant secretary for the committee become heavily involved in the process whereby the Prime Minister and his senior cabinet colleagues evaluate programs according to priorities they have developed. We have discussed how difficult it is to get the Cabinet to establish priorities and to live by them. For instance, the ambitious 1974 effort foundered when departments dusted off their pet proposals instead of responding to the Cabinet's priorities. The difficulty of that priorities exercise, along with economic pressures, forced the government to abandon its four-year plan. Yet, as one officer in the PCO told us, Trudeau still firmly believes that the government must do all in its power to plan. The same officer quoted Trudeau's recent exhortation to a committee of deputy ministers: "We aren't here just to manage departments; we want to see change."

The deputy for Plans and the assistant to the Priorities and Planning committee attempt to predict problems which might arise within the next two years and to encourage Cabinet to respond to them. Priorities and Planning is, thus, an executive committee for the Cabinet as it attempts to grapple with the projections. The committee also engages in more routine, year-long executive-committee duties; for example, it develops the expenditure guidelines for each fiscal year. It also evaluates each legislative proposal in light of over-all government objectives. Thus, the officials who make long-range projections find that their time is devoted frequently to helping Priorities and Planning, as the executive committee of the Cabinet, solve day-to-day problems. Some PCO officials, in fact, complained that the Plans division has become too involved in the day-to-day concerns of the Priorities and Planning committee.

The assistant secretary for Planning Projects is responsible for long-range planning, yet he is also called on to handle day-to-day problems. His section is supposed to prepare briefs for Priorities and Planning based on long-term analysis of public policy issues. Yet, the assistant secretary's group also resolves labour disputes for ad hoc cabinet committees, which are frequently formed, and takes on other such special assignments. For instance, it attempted to develop post-anti-inflation-program machinery for government consultation with corporate, labour, and consumer groups during 1976–77. Thus, even the section of the PCO specifically designed for long-range analysis finds that such projects must often take a back seat to firefighting.

Another cabinet committee, Legislation and House Planning, reviews bills before they are submitted to Parliament, and sets the schedule for and monitors their progress through Parliament according to the legislative goals of the government. The assistant secretary for this committee and his officials make sure that the original policy intentions of the Cabinet are met by the bill as drafted. The chairman of the committee, the president of the Privy Council, calls upon his own resources as government leader in the House of Commons to attend to the scheduling and political aspects of the passage of bills through Parliament.

An assistant clerk of the Privy Council serves the Cabinet in its capacity of approving orders-in-council, that is, formal instruments containing either appointments or regulations. This office, which really only performs the legal and clerical processing implied by Pitfield's title as Clerk of the Privy Council, reports to the assistant secretary for Legislation and House Planning.

Four offices which come under the aegis of the deputy for Plans perform important service functions within the PCO. First is a secretariat under the direction of the assistant secretary to the Cabinet (public information) which monitors public access to government information. Second is a machinery-of-government office. Headed by a senior assistant secretary, it serves as the PCO's "department of political science". The office advises the

Prime Minister and Cabinet on the structure and functioning of Cabinet, the reorganization of departments, Crown corporations, and agencies. The office also maintains liaison with Government House, the Governor General's office, on such matters as the honours and awards system, and royal visits.

Also under the senior assistant secretary (Machinery of Government) is the Senior Personnel Secretariat. Headed by a director, it has led a somewhat double existence. Originally established under Gordon Robertson to help him select nominees for senior civil-service appointments, the office became part of the Federal-Provincial Relations Office when Robertson was appointed FPRO secretary. At the time, senior public servants feared that Michael Pitfield, because of his relative youth and close ties to the Prime Minister, might apply the merit and seniority criteria less evenhandedly than Robertson had. Thus, the director for Senior Personnel still reports to Robertson regarding recommendations for individual appointments. But, since senior-personnel management is a matter of cabinet policy, the office now works for Pitfield. Thus we see that the Senior Personnel Secretariat has returned to the PCO.

The final secretariat attached to the Plans division is the Office of the Legal Advisor. This office provides routine advice to the PCO, especially the orders-in-council unit, Legislation and House Planning, and Machinery of Government. The office, whose officials all belong to the Department of Justice, rarely involves itself in the daily operations of the PCO. Indeed, it is located in a building several blocks down Wellington Street from the Langevin Building (which houses most of the PCO). As we noted above, Michael Pitfield has acquired the full-time services of a special legal counsel who directly handles the PCO's most pressing and critical legal problems.

In sum, the PCO serves the Prime Minister and the Cabinet in two ways. First, it assures that the decision-making process operates as smoothly as possible. Second, it assures that this process promotes the legislative program which the government has adopted. The PCO fulfils its purpose when it succeeds in integrating seemingly conflicting departmental objectives and programs. To point out what role the PCO should play, one officer told us how it once failed:

If we undermanage the decision process we wind up with an issue like the decision to buy the Lockheed surveillance aircraft where integration simply did not take place. You have, in other words, a lot of shilly-shallying where the right hand doesn't know what the left hand is doing and the government begins contradicting itself every time a minister from one of the disputing departments appears before the TV cameras. That's not the way to proceed. Rather, you enshrine within the Cabinet the principle, in this case Canadian sovereignty, and accept the fact that this is going to cost a lot of money. Then you work on the details, after consensus has developed about the principle and the expense.

Most officers realize, however, that they cannot simply enshrine a principle and expect other departments to co-operate. This is where the PCO's lobbying becomes vital. One officer describes its role as "keeping the adrenalin flowing":

Every so often you find that for various reasons — most of them good — a system such as ours is given to a lot of inertia — both natural and cultivated. A central agency such as ours is meant to be constantly at war against inertia.

Sometimes, however, mere prodding does not work; PCO officers must occasionally pull rank. For example, they might inform the Prime Minister of an impasse and suggest a way of resolving it: "If a minister and his officials are dragging their feet on something that is dear to the PM's heart, we might try to get a letter out of him to the minister saying, in effect, 'get off your ass'."

The aggressive tone of these remarks notwithstanding, the PCO often fails to accomplish integration. We have already discussed how stretched the analytic capabilities of the PCO are. Officials frequently complained that they were underfunded and understaffed, especially in resources for in-depth analysis. These PCO officials, however, often expressed an overly zealous attitude to their work, which can be counterproductive. The point was made by an official in the TBS:

Once I had an extremely frustrating experience with PCO. I was
working on a project involving senior officials in various departments.
I had worked out the details with the deputy ministers of all the
departments and with [the ministry responsible for the issue our
respondent was interested in]. So I sent the proposal off to PCO for their
stamp of approval. It was rejected by some pipsqueak fresh out of
graduate school because there were "jurisdictional problems"; the
project encroached on the responsibility of [the same ministry]. Hell,
I had made it clear that [they] supported the proposal. I decided that it
wasn't worth the trouble trying to fight PCO. Those guys draw the wag-
ons in a circle to protect their own. But this thing really infuriated me.

Respondents in the other central agencies often gave similar
accounts of PCO second guessing, even meddling. Finance officials frequently complained that the PCO intervenes too often
in economic matters, especially development of the budget. TBS
officials told us that they are frequently frustrated in their
efforts to review new expenditure programs. PCO officials, said
TBS respondents, will help some new programs, which some key
ministers back very strongly but which are not likely to stand up
to TBS scrutiny, win approval in principle from the Cabinet.
Faced with such a fiat, TBS officials believe that they are unable
to exercise fully their responsibility for control over expenditures. Thus, the PCO on occasion reverses the meticulously
prepared proposals of experts in other departments, or helps
launch programs which they know to be vulnerable to criticism.
Overruling expert opinion is a ministerial prerogative. Insofar as
the PCO advises the Prime Minister and the Cabinet about what is
acceptable and what would be rejected, it partakes of the
headiest and, perhaps, most legitimate of political-administrative
functions. Officials in the PCO participate in and encourage the
search for accord among contesting parties. They have a sufficient substantive grasp of most questions to understand what are
the main obstacles to accord and, once an agreement is reached,
to communicate its substance to Prime Minister and Cabinet.
However, we believe that PCO officials should never duplicate
work done by other departments. If they operate as super-
analysts with insight superior to that of officials in other depart-

ments and agencies, they overstep both their capabilities and authority.

THE FEDERAL-PROVINCIAL RELATIONS OFFICE

Michael Pitfield replaced Gordon Robertson as Clerk of the Privy Council in 1975. Robertson, who had been clerk for over ten years, took a PCO secretariat for Federal-Provincial Relations and retained his status as a secretary to the Cabinet. The secretariat became the Federal-Provincial Relations Office (FPRO). Since then the FPRO has mushroomed into a full-sized central agency with over forty professional staff members. The senior professionals include: two deputy secretaries (the same number as the PCO); three assistant secretaries; a constitutional advisor; and four directors.

The November 15, 1976, Parti Québécois victory contributed indirectly to the tremendous expansion of the FPRO. Donald Thorson, formerly Deputy Minister of Justice, and one of the deputy secretaries, Paul Tellier, joined the office subsequently to work on the problem of Canadian unity. Thorson served until Summer 1978 (followed by Carter) as a special constitutional advisor with responsibility for the development of proposals for constitutional reform. Tellier heads a secretariat which works on problems of national unity, in particular those which arise between Ottawa and Quebec. Tellier directs as well the notorious counter-propaganda group which Trudeau established in response to separatist propaganda from the Quebec government.

The rest of the FPRO operates as a single division and assists the Cabinet on day-to-day matters which fall under the general description of "federalism". Since Gordon Robertson spends the vast majority of his time on senior appointments, national unity, and other special assignments from the Prime Minister, the other deputy secretary in FPRO supervises the division's work. Until 1977, FPRO served essentially as the secretariat for the Cabinet's Federal-Provincial Relations committee. At present, that committee has, in practice, merged with Priorities and Planning. The division's tasks usually involve more than simply management of the Cabinet's or Priorities and Planning's work related to

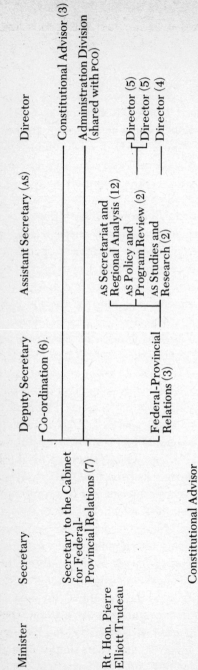

FIGURE 3.3
FEDERAL-PROVINCIAL RELATIONS OFFICE (FPRO), JUNE 1978

Minister	Secretary	Deputy Secretary	Assistant Secretary (AS)	Director

Rt. Hon. Pierre Elliott Trudeau

Secretary to the Cabinet for Federal-Provincial Relations (7)

Co-ordination (6)

Federal-Provincial Relations (3)

AS Secretariat and Regional Analysis (12)
AS Policy and Program Review (2)
AS Studies and Research (2)

Constitutional Advisor

Constitutional Advisor (3)
Administration Division (shared with PCO)
Director (5)
Director (5)
Director (4)

(Numbers in parentheses denote number of professional staff members, including personal staff, reporting directly to unit head.)

federal-provincial matters. It handles as well all official communication between the Prime Minister and provincial premiers, selects those issues before Cabinet which the secretariat wishes to review thoroughly, co-ordinates communication from several departments on federal-provincial matters, solicits opinions from provincial governments, briefs the Prime Minister on important issues, and provides a secretariat for federal-government delegates to federal-provincial conferences.

Three assistant secretaries report to the deputy secretary for Federal-Provincial Relations. The assistant secretary for Regional Analysis manages the technical support staff for the Priorities and Planning cabinet committee when it works on federal-provincial matters and provides analyses of attitudes in various provinces regarding major federal-provincial issues. The assistant secretary for Policy and Program Review directs the "operations" section of FPRO. His unit follows the "desk" form of organization — that is, officials assume responsibility for such sectors of government operations as social policy, transportation, urban affairs, resources, and economics and finance. The officials then review all proposals before Cabinet to see if they harmonize with provincial programs and federal-government policy. The officials' reviews can result in difficulties for a department which has failed to work closely with FPRO on a matter which concerns federal-provincial relations. The assistant secretary for Studies and Research runs FPRO's "think tank" which presents briefs on problematic aspects of federal-provincial relations in general; for example, this unit helped develop the government's proposals for constitutional reform.

THE DEPARTMENT OF FINANCE

Check your university calendar's listings for the Department of Economics. You will find listed such courses as Canadian Economic Development, Monetary Economics, International Trade and Institutions, Public Finance, and Regional Economics. If you obtained a Government of Canada Telephone Directory and looked under Department of Finance, you would discover strik-

ingly similar titles for departmental divisions: Tax Analysis and
Commodity Tax, Economic Development, Government Finance,
Economic Analysis, Structural and Long-Range Analysis, and
International Economic Relations. Thus, as we rode the elevator
to the top four floors of the twenty-seven-storey Place Bell
Canada, Ottawa's tallest building, we stood pensively. The
physical heights called to mind the immense power of the world
of finance. Judging from our first respondent's remarks about
what he would miss most if he left his department, we believe
that Ottawa bureaucrats frequently experience similar anxiety as
they ride to the top floors of Place Bell Canada:

We are the economics powerhouse in Ottawa. Do you think I stay here
because I like the pressure and the hours? No, it's because I work in the
best economics department in the country, have the type of resources
and staff with which I can really do economic analysis, and, above all,
have a chance to be in on decisions which have a tremendous impact on
the economy. Departments are constantly coming up here with ill-
conceived ideas which would either screw up the economy and/or
employ an economic instrument, like taxation, for a social or cultural
goal. I find it satisfying and exciting to see these policy proposals shot
down by our boys purely on the grounds of economics.

To appreciate fully the pervasive influence of Finance in
matters concerning economics, one must keep two things in
mind. First, the department serves the Minister of Finance in his
capacity as the member of the Cabinet responsible for managing
the economy. Thus, the department participates in development
of all policies which have an impact on the state of the economy.
Its officials begin to work with other departments at the earliest
stages of policy development. Their advice must take as comprehensive a shape as possible:

Our first requirement is to look at issues that the government is trying
to grapple with in as scientific a way as possible. We have to clarify the
nature of the problem in economic terms and relate it to the interface

with other issues. Since we are advising a minister, we have to be aware of the political implications as well.

The department also oversees several economic-policy programs which other departments must administer and/or adhere to. As one respondent put it:

The department is a Department of Economics with teeth. That is, it has responsibility for setting the fiscal framework within which the government of Canada must live, drafting the budget, developing tariff and tax policy, and managing a number of financial programs. In these sectors of activity, other departments have to follow our constraints and/or win our approval for whatever new arrangements they desire.

Thus, Finance both advises on policy and oversees legislation-based programs. For this reason it has two main modes of operation. As advisor, it stresses economic analyses of policy. Several Finance officials contrasted such review of policy proposals with that done by the Treasury Board Secretariat. They pointed out that the departments give Finance better information. Ideally, Finance attempts to analyse a department's policy before its proposals are submitted to Cabinet. Its advisory role is, then, a long-term one and is not limited to those specific economic instruments for which it has primary responsibility, such as the budget and taxes.

In performing legislation-based activities, Finance either maintains close surveillance of programs, such as those involving management of the public debt or government investments, or advises the minister on policy decisions which come under his aegis by virtue of his responsibility for shepherding the budget and related legislation through the Cabinet and Parliament. In the latter case, Finance must be careful to protect the integrity of what it considers to be economic instruments. For instance, although Revenue Canada administers tax policy, Finance oversees all uses of taxation as an economic instrument. The department's tactics vary according to its relative power in any particular instance. For example, by working through interdepartmental panels and Cabinet and its committees, Finance has been able to thwart all efforts by the Department of Health and Welfare to employ the income-tax structure as a means for providing a guaranteed annual income to all Canadians. However, with respect to the *Time–Reader's Digest* bill, Finance found itself in a weaker position. The bill, advocated by cultural nationalists, sought to abolish tax exemptions for Canadian advertisers in Canadian issues of certain U.S.-owned publications. *Time* and *Reader's Digest* stood to lose the most from the bill; Canadian magazines such as *Maclean's* believed they would gain advertising through the measure. Although Finance opposed the bill on the grounds that it constituted a cultural use of an economic instrument, the nationalists won the day in Cabinet. Eventually, Finance sponsored the bill, but only to protect its traditional jurisdiction for developing tax legislation. The department, however, left the onerous task of guiding the bill through Parliament to the Secretary of State and the Minister of Revenue. It was, therefore, much more difficult for this bill to win approval than most of the tax bills sponsored by Finance.

Thomas Shoyama, as deputy minister, heads the Department of Finance. Born in 1916, he joined the federal civil service in 1964, after serving for almost twenty years in the Saskatchewan public service. Shoyama thus has spent most of his bureaucratic career serving a socialist government, the CCF (later NDP) in Saskatchewan. As deputy minister of Finance he has been much more open to government intervention than his predecessors. His collegial style is well suited to Finance's advisory role *vis-à-vis* other departments.

Almost seven hundred people, more than half of whom are professionals, assist Shoyama. Six officials, two of whom head units attached to the deputy minister's office, report directly to him. An associate deputy minister manages the department's day-to-day operations, allowing Shoyama more time for interdepartmental and cabinet-committee work. An information officer serves essentially as public-relations director for the entire department. His role is particularly crucial in Finance because he and his sizeable staff draft and document the annual budget speech of the Minister of Finance, so important in the hierarchy of government policy statements. The remaining four officials who report to the deputy are assistant deputy ministers responsible for the four branches of the department.

The first branch is Tax Policy and Federal-Provincial Relations. Its assistant deputy minister advises the deputy minister on tax policy, on federal-provincial fiscal arrangements, and on the department's view of social policy. Two sub-divisions develop tax policy: Tax Analysis and Commodity Tax, and Tax Policy — Legislation. Each tax division houses economists, lawyers, and accountants. The economists attempt to gauge the economic impact of tax·policy, including its distributive and allocative effects. The lawyers and accountants advise on the structure of tax law, assuring that its provisions actually meet the requirements of government policy. Two other divisions, Federal-Provincial Relations, and, under it, Municipal Grants, have direct responsibility for administering fiscal arrangements between the federal government and provinces and municipalities. They also review proposals from other departments regarding these arrangements. Since fiscal arrangements with the provinces comprise a major portion of the current structure of Canadian federalism, the Federal-Provincial Relations division in particular plays a major advisory role both before and during federal-provincial conferences. Finally, a division reviews social and manpower policy. Because the BNA Act and its amendments assign most responsibility in these fields to the provinces, the federal government's involvement in these areas passes through an intricate web of federal-provincial arrangements whereby the federal government grants funds or tax powers in exchange for the provinces' initiating and maintaining desired programs. The Social Development and Manpower Policy division monitors these arrangements and the development of new ones.

The second branch is Economic Programs and Government Finance. It provides advisory and administrative services. Two divisions, Economic Development and Resource Programs, review proposals put forward by other departments in terms of

FIGURE 3.4
DEPARTMENT OF FINANCE, JUNE 1978

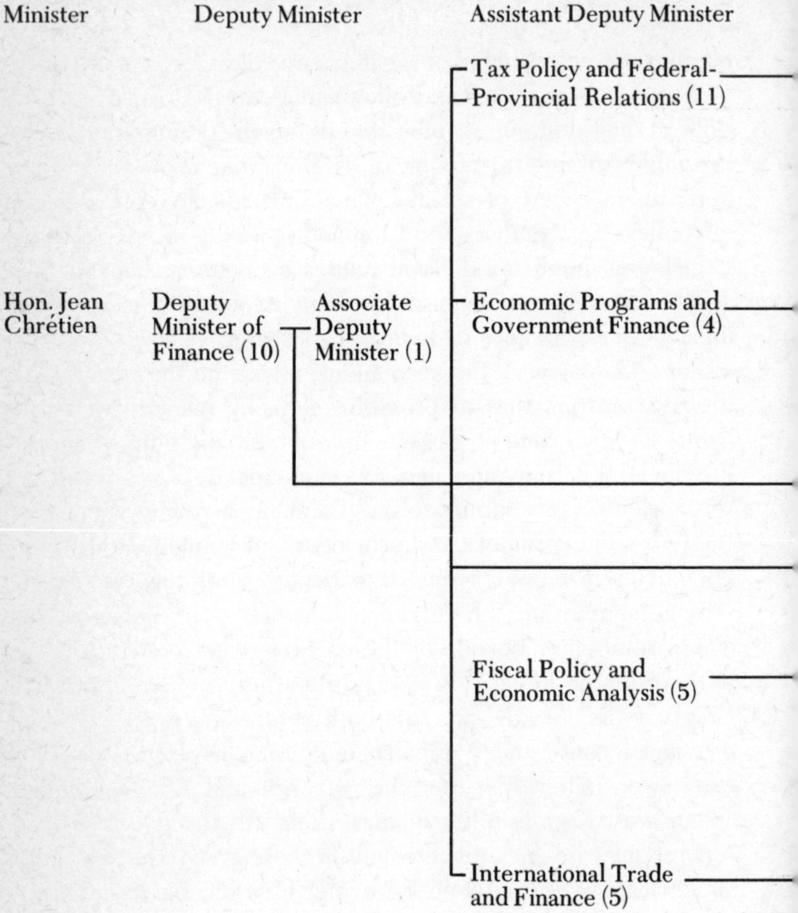

Minister	Deputy Minister	Assistant Deputy Minister

Hon. Jean Chrétien

Deputy Minister of Finance (10)

Associate Deputy Minister (1)

Tax Policy and Federal-Provincial Relations (11)

Economic Programs and Government Finance (4)

Fiscal Policy and Economic Analysis (5)

International Trade and Finance (5)

(Numbers in parentheses denote number of professional staff members, including personal staff, reporting directly to unit head; "–" indicates that staff is divided into sub-units reporting to chiefs, etc., e.g., 10–3 means 10 professionals in 3 sub-units.)

Director

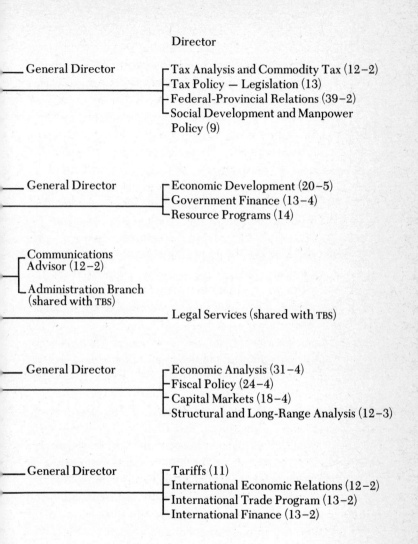

General Director
- Tax Analysis and Commodity Tax (12–2)
- Tax Policy — Legislation (13)
- Federal-Provincial Relations (39–2)
- Social Development and Manpower Policy (9)

General Director
- Economic Development (20–5)
- Government Finance (13–4)
- Resource Programs (14)

- Communications Advisor (12–2)
- Administration Branch (shared with TBS)

Legal Services (shared with TBS)

General Director
- Economic Analysis (31–4)
- Fiscal Policy (24–4)
- Capital Markets (18–4)
- Structural and Long-Range Analysis (12–3)

General Director
- Tariffs (11)
- International Economic Relations (12–2)
- International Trade Program (13–2)
- International Finance (13–2)

their probable effects on the economy, in order to advise the
Minister of Finance on the position that the department should
take in Cabinet and its committees. These divisions' contribution
is akin to what one might expect from an economic-planning
commission. Officials guide departments in such a way that
economic aspects of proposals are brought within the requirements of the economy, as Finance sees them. The administrative
division of this branch is Government Finance. It monitors
government investments in Crown corporations, the capital
budgets of the corporations, and their investment of funds in the
private sector.

The third branch is Fiscal Policy and Economic Analysis. It
fulfils the pre-eminent Finance department function — advising
the minister on management of the economy. As one official in
the branch said to us: "We provide the central macro-economic
intelligence services, for stabilization." While other officials
there might describe their roles differently, nevertheless this
branch, more than any other, helps the minister perform his
chief role by developing general economic, fiscal, and financial
policy for the government.

This third branch has four divisions. Economic Analysis keeps
abreast of economic conditions in the country, provides forecasts
of economic performance, and conducts regional analyses. The
Fiscal Policy division, a group of twenty-five professionals,
performs a number of key staff functions. It forecasts government revenues and expenditures. According to how the government might want to influence the economy, it drafts macro-
economic policy, in particular the annual fiscal framework. It
then directs other departments in the over-all spending level for
a fiscal year. Finally, an intergovernmental and regional unit in
the division assures that the fiscal framework considers the plans
of the provinces. A Capital Markets division comes the closest to
an executive unit within the branch. It manages the public debt
and borrowing. However, it also monitors capital flows within
the economy and the performance of financial institutions. Thus,
this division drafted most of the Bank Act's major revisions now

before Parliament. The final division, Structural and Long-Range Analysis, develops the long-term scenarios of the economic impact of other departments' policy proposals. The division's observations are based on economic projections as far as fifteen years into the future. The division tries to assure that various departments' long-term goals are within the realm of the possible, that is, what the country is likely to be able to afford.

The fourth branch is International Trade and Finance. Its four divisions handle Canadian economic and financial policies which relate to external affairs. The Tariffs division reviews the customs tariff structure and related policies in much the same way as the Tax branch reviews taxes; that is, Revenue Canada administers tariffs, and the Tariffs division in Finance develops the underlying policies and the legal framework for it. The International Economic Relations division advises the minister on the economic implications of international trade and investment policy. These policies concern such diverse issues as Canada's relations with GATT (General Agreement on Tariffs and Trade) and the federal government's Foreign Investment Review Board. The International Programs division concerns itself with development of trade. The division operates mainly through participation on the boards of trade-related agencies such as the Export Development Corporation and the Canadian International Development Agency (CIDA). It thus provides a link between the economic policy being pursued by Finance and the activities of several governmental agencies. Finally, the International Finance division monitors Canada's balance of payments, forecasts international financial developments, and advises on relations with international organizations with which the Minister of Finance is heavily involved, such as the International Monetary Fund and the Organization for Economic Co-operation and Development (OECD).

Thus, through its advisory and administrative roles, Finance is intimately involved in developing and implementing economy-related policies, and thus, in many respects, dominates the economics field. However, some officials have indicated to us that recently the PCO poses a threat to Finance's hegemony. One official said this threat developed in 1975 when Shoyama's predecessor, Simon Reisman, stepped down:

In the old days, Finance, through the national budget, acted almost unilaterally. Now, in the Trudeau era, PCO has tried to appropriate ultimate responsibility for the budget, which must, of course, be reviewed by the Economic Policy, and the Priorities and Planning committees of the Cabinet. We are getting to the point where the budget is going to have to be negotiated through the entire Cabinet. Much of this is PCO's doing.

As noted above, the installation of mandatory wage and price controls, which Reisman fought, illustrates how the PCO (along with the PMO) recently forced Finance's hand. However, such challenges to Finance are episodic at worst. In the normal course of the economic-policy process, Finance continues to dominate.

THE TREASURY BOARD SECRETARIAT

Although spawned by the Department of Finance in 1967, TBS has since grown considerably. The Treasury Board, of course, reviews departmental estimates as they relate to fiscal policy, and also monitors the implementation of administrative and personnel policy in the federal government. All of TBS used to report to one head, the secretary of the Treasury Board — a deputy-minister-level official. Recently several functions of the secretariat, i.e., those relating to financial administration and efficiency evaluation, have come under the direction of an additional deputy-minister-level official, the Comptroller General.

The deputy secretaries reporting to the secretary of the Treasury Board head four units, the Program, Administrative Policy, Personnel Policy, and Official Languages branches. The Program branch consists of some sixty professional staff who review the estimates of departments and agencies as regards the allocation of resources — both of dollars and person-years. Through the deputy secretary for the Program branch, its officials are also involved with drafting the fiscal framework each year. The branch is organized into eight divisions, three of which perform service functions for the others. The remaining five review divisions actually carry out the branch's mandate. Each review-division director manages a team of analysts who are responsible for the programs of specific departments or agencies. The divisions are Industry and Natural Resources; Defence, External, and Cultural Affairs; Social and Manpower Policy; Transportation, Communications, and Science; and General Government Services; in organization, they differ considerably from the PCO's cabinet-committee secretariats. The size of the TBS's Program branch permits much more specialized analysis of proposals than does that of the Operations division in the PCO.

Program branch is busiest from May to July when, as part of the budgetary cycle, it conducts its annual program review. During this review officials attempt to ferret out programs or units which are overly funded or staffed and/or which are simply not accomplishing what they were mandated to do. The officials do not usually recommend that a program or a unit be cut out. They often, however, suggest reductions in funds or person-years. If the program or unit appears to be badly managed, officials may suggest that an interdepartmental panel or the OCG's evaluation units re-examine it entirely. Two officials in the Program branch describe what their reviews aim for:

If we see an ineffective unit, we'll cut it out. (Pause.) Well, perhaps that's a bit too strong. Even if we wanted to, it would make no sense to just cut out a unit. A department can use slippage and attrition to make it appear that they have responded to us when actually they haven't. But, we can flag a problem.

You become sort of an investigative journalist here. It's a seat-of-the-pants operation. If I sense that something is wrong with a program, I'll get one of my analysts to look it over. He doesn't have much time, but he can at least find what the hell is going on. If he finds that it's in trouble, I will call for an evaluation. I did this recently with a

FIGURE 3.5
TREASURY BOARD SECRETARIAT (TBS), JUNE 1978

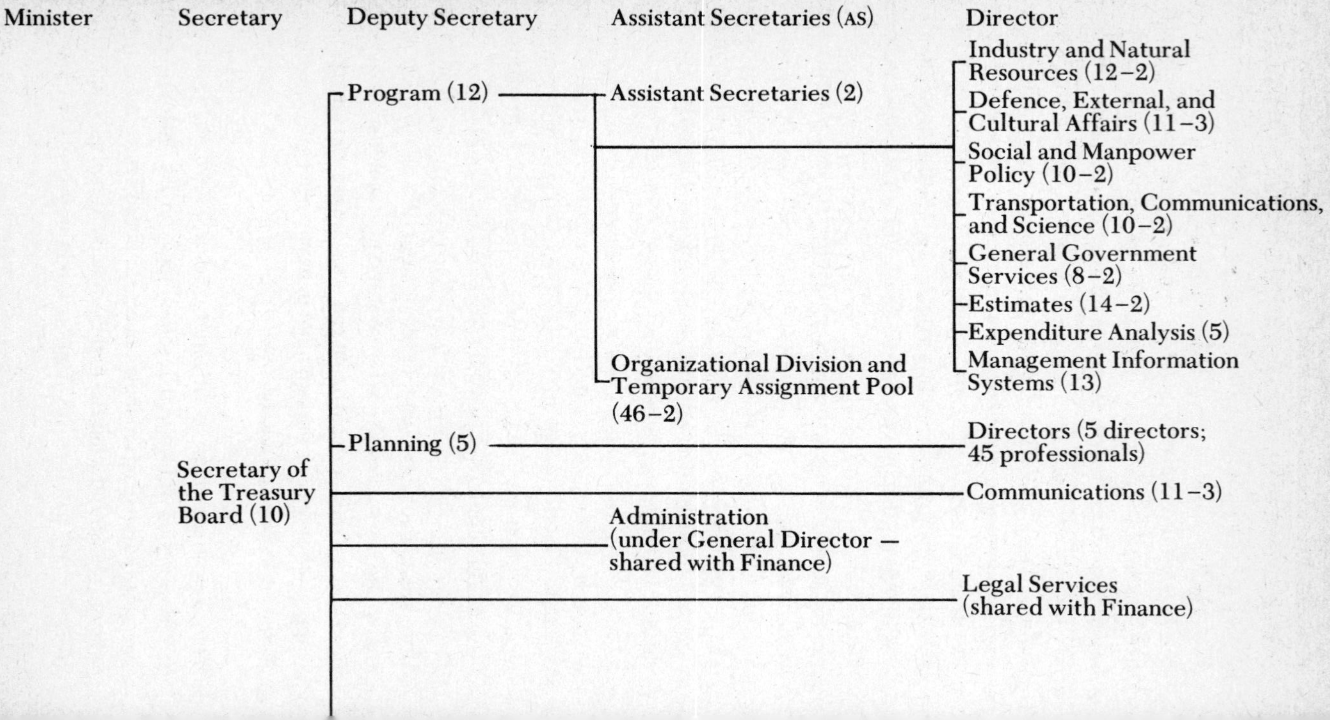

Minister	Secretary	Deputy Secretary	Assistant Secretaries (AS)	Director

Program (12) — **Assistant Secretaries (2)** — **Director**
- Industry and Natural Resources (12 – 2)
- Defence, External, and Cultural Affairs (11 – 3)
- Social and Manpower Policy (10 – 2)
- Transportation, Communications, and Science (10 – 2)
- General Government Services (8 – 2)
- Estimates (14 – 2)
- Expenditure Analysis (5)
- Management Information Systems (13)

Organizational Division and Temporary Assignment Pool (46 – 2)

Planning (5)
- Directors (5 directors; 45 professionals)
- Communications (11 – 3)

Secretary of the Treasury Board (10)

Administration (under General Director — shared with Finance)

Legal Services (shared with Finance)

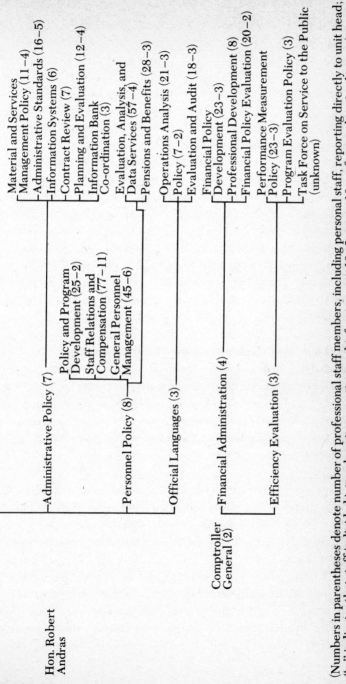

Hon. Robert Andras

Administrative Policy (7)
├─ Material and Services Management Policy (11-4)
├─ Administrative Standards (16-5)
├─ Information Systems (6)
├─ Contract Review (7)
├─ Planning and Evaluation (12-4)
├─ Information Bank Co-ordination (3)

Personnel Policy (8)
├─ Policy and Program Development (25-2)
├─ Staff Relations and Compensation (77-11)
├─ General Personnel Management (45-6)
│   ├─ Evaluation, Analysis, and Data Services (57-4)
│   └─ Pensions and Benefits (28-3)

Official Languages (3)
├─ Operations Analysis (21-3)
├─ Policy (7-2)
├─ Evaluation and Audit (18-3)

Comptroller General (2)

Financial Administration (4)
├─ Financial Policy Development (23-3)
├─ Professional Development (8)
├─ Financial Policy Evaluation (20-2)

Efficiency Evaluation (3)
├─ Performance Measurement Policy (23-3)
├─ Program Evaluation Policy (3)
├─ Task Force on Service to the Public (unknown)

(Numbers in parentheses denote number of professional staff members, including personal staff, reporting directly to unit head; "-" indicates that staff is divided into sub-units reporting to chiefs, etc., e.g., 10-3 means 10 professionals in 3 sub-units.)

department. I went over to their senior people and said, 'Look, you guys had better do something here.' They agreed and I got the Planning branch to help them design a study.

When not occupied with program evaluation, the branch reviews requests for expenditures which require Treasury Board approval. It also advises the Treasury Board regarding policy proposals before Cabinet which involve new expenditure pro- grams. Since Janury 1976, the TBS has had access to all cabinet documents which the president of the Treasury Board requests. This practice reduces the informational edge that the PCO has over the TBS by virtue of the fact that the former is the first to see cabinet documents. This new system complements an addi- tional innovation whereby a cabinet minister who sits on the Treasury Board is designated to represent the board's point of view in each committee. One official pointed out to us that such access gives him invaluable lead time in which to prepare challenges to poorly worked out proposals:

Recently a proposal came up that I knew I had to get stopped. We didn't have time to do an analysis of our own. We did have time, however, to raise enough questions that it was referred to an interdepartmental panel. Of course, they didn't do an objective study either. An interdepartmental conspiracy developed to kill the proposal. But, if I hadn't seen that thing coming down the pike when I did, it might have gotten through Cabinet.

Departments often try to get cabinet approval in principle for a program, pending a Treasury Board ruling. Thus, TBS officials' early access to cabinet documents considerably strengthens the Program branch's ability to control questionable allocations to new programs.

The Treasury Board must approve and monitor administrative policy in all departments and agencies. The Administrative Policy branch conducts the analytic and advisory work for this task. The branch monitors several aspects of administration. Officials in Program branch often call upon it to check into one or another aspect of a department's management. The branch's on-going work includes review of submissions for acquisition of goods and services; and setting and monitoring policies for acquisitions, employee and administrative services, and data-processing systems. As we interviewed in this branch, we were struck by how routine its work is. Unlike the aggressive Program branch, its motto, as expressed by half our respondents there, is *probity and prudence.* As one official put it:

Take a seemingly insignificant thing like travel. With the size of government there is a lot of travel. We have to ask whether travel is related to program objectives across the board. If it isn't, we are the ones to call for a stiffening of regulations. We have to assure as well that there is a communality of treatment for people who need to travel. In large part, this function concerns our developing standards that people know about and adhere to.

One respondent indicated that more than probity and prudence is involved in the review of administrative practices; that is, branch officials look for problems which might cause the government some embarrassment: "There has to be a central look at how departments are entering into contracts and making acquisitions. We are trying to avoid nasty headlines."

Whatever our officials' views of why they conduct their surveillance, a majority of them felt that much of their work is futile — mainly because they have insufficient means at their disposal whereby deputy ministers may be held accountable for the management of their own departments. We will return to this issue of accountability later in this section when we examine the recent reorganization of the TBS, including the creation of the Comptroller General's office.

The Treasury Board employs all personnel in the government. The TBS's Personnel Policy branch houses the six divisions responsible for personnel management in all government departments and agencies, and this branch advises the board on policy. Much like administrative policy, personnel policy is a concern which evolved from the board's central function. Personnel is most active when general expansion or tightening of the fiscal framework occurs, or when specific personnel policies pose serious difficulties. As a result, officials in this branch have much less exposure to the board than, certainly, officials in the Program branch. They attempt as much as possible to use conventional authority to bring departments into line when personnel difficulties arise. The board, after all, primarily concerns itself with control of expenditures. One division of the branch assists the deputy secretary in developing policy; one is concerned both with long-range issues and with proposals which are under review. Another division provides analytic services to the whole branch. The operations side of the branch consists of three divisions: Staff Relations and Compensation, General Personnel Management, and Pensions and Benefits. Staff Relations, unlike the others, has an ongoing and virtually direct relationship with the president of the Treasury Board. This is so because the division serves as the working unit which negotiates collective agreements with public-service unions. All such agreements must win approval from the Treasury Board.

Officials in Personnel Policy, like those in Administrative Policy, often registered concern about maintaining the accountability of departments. Officials here, however, stressed the need to bring the deputy minister's management of personnel in line with policy. Generally, however, Personnel Policy officials seem better equipped to cope with their recalcitrants. Two officers explained particularly well their approach:

Even when the Prime Minister makes exhortations he's not particularly effective with the deputy ministers. So, we simply continue to enunciate the policy and require the departments to make reports. They co-operate with what is reasonable. We can't fire deputy ministers, but we can get compliance through reasonableness.

There is a lot more authority attributed by others to our function than we have in fact. We have implicit functions which stem from the purse control, that is, what the Program branch is most involved in, which really are overblown by others. That's why we are called in so much by

other departments. We know how one gets authority and resources to
do something in the personnel field. It's a culture we have here at TBS,
and people in departments have to know about it to get things done.
This is where the trade-off comes. They listen to us because they know
that they have to work with us.

A branch can increase accountability if officials understand that
the TBS cannot bring deputy ministers to their knees, but *can* get
departmental officials to listen to reason.

Finally, under the secretary of the Treasury Board, the Official Languages branch assures that the Official Languages Act
and the subsequent parliamentary resolutions are being adequately implemented. It also develops revisions in bilingualism
programs so that the objectives of the Act might better be
fulfilled. The responsibility for official-languages policy in the
public service at one time resided with the Secretary of State
Department. But enforcement required more clout and the
Treasury Board, as the employer of all public servants, possessed
exactly the type of power needed. The Official Languages
branch, which came to the TBS as a single division, has grown to
three — namely, Policy, Evaluation and Audit, and Operations
Analysis.

Some genealogy is required as we shift our attention from the
branches which report to the secretary of the Treasury Board to
those which report to the Comptroller General. We can trace
the genealogy by looking in the Government of Canada Telephone Directory. In 1975, under Administrative Policy, "Financial Administration" was simply a division headed by a director.
In the following year, the directory indicated that the same
division was headed by an assistant secretary. The Fall directory
further revealed that Financial Administration had become a
branch of the TBS headed by a deputy secretary. Though a small
seed in 1975, the unit has grown with exceptional speed. Today
Financial Administration forms part of a new secretariat under
the Comptroller General, a deputy-minister-level official who
reports directly to the president of the Treasury Board. Financial
Administration, moreover, has drawn to itself other divisions of

the old TBS, namely those responsible for performance-measurement policy, program-evaluation policy, and a task force on
service to the public.

We noted above the tremendous concern among officials in
Administrative Policy and Personnel Policy that managers within
departments, in particular deputy ministers, simply are not being
held accountable for what they do. We also noted the scepticism
of Program-branch officials over whether expenditure or manpower cuts ordered by the Treasury Board are actually carried
out. The elevation of Financial Administration to a branch of the
TBS came from a realization throughout the central agency that
something had to be done to improve the monitoring of expenditures and administration. In 1976, the Auditor General — who
reports directly to Parliament — found that financial administration throughout government was in a sorry state indeed, particularly in such Crown corporations as Atomic Energy of Canada Limited. He urged that a Comptroller General be appointed
to improve financial administration. Michael Pitfield and the
then secretary of the Treasury Board, Gordon Osbaldeston,
balked at this proposal because they feared that it would
undercut the influence of deputy ministers. They gave in,
however, when evidence emerged of the extent to which Atomic
Energy of Canada Limited had misadministered funds. MPs and
the media reacted vociferously, and reorganization to make
Financial Administration the core unit of a new central agency
under the Comptroller General began early in 1977. The Performance Measurement Policy and Program Evaluation Policy units,
which used to be housed in the old Planning branch in the TBS,
followed Financial Management to the aegis of the Comptroller
General, as did the newly created task force on service to the
public.

These reorganizational moves raise an important question. Do
financial management, performance-measurement policy, and
program-evaluation policy really demand an agency all to themselves? Or could the government have tightened up the existing
TBS organization, instead of creating yet another central agency
in an era which has seen these offices proliferate almost as

quickly as programmatic departments? As we have seen, Finance begot the TBS in 1967 and the PCO begot the FPRO in 1975, and in 1978 the TBS gave birth to the OCG. What exactly is the division of responsibilities between the TBS and the OCG?

Financial Administration controls the way in which resources are spent rather than how they are allocated. Essentially, it is program-oriented accounting. The Treasury Board has responsibility for both aspects of control, but has traditionally stressed review of allocations. When we were conducting our interviews, Financial Administration was just starting up as a branch and the 1976 Auditor General's report had not come down. The branch was developing guidelines for financial administration, financial systems, and reporting of departmental accounts, to be used throughout the public service. It was disseminating these standards and evaluating their implementation. Our respondents, however, reported serious difficulties in their work. They lacked control over appointments to senior financial-administration positions within departments, which meant that a number of people without sufficient training in financial administration were being assigned to departmental posts. Moreover, they encountered much resistance to the guidelines they set up. One official's comments were reminiscent of what we had heard in other branches of the TBS. Coming from someone in the branch responsible for accountability for expenditures, his words alerted us to a serious malaise: "We have fine leadership and adequate staff now, and we have a strong mandate. Yet, there is a problem of accountability throughout government. It's hard getting people to operate in a way whereby there is accountability."

The Office of the Comptroller General also houses two former units of the old Planning branch — Performance Measurement and Program Evaluation. The Planning branch, conceived and developed by Douglas Hartle, lost the rationale for independent existence and was abolished in the Fall of 1978. At the same time, Harry Rogers, the first Comptroller General, announced that the OCG will split Program Evaluation into two streams: first, evaluation of "major programs", such as defence, agriculture, employment, or immigration, will be highly general and the findings will be reported periodically to Parliament; second, the results of more specific and rigorous evaluations employing "the best empirical methods to date" will be confidential, being restricted to the internal use of the Treasury Board and the Cabinet. The division of responsibilities between the TBS and the OCG is as follows: the TBS is responsible for personnel policy, including the use of official languages in the public service, and for the allocation of expenditure budgets, person-years, and other resources in the public service; the OCG is responsible for financial management, i.e., control of spending in the public service, and for evaluation of departmental programs and performance.

Conclusion

This chapter has given a profile — based on central agents' responses to questions about their roles and functions — of what central agencies do. We have found that central agencies differ considerably in their functions. We have found as well that their officials bring to their work role perceptions which differ greatly from agency to agency. Not surprisingly, there seems as well to be a correspondence between the role orientations of officials within a given agency and its apparent mandate. There is also an observable consistency between the satisfaction of officials with their agency's performance and what we have been able to discern about that agency's current ability to fulfil its mandate. The next chapter will look at the officials' socio-economic backgrounds to ascertain the degree to which the differences between agencies might correspond to factors in our respondents' backgrounds.

4 On the Road to the Mountain: Socio-economic Backgrounds

Many students of Canadian politics have read the works of John Porter, Robert Presthus, and Wallace Clement.[1] Their studies of the relationship between social stratification and power in Canada contain a wealth of information on the socio-economic composition of Canada's elite groups. Clement, for example, found that the business elite in Canada come mostly from families which are upper class, central Canadian, and British or French.[2] The vast majority of them, 85 per cent, received university education, many at "prestigious" institutions, such as McGill, Harvard, and the University of Toronto.

The socio-economic backgrounds of the elite can profoundly affect how they view their work. Porter, Presthus, and Clement all point out that many top politicians in Canada come from the business world and return to it once their service in government is complete. They note that this circulation of the business elite in and out of politics accounts for the marketplace orientation of many Canadian political leaders.

This chapter seeks to ascertain the nature of the socio-economic backgrounds of the individuals who served in the five central government agencies at the time of our interviews, in 1976. We find that central agents' socio-economic backgrounds resemble those of the country's general populace much more closely than do the backgrounds of bureaucratic elites in other advanced liberal democracies for which we have comparable data. Moreover, in the past decade Canada has seen a remarkable influx of bureaucrats representing segments of the populace traditionally excluded from senior positions in the public service.[3] Finally, the chapter contrasts the socio-economic backgrounds of senior officials in the five central agencies in an attempt to delineate any differences which might correspond to the roles of the agencies.

Central Agents: Some Typical Profiles

John Porter's study of social class and power in Canada attempts to typify the composition of various elite groups. Based on a cross-section of deputy ministers, associate and assistant DMs, and directors in the "most important departments", his 1953 data indicate that the senior civil service in Canada was just a cut below the business elite in terms of the conventional measures of socio-economic status.[4] The vast majority (79 per cent) graduated from university. Indeed, some 44 per cent had attended graduate or professional school. From one standpoint the senior officials represented an even more elite group than the business leaders of the time (1953), in that about 18 per cent of the former had taught university at some point in their careers. Porter reports that French Canadians found it almost as difficult to rise to senior positions in the civil service as they did in the business world; non-conformist Protestants (i.e., non-Anglicans) and Catholics, however, found it relatively easy to rise to the senior posts, although they were proportionately much less numerous than in the population generally. Porter does not even mention whether Jews or other ethnic groups were among the senior officials in 1953. Finally, a somewhat greater number of senior officials than members of the business elite came from middle-class rather than upper-middle or upper-class families and from non-elite schools. Porter's findings suggest that the bureaucratic elite was slightly more open than the business elite to individuals with middle-class backgrounds and to non-Anglicans.

Our findings reveal, through our 1976 study of respondents' backgrounds, that the relative openness which Porter discovered has increased considerably since 1953. Before proceeding with the analysis, however, let us look at profiles of the *types* of person whom we encountered while interviewing in the central agencies. Because we firmly promised all respondents that we would not reveal their identities, we have developed representative profiles. That is, we will give the reader an idea of the types of person who fill central-agency posts without revealing the details of particular respondents' backgrounds. As in fiction, any similarity between our profiles and an individual respondent's background is coincidental. Yet, the following types would certainly have to appear in any novel which purported to convey a sense of who minds the shop in central agencies.

Geoffrey "Jeff" Dawson (b. 1942) was born in Swift Current, Saskatchewan, of parents who traced their ancestry to western Ontario, and, before that, to Northern Ireland. Dawson grew up in Swift Current where, throughout his teens, he helped his father in a small family business, a clothing store. Dawson's parents distinguished themselves in particular as members of the United Church and the Liberal party. Dawson, a particularly gifted young man, became totally dedicated to politics by his mid-teens. He became even more dedicated when many adults, especially customers he charmed in the store, told him that he was going to be prime minister one day. He believed this strongly when he went off to the University of Saskatchewan. There events did indeed point to a promising political future. Dawson became president of the Young Liberals at the University of Saskatchewan in his second year. Through that post he got to know a number of top people in the national party organization. After graduating in 1964 with an honours BA in political science, Dawson went on to Queen's University for graduate studies. During a summer job in Ottawa, he had impressed a number of people. Finishing his MA in 1965, he planned to go to law school until he won a last-minute chance to serve as an executive assistant to a cabinet minister. After two years in that post, Dawson found that he needed training in administration, so he moved to Harvard University to begin a graduate course in management. After finishing his work at Harvard, he returned to Ottawa and a position in the PMO where he has subsequently served in a number of capacities. Dawson wants eventually to run for election to the House of Commons. He finds himself, however, in a bit of a bind. The prospects of a Liberal operative winning a seat in his native Saskatchewan do not look at all good, and he would have to compete with local aspirants for a nomination in Ontario. For the time being, the PMO provides him with an opportunity to be as much involved in the Liberal government as any party member — except, of course, some top cabinet ministers — can be. If there is a shift in Liberal-party fortunes in Saskatchewan, he will return there to run for the House so that he can get on track for a cabinet post.

Michel Desjardins (b. 1930) grew up in an upper-middle-class family in Montreal where his father was a lawyer. For his high-school degree and classical BA, Desjardins went to Collège Brébeuf, the elite Jesuit school and alma mater of Pierre Elliott Trudeau. He then went on to law school at the University of Montreal. After attaining his degree, Desjardins joined a large law firm in Montreal. In 1970, he had an opportunity to work for the Department of Justice in Ottawa. Since then he has served there as counsel to two departments, and in 1975 he joined the PCO as an assistant secretary. Desjardins has worked hard both as a legal counsel and as a secretary to a cabinet committee, and has impressed people in Ottawa. He will, thus, probably be named an assistant deputy minister either in the Department of Justice or the ministry of the Solicitor General in a few years.

Edmund Jones (b. 1941) grew up in one of Toronto's most elegant neighbourhoods, Forest Hill, right across the street from Canada's most exclusive prep school, Upper Canada College. He received his high-school education at UCC, and then moved to the prestigious Trinity College of the University of Toronto. Graduating with an honours BA in political science, Jones went on to Harvard where he studied international relations. Completing his PhD in 1967, he went immediately to the Department of External Affairs where he worked on disarmament questions. In 1970, Jones came over to the PCO to join the cabinet-committee secretariat. Since then he has risen through the ranks to a senior post. Considered a PCO "whiz kid", Jones will probably stay with the agency until he is ready to become a deputy minister in an operational department.

Richard Dwyer (b. 1928) comes from a middle-class Catholic family in Montreal West. He went to Loyola High School and

College. He received his BA in 1950 and joined the Royal Canadian Air Force for duty in Korea. After the war, he returned to Montreal and started a graduate course in history at McGill. While enrolled in the course, he heard through a friend of some openings in the public service and left McGill to take a job with the Defence department. In 1960, he left Defence to join the Department of National Revenue where Robert Johnston was deputy minister. Since then Dwyer has followed Johnston, first for a thirteen-year term in the PCO and then to the FPRO. In a sense, Dwyer owes his success to Johnston. The real key to Dwyer's success, however, is that he has cultivated to perfection a quality which Johnston very much admires and would like to have for himself, that is, total bureaucratic anonymity. Dwyer plans to retire in the next year or so and find an executive post in the private sector.

Stephen Pohl (b. 1940) emigrated from Germany with his parents in 1949. His father was an electrician. Pohl went to Central Collegiate Institute in Calgary. Graduating at the top of his class, he won a scholarship to the University of Alberta where he received his honours BA in economics in 1962. From Alberta, Pohl went to Yale University for his PhD. He took a teaching post at McMaster University in 1967. In 1972, a former colleague who had moved to Finance recruited him to join the department as a senior analyst. Pohl has risen to the directorship of his division. Since there are not many higher positions for economists and he has already advanced much more rapidly than most others of his age, Pohl will probably find himself frozen at the level of director unless he takes a position outside of Finance.

Thomas Holt (b. 1936) comes from London, Ontario, where his father was stationed as a locomotive engineer with Canadian National Railways. Holt went through the London public schools, and attended Victoria College at the University of Toronto. In 1958, he graduated with an honours degree in mathematics. He found a job with IBM, which sent him to Stanford for a two-year graduate program in computer science. When he returned to Canada, Holt worked for IBM in Ottawa. In 1962, the Dominion Bureau of Statistics (DBS) offered him a much better salary than

IBM, so he joined the public service. He took a leave of absence from 1968 to 1970 to do further graduate work at the London School of Economics. Upon returning to Ottawa, the Department of Finance hired him to help develop computer-based simulations of the economy. He has risen to the rank of assistant deputy minister in Finance.

Milton Rubenstein (b. 1922) came to Canada from New York City when he was five. His family moved into the College and Spadina district of Toronto. Rubenstein was exceptionally bright; he went to the nearby University of Toronto School, where he ranked high in his class throughout high school. He then went to University College at the University of Toronto and majored in economics. Graduating in the middle of the war (1943), he joined the Royal Canadian Army as a private and rose to the rank of Captain. He spent most of his time overseas as an intelligence officer. Returning to Canada in 1946, Rubenstein went to Queen's University for a graduate degree in economics. He joined Industry, Trade, and Commerce as an economist in 1948 and has since served in several departments. Rubenstein joined the TBS four years ago and now holds the rank of assistant secretary.

Jacques Forget (b. 1939) was born in Gâtineau, Quebec. His father, a small contractor, moved the family to Ottawa in 1950, where they lived in a bilingual section of Sandy Hill. Forget went to the University of Ottawa School. After graduation from high school, Forget ventured across the province to the University of Western Ontario, mainly because he wanted to learn how to work in an English-speaking milieu. Receiving a business degree in 1961, he joined the public service because he wanted to return to Ottawa, and "the only business in Ottawa is government". He trained to become a chartered accountant while in the public service. His advancement to the senior levels has been aided by the recent stress on financial administration in Ottawa. As a director in the Financial Administration branch of the new OCG, Forget enjoys the challenge of upgrading financial administration throughout government.

These sketches indicate how officials in the senior ranks of central agencies have quite different backgrounds than earlier typologies of the bureaucratic elite suggest. We will see, for instance, that in 1976 those individuals who became senior officials in central agencies represented Canadian society much more accurately than did those in Porter's 1953 group and, moreover, that different agencies recruit different types of individuals.

Who Are the Superbureaucrats?

A growing body of literature on senior officials in other advanced liberal democracies suggests a number of trends in recruitment which may appear in our central agents' socio-economic backgrounds. Robert D. Putnam, for example, studied legislators and bureaucrats in Italy, Germany, and Britain. He reported that senior officials in those countries still come predominantly from the middle and upper classes.[5] Indeed, even the younger officials, who showed great promise of reaching the senior ranks, overrepresented the middle and upper classes. Putnam found, however, that recruitment patterns differ from country to country. Along classic lines, Germany and Italy still prefer senior officials with backgrounds in law, presumably because they are in the best position to make administrative decisions. Britain, on the other hand, maintains a strong partiality for men of letters from "Oxbridge", to fill high posts.

Ezra N. Suleiman studied senior officials in France. He found that the overwhelming majority of these public servants came to Paris for part of their education;[6] one-third attended elite Parisian lycées; and the vast majority passed through l'École Nationale d'Administration.[7] Among the graduates of this spawning ground for the political-administrative elite in France, he found few with relatively humble social origins who gain entrance to the three corps which supply most senior civil servants for government departments and agencies.[8] He found that, through a number of degrees of screening, the French recruitment process, intentionally or unintentionally, excludes those who have relatively humble social origins and/or who have not received their education at prestigious institutions.

Closer to home, in the United States, we find some of the same trends. Mann, Stanley, and Doig studied the social origins of senior political administrators in the U.S. federal government from 1933 to 1965. They found that these officials came disproportionately from large cities in the East and most often were well-educated, middle-aged Protestants.[9] Joel D. Aberbach and Bert A. Rockman, in a later study, distinguished between the political appointees and career public servants among senior political administrators in the U.S. federal government. They found that political appointees bring higher-status backgrounds, including more prestigious degrees, to Washington than do career officials.[10] Yet both types of senior officials come disproportionately from the Washington–New York axis along the eastern seaboard.[11] Aberbach and Rockman found as well that career civil servants studied social or management sciences in university more often than appointees did.[12] Appointees more frequently received their university training in law. These findings confirm three phenomena indicated by Canadian data. First, the socio-economic backgrounds of career officials in the United States suggest that recruitment of political administrators in North America is more open than in Europe. Second, in Europe and North America, senior officials tend to come disproportionately from the metropolitan centres; this trend appears to persist in the United States, for example, despite efforts to recruit more broadly. Third, in comparison to their counterparts in Italy's and Germany's classic bureaucratic systems, North American career civil servants, who have training in fields other than law, find access to senior positions relatively easy.

Two studies indicate that, much like the U.S. system, the Canadian public service has opened up in recent years. P. J. Chartrand and K. L. Pond surveyed virtually all senior officials in Canadian government in 1967.[13] With respect to education, they found that the social and management sciences and law accounted for the greatest number of degrees (31 per cent). Yet senior officials also held degrees in the fine arts and humanities (9 per cent), economics (24), natural science (27), and engineering (8). In addition, their survey destroyed one myth — that

Queen's University in Kingston feeds more individuals into the senior ranks than other schools.[14] The University of Toronto produced the most senior officials. Queen's, in fact, ranked a mere fifth, while, in 1967, 22 per cent of senior officials took their bachelor's degree at Toronto. Following Toronto in the top four were the University of Manitoba, the University of British Columbia, and the University of Alberta. Since three western-province universities were found to outstrip Queen's in producing senior officials, it appears that high Canadian posts are now quite accessible to those from the "hinterland". Chartrand and Pond also found that senior officials often got their MAs and PhDs in the United States, although the University of Toronto and McGill University still sent the largest numbers of MAs and PhDs to senior positions.

The following year, 1968, Robert Presthus interviewed senior officials in Ottawa and Washington. He and William Monopoli report that only 40 per cent of Canadian respondents came from upper-middle-class families.[15] They found as well that those with graduate degrees in the humanities and natural sciences gain access to senior bureaucratic posts more frequently in Canada than in the United States. These Canadian studies suggest that (1) Canadian officials now often come from middle- and lower-income families and from a fairly broad spectrum of academic and professional disciplines, and (2) that the Canadian civil service draws a better geographic cross-section of university graduates than the American service does.

Our senior officials in central agencies are, presumably, men or women who have passed through several preparatory stages and through certain socio-economic processes of elimination. Apart from the merit system, the recruitment pattern for prime posts still favours those with high-status backgrounds. Accordingly, we might expect a disproportionate number of central agents to be older British Protestants from big central-Canadian cities who were educated at elite institutions. However, our data on central agents' socio-economic backgrounds present strong evidence to the contrary. We find, for example, that central agents averaged forty-five years of age (see Appendix II), whereas in 1967 senior officials in the federal government over-all averaged fifty-one years of age. With the rapid growth of the civil service since 1967, a more recent study of all senior officials might yield a lower average age. But, we have found too many "high fliers"[16] in the five agencies under scrutiny to maintain that central agents have gotten where they are only after several years of service in operational departments. Indeed, it appears instead that central agencies contain many young protégés who are being groomed for the higher executive posts in operational departments. That only 22 per cent of our central agents are fifty-one years or over supports this hypothesis.

We might also expect senior officials from Ontario, and, perhaps Quebec, to move into central agencies more easily than others because these areas are closer to the seat of power and are more urban. We might expect the same of officials from Toronto and Montreal, Canada's two main financial, industrial, and cultural centres. In fact, Ontarians (38 per cent of central agents) benefit much more from their proximity to Ottawa and the sophistication of their society than do Québécois (only 15 per cent). Even Westerners have easier access than Québécois (22 per cent vs. 15). Four per cent of our officials come from the Atlantic provinces, a figure far short of these provinces' proportion of the nation's population. On the other hand, immigrants, especially those from Great Britain, hold an exceptionally large proportion of positions in central agencies (21 per cent). Fifteen per cent of our central agents come from Toronto and 10 per cent from Montreal, which suggests only a very modest tendency towards recruitment from the nation's two main metropolitan centres. Thus, our data indicate that, insofar as recruitment favours people from particular regions, Ontarians and Westerners are the principal beneficiaries. The tendency parallels Chartrand and Pond's finding that senior officials mostly received their BAs from universities in Ontario and the West.

According to our prediction that individuals with elite backgrounds are favoured for senior central-agency positions, we might expect to find among respondents vastly disproportionate numbers of English and French Canadians because they are members of Canada's two charter groups. Indeed, Porter found in 1953 that those who belonged to neither group rarely assumed high posts in any sector of Canadian life. But this situation has changed somewhat in the past twenty-five years. For instance, Kornberg and Mishler found in 1971 that a considerable proportion of MPs belong to non-charter groups, while Campbell found in the same year that Senators, who are considerably older than MPs, and, therefore, represent an earlier generation of politicians, rarely belong to the non-charter groups.[17] In this present study, we find that 20 per cent of senior officials have parents who belong to non-charter ethnic groups, a dramatic improvement over Porter's 1953 data. At the same time, the 20 per cent and 23 per cent of central agents with French fathers and mothers represent a considerable improvement for Canada's second charter group over Porter's 1953 figure of 13 per cent. As Kornberg and Mishler's and Campbell's studies discovered a generational difference between MPs and Senators, so our findings here suggest that the ranks of the bureaucratic elite have opened up in the past twenty-five years, especially to non-charter-group Canadians.

As part of the trend towards greater access, we might expect to find more Catholics and Jews among the senior officials in central agencies. The Catholic population might have gained especially through greater access for the French and continental Europeans; Jews might have benefited from greater access for non-charter-group Canadians. Our findings, in fact, support these predictions; there are as many Catholics as Protestants in central agencies — 38 per cent each. Moreover, Jews comprise almost 9 per cent, whereas Porter reports none among senior officials in 1953. Thus, our findings indicate some healthy trends. It is interesting that just over 15 per cent of our respondents said that they do not identify with a religious group. This figure greatly exceeds the proportion found in 1971 of non-religious Canadian legislators.[18] This probably reflects a new climate in the bureaucracy which allows officials to register with candour their lack of religious beliefs without fearing that they have failed to live up to a traditional norm. Legislators, on the other hand, might feel obligated to register adherence to some organized religion.

So far, data from our respondents do not support our predictions about senior central agents' ages, areas of origin, or ethnic, religious, and socio-economic backgrounds. Indeed, we have found that central agents have "humbler" origins than previous studies have indicated. This observation is further confirmed by their fathers' educational and occupational histories. Only 37 per cent of central agents' fathers attended university, while 29 per cent never even attended high school. In addition, although 30 per cent of central agents' fathers had professional or technical occupations and 36 per cent were businessmen or managers, a fairly large 34 per cent had clerical or blue-collar jobs. The figures fall within the bounds of comparable data on the family backgrounds of senior officials in the United States and Canada.[19]

What factor, then, has provided central agents with the edge over others for advancement in the civil service? It appears to be education. A larger proportion of central agents than of other senior officials finished university and obtained graduate degrees. We find, in fact, that 91 per cent of our respondents have at least a bachelor's degree, an 11 per cent increase over Chartrand and Pond's figure covering senior officials in all departments. (This increase may be explained in large part by a tightening of recruitment standards throughout the civil service.) Central agencies, however, appear no more selective than the rest of the public service about which schools their senior officials come from. Thirty-six per cent of our respondents received their undergraduate degrees from "elite English schools", a category including the University of Toronto, McGill, Queen's, and Dalhousie. As was the case among Chartrand and Pond's officials, the University of Toronto supplied the largest proportion of undergraduate degrees (23 per cent).

When we look at central agents' studies beyond the baccalaureate degree, we see just how much they have stressed academic achievement. Seventy per cent of our respondents have graduate degrees, more than double Chartrand and Pond's figure for all senior officials. Most of the senior officials with graduate degrees received at least one from a foreign university. Our officials even differ from Chartrand and Pond's in that slightly more of them went overseas for graduate work than went to the United States (thirty-one have foreign degrees, seventeen from overseas, and sixteen from the United States). This is probably so for two reasons: first, there are many immigrants among our central agents; and second, our respondents seem somewhat to prefer some top British schools to those of comparable status in the United States. For example, more received graduate degrees from Oxford and the London School of Economics than from Harvard and Yale. Finally, although central agents do not appear to have done their university studies at more elite institutions than Chartrand and Pond's officials, they represent a narrower spectrum of academic disciplines. A large majority (65 per cent) received liberal-arts undergraduate degrees, mainly in economics and political science. Among all central agents, 36 per cent earned graduate degrees in liberal arts and 14 per cent obtained law degrees. The largest number received graduate degrees in economics (28 per cent). Less than 10 per cent took natural science and business programs. Central agencies tend to hire economics graduates because these agencies, especially the Department of Finance and the TBS, play critical roles in managing the economy and government expenditures.

We looked at our officials' memberships in professional associations and social clubs to see if memberships reflect current high professional and social status. Some 30 per cent of our respondents belong to one professional association and 26 per cent belong to two or more. Forty-four per cent, however, belong to none. Only 41 per cent of our officials said they belong to social clubs. Few were members of the prestigious and exclusive men's clubs such as Le Cercle Universitaire, or the Rideau Club (which one respondent said he "would not be caught dead in because it is a hotbed for lobbyists"). Most "joiners" belonged to recreational clubs, but, as with social clubs, only a small number held memberships in the most expensive and most esteemed clubs such as the Rockcliffe Tennis Club. Bureaucratic propriety and, certainly, the absence of the fat expense allowances common in the business world seem to dictate that central agents join less costly and less prestigious clubs, and for recreation, not for a place to entertain and to make contacts.

So far, we have seen that recruitment to senior posts in central agencies is relatively open, more like the American system than the European varieties. That is, a significant number of Canadian central agents come from almost every socio-economic group and have attended non-elite as well as elite universities. Two things, however, distinguish central agents from other senior officials in Canada: they have obtained more graduate degrees, and they have specialized more often in economics, a discipline currently in great demand given the federal government's preoccupation with economic matters.

Interagency Differences

Let us not assume that the five central agencies recruit senior officials with certain socio-economic backgrounds in equal proportions; in fact, different agencies tend to take on different types. As we have seen, Finance markedly prefers economists (Chapter 3). Economists are in demand in the TBS as well, particularly in branches such as Program and Planning where cost-benefit analyses are conducted. The PMO recruits its "exempt staff" from outside the public service and at least as much on the basis of proven political talents as of academic or professional skills. In this section we probe some of the differences among agencies in officials' backgrounds, and ask whether the backgrounds vary in relation to the agencies' roles.

With respect to region and city of origin, some hypotheses immediately come to mind. Mainly because of the shortage of Liberal MPs from the West, the PMO appears to favour officials from that area, especially Alberta, the home province of Jim Coutts, Ivan Head, and Joyce Fairbairn. We expected the PCO to recruit disproportionately from Montreal because this is the home town of both the Prime Minister and Michael Pitfield. It struck us that very few individuals raised in Quebec work in the senior ranks of the Finance department.

Several cross-tabulations (Appendix II) support the view that certain agencies are partial to individuals from certain regions and cities. The cross-tabulations fail, however, to support the expectation that Westerners gravitate more to the PMO than to other agencies. The data do indicate that the Westerners have disproportionate access to Finance; this agency seems to account for a great deal of the imbalance among departments' recruitment. Among those whom we interviewed in Finance in 1976, only one grew up in the Maritimes and none grew up in Quebec. On the other hand, the department houses the largest proportion of immigrants among the five central agencies. Our findings only moderately suggest that Torontonians go to the TBS more than to other agencies. Montrealers, on the other hand, find their way much more often into the PMO, the PCO, and the FPRO than into other agencies.

What we have already learned from differences in region of origin suggests some imbalances in the recruitment of individual agencies along ethnic lines. For example, officials with French-Canadian fathers and mothers were totally absent from positions at the level of director or above in Finance at the time of our interviews, but officials who belong to neither of the charter groups have greater access to Finance than to any other agency. There are *only* "charter-group" officials, however, in the PMO. Thus, it appears that, although they may market their academic and professional skills to a highly technical department like Finance, non-charter-group members might lack the political contacts for posts in the PMO. The relatively large proportion of Catholics in the PMO/PCO/FPRO and their small numbers in Finance make sense — the church-run educational system, which provided most of our Catholic officials, stressed the humanities to the detriment of specialized training in the social, management, technological, and natural sciences.[20] Thus, we would have expected Catholics to gravitate to the PMO, the PCO, and the FPRO, all of which call upon generalists' aptitudes more than Finance, which demands expertise in economics, or law, or accounting.

These observations lead us to consider educational and

occupational family differences. To see if respondents from families of higher socio-economic status have better access to any particular agency, this study compared the educational and occupational backgrounds of central agents' fathers. The results of the analysis say that in only two ways does such a bias show. First, respondents whose fathers never went to high school tend somewhat to be in the TBS; those whose fathers at least completed high school most frequently are in the PMO, the PCO, and the FPRO. What about the officials themselves? Do their own educational backgrounds determine which agency they enter? Not with respect to undergraduate degrees, at least. For instance, no central agency displays a marked preference for graduates of elite English or French schools. Graduates of elite English schools, however, find their way to the PCO somewhat more often than other officials, although this difference is not statistically significant. There is also some evidence that individuals who took their undergraduate degrees in science faculties tend more than others to obtain positions either in the PCO or the TBS. Among those with undergraduate degrees in liberal arts, officials with economics BAs clearly work most often in Finance, and officials with political science BAs hold marginally more positions in the TBS. The PMO, the PCO, and the FPRO have drawn the greatest proportion of officials with U.S. graduate degrees. Finance, which employs a greater number of immigrants than any other central agency, has the highest proportion of officials with overseas graduate degrees. The fields in which graduate degrees were taken indicate that lawyers go most often to the PMO, the PCO, and the FPRO; business-administration graduates very frequently go to the PMO; and economists tend to go to Finance. All this stands to reason. Insofar as lawyers fit the generalist, rather than specialist, mould they meet PMO, PCO, and FPRO requirements for advisory work in wide-ranging policy matters and secretariat work in the processing of proposals through Cabinet. Business administrators provide the managerial expertise necessary in the PMO to assure that the various switchboard functions run efficiently and effectively.

Conclusion

In this chapter we have contrasted the socio-economic backgrounds of our central agents with those of the elite in Canada and elsewhere. We have also compared the socio-economic backgrounds of central agents in our five agencies with each other to find if there are any differences which relate to the various missions of the offices. We noted that the Canadian bureaucratic elite represents the general populace better than the senior levels of public service in almost any other advanced liberal democracy. Moreover, perhaps because our central agents include several "high fliers" who represent the new breed of the bureaucratic establishment, their backgrounds reflect very dramatically how the ranks of senior officials in Canada have become more open to previously underrepresented groups, especially Catholics, non-charter ethnics, and Jews. Indeed, our finding that 44 per cent of their fathers never graduated from high school highlights how our respondents have experienced rapid upward mobility. These officials benefited more from educational achievement than from anything else. In fact, of all characteristics, earning a graduate degree delineates our respondents' backgrounds most sharply from those of senior officials previously studied in Ottawa. Further, our central agents need not have received their education at an elite prep school or university to begin graduate work. Most of our respondents went to public high schools and received their BAs at non-elite universities. Thus, educational achievement has proved to be an immensely useful vehicle for those from less-elite socio-economic strata to break into the bureaucratic elite. The immense growth of the federal government, especially in the past twenty years, has provided a seller's market for "whiz kids".

This study has found as well that some central agencies recruit individuals with generalized university backgrounds, while other agencies hire people with specialized training. As the economics department of any leading university might do, Finance has sought out and hired top talent in economics, wherever it may be found. The department has recruited heavily from the western provinces and among immigrants; at the time of our interviews it totally excluded French Canadians from its posts at the level of director or above, no doubt because church-run schools and colleges, at least before 1960s reforms, failed to produce specialists in significant numbers. By the same token, the generalists, namely the political-science and law graduates, go disproportionately to the TBS and the PMO/PCO/FPRO, respectively. There they appreciably swell the proportion of French Canadians and Catholics in these offices.

In conclusion, we have seen that educational achievement, combined with rapid growth in the federal government, has helped to open the senior bureaucracy to several previously underrepresented groups; and that among the educational achievers, specialists, primarily economists, tend to go to Finance and generalists tend to go to the other four agencies. The next chapter will look more closely at our officials' careers in government. Compared with senior officials in other countries, how did central agents enter the public service and rise through the bureaucracy to their present positions? Is the specialist-generalist phenomenon reflected in advancement through posts within specific central agencies?

Ascending to and Remaining
on the Peak:
Career Paths and Orientations

Max Weber, the classical sociological theorist, viewed the bureaucratic career as a vocation.[1] That is, one would decide early
in life upon a career in the public service, find a suitable position
after adequate preparation (in Weber's day, studies in law), and
then work to achieve the life-long ambition of rising as high as
possible in the bureaucracy. One would never think of leaving
government service for a position in the corporate or political
world. Nor would an outsider, at midpoint in his career in the
business world or academe, be foolish enough to try to enter
government service for the purpose of advancement.

The sanctity of the bureaucratic vocation, like that of many
other careers, has eroded somewhat during the twentieth cen-
tury. In Canada, we find little evidence that bureaucrats consider their work as a vocation. Indeed, this chapter will show that
the career paths and orientations of Canadian bureaucrats deviate sharply from those of public servants in several European
countries. Furthermore, even though central agents are at the
hub of the Canadian public service, they appear to have tran-
scended the limits of classic bureaucratic careers and thinking
more than other senior officials in Ottawa.

We begin by looking at comparative and Canadian literature
on the subject to see the routes and detours classic bureaucratic
careers often take. We shall analyse our central agents' pre-
government careers, their motives for the transition from the
private to the public sector, their career routes within government, and their orientations towards expertise, individual goals,
and personal satisfaction. When and why did our central agents
get into the public service? And did they come into central

agencies especially from certain departments? The chapter then examines whether the specialist-generalist dichotomy influences the career routes of central agents; finally, it asks whether our officials' responses to questions on their career goals and satisfaction with the public service tally with classic views of bureaucratic career goals.

The Bureaucratic Vocation

Among advanced liberal democracies, Italian and French senior officials come up the most stratified career ladders. In 1971, Robert Putnam found that no fewer than 95 per cent of senior Italian officials began their bureaucratic careers before 1943.[2] Putnam found, further, that over 80 per cent of the officials served their entire careers in their current department. Clearly, Italian officials' progress in the bureaucracy depends greatly on seniority in a single department. Ezra N. Suleiman's research has uncovered ways in which the French bureaucratic career is similarily stratified and, thus, vocational. He reports, for instance, that senior officials whom he interviewed were "early bloomers". That is, 25 per cent maintained that they decided upon a bureaucratic career before adolescence, and 40 per cent asserted that they made their decision before entering university.[3] Further, many of Suleiman's respondents explained their choice of a bureaucratic career in terms of a calling to public service.[4] Unlike Italian bureaucrats, the French officials did not usually stay in one public-service department. Practically all of them, however, belonged to the three corps of the bureaucracy (i.e., Inspection des Finances, Cour des Comptes, and Conseil d'Etat) which traditionally supply senior executives.[5] Rarely did they report having worked outside government before joining the public service.[6]

John Porter's analysis of 1953 career data for Canadian senior officials throughout the public service yields little evidence of such stratified bureaucratic career routes.[7] Only one quarter of Porter's senior officials had spent their entire careers in the service; almost two-thirds came directly from outside government to senior posts. Business and politics supplied the greatest proportion of outsiders, but universities and the armed services supplied their shares as well.

P. J. Chartrand and K. L. Pond's 1967 data amplify Porter's findings. By 1967, only 15 per cent of the senior officials had spent their entire careers in government.[8] Almost one-third of the officials who came to government from the private sector entered at senior levels. In sharp contrast to Italy's top bureaucrats, Canadian officials actually improved their rate of advancement in the public-service hierarchy by changing departments often.[9] Indeed, those who made at least four changes during their careers most rapidly obtained the highest posts.

Both Porter and Chartrand and Pond data suggest, therefore, that the careers of senior officials in Canada do not fit the mould of bureaucratic stratification. Many officials get their start in their career outside of government. Outsiders move with relative ease into senior posts. Once inside government, officials often obtain advancement by moving from department to department. Seniority within a particular department is, thus, not a firm prerequisite for promotion to senior posts. None of these data, however, tell us whether central agents' careers fit this over-all pattern or deviate markedly from it. The section which follows considers this question.

Our interest in officials' own views of the importance of expertise in their work relates to the classic view of the bureaucratic career. Max Weber, for instance, maintained that public servants' expertise distinguishes them most from other participants in the policy process.[10] Officials, in Weber's view, base their roles in the policy process and administration on immense knowledge of the technical aspects of issues rather than on political authority.[11] Presumably, this expertise was accumulated through formal education and research, as well as career experiences in bureaucracy. Robert Putnam has given this Weberian assumption its most recent and rigorous test. He has found among Italian, German, and British senior officials clear evidence that "technicians", i.e., natural scientists, political scientists, econo-

mists, and management experts, tend more than "non-techni-
cians", i.e., humanities graduates and lawyers, to keep informed
in their fields by reading relevant professional journals and to
maintain some sense of identification with a profession independent of their career either in their agency or the civil service.[12]

Putnam has none the less challenged the assumption that a
technician's speciality influences his attitude to work. Although
the assumption relates ultimately to a technician's interaction
with others in the policy arena, on the most fundamental level, it
concerns his view of what individual goals may be sought and
what personal satisfaction may be derived from public service.
The technician, convinced of the utility of his values, believes
that expertise must supplant politics. Hence, he uses his expertise
in his job and derives the greatest satisfaction when it affects
decisions.[13] A technician, then, has neutral or even negative
views of political roles *per se*. Putnam reports, in fact, that among
the senior officials he studied in Italy, Germany, and Britain, only
natural scientists actually display a clear aversion to the world of
politics. On the other hand, in Britain and Germany, social
scientists (i.e., economists, political scientists, and "other") indicate the strongest tendency to incorporate political goals and a
commitment to political efficacy into their views of the bureaucratic role.[14]

Putnam's findings with regard to social scientists might have fit
his hypothesis better if political scientists had been excluded
from the category. In Canada, at least, it is questionable whether
training in political science, or even in public administration,
actually imparts expertise for government service beyond what
any liberal-arts degree provides.[15] Unfortunately, Canadian studies of bureaucracy have not systematically analysed expertise
and technocratic role perceptions among senior officials in
Ottawa. However, as previously noted, the Finance department
recruits specialists (economists) disproportionately, whereas the
other central agencies take on more generalists (political scientists and lawyers); therefore, we might expect officials to register different views of their bureaucratic vocation depending on
which agency employs them.

Central Agents

We asked our central agents a number of questions to ascertain how and why they got into government, what they did before entering, how they have advanced up the career ladder, and the nature of their views of expertise, individual goals, and personal satisfaction. First we asked when they decided to join the public service. Only 27 per cent said they chose their bureaucratic career either before graduating from university or immediately afterwards. The remainder said they chose their present careers after spending some time outside the public service. We then probed to find if their motives for entering bureaucracy reflected vocation-like goals. We expected that among central agents (whose positions, of all senior posts in government, require relatively great sacrifices because of the hours and strain) vocational elements might prevail in their descriptions of how they entered the public service. In other words, we expected that these officials would tend to be more zealous than other Canadian officials.

Our respondents proved to be zealous, but in quite a different way than we expected. The largest percentage of them said they entered public service for reasons which relate more to career success and management skills in general than bureaucratic service in particular. Some 60 per cent pointed out that they came to government because they could not find a satisfactory position in the private sector or were unhappy with the one they had. As expressed by one respondent:

I was working for ＿＿ and I got into a disagreement with the president over the company's future. Just at that time, the Department of ＿＿ approached me to do some work for them and I grabbed the chance to get out.

Another respondent attributed his move to connections which he lacked elsewhere:

I had been outside of Canada for six years. All of my friends had moved to Ottawa. One of them, a Minister, asked me if I would like to do some work for him. It was the best offer to come along.

The second-largest percentage (27 per cent) said that the sheer challenge anticipated in a government career attracted them to public service. The respondents here used the most effusive language, conveying above all excitement at being at the centre of things:

What attracted me and kept me in was the idea of being at the centre, doing immensely interesting work. The whole process of governing absorbs and interests me immensely as well as the whole process of power and influence as it is exerted in government operations.

I was fed up with being on the outside. I wanted to do a professional job, but with the feeling that I was being heard. I got tired of the pettiness of the private sector.

These two motives express a desire for career advancement and an attraction to the centre of power. We might expect the former, in so far as from Chapter 4 we know that our officials have experienced a great deal of socio-economic upward mobility. But an attraction to power strikes us as somewhat atypical of bureaucrats, at least if we accept Weber's view that officials simply wish to lend their expertise to government. Contrary to Putnam's positive findings regarding the Weberian hypothesis, our central agents appear to have crossed the line between the detached specialist and ambitious political administrator to an unusual degree.

We did find, in addition to career advancement and an attraction to the centre of power, at least some reference to more classic bureaucratic motives. Twenty per cent of our respondents, indeed, evinced an idealism which would have warmed Weber's heart:

I joined the government directly from university. I came because I had a strong predilection to public service, which perhaps may be traced to my Scottish-Presbyterian background. It was and still is a high value for me to serve my country.

I believed that government was the saviour of the world, that it could better society.

Along similar although less idealistic lines, many of our central agents said that they entered government because of their expertise. Some 16 per cent thought that they could contribute in a particular policy sector; 12 per cent believed that their academic training equipped them for a particular type of analysis; 10 per cent reported that their speciality outside of government involved a skill needed in the public service. Thus, although we found many respondents who especially esteemed career advancement and power, some valued government service in and of itself, and expertise within some substantive field.

Since such a large proportion of our central agents started their careers outside the federal government, we wanted to know where they had worked before joining the Ottawa public service. Most had spent time in the business world: 15 per cent in private corporations, 8 per cent in law firms, 7 per cent in consulting firms, and 5 per cent in accounting firms. Yet academe provided its share of central agents as well. Fully 23 per cent of our respondents had worked previously in universities. Far down in the ranking of sectors in which our respondents spent part of their careers, we found that high schools produced 4 per cent, public-interest organizations 2 per cent, and the church ministry 1 per cent. Thus, within the private sector, corporations and professional firms or universities sent most of our respondents to the public service. The large proportion of former academics reinforces our assertion (Chapter 4) that our respondents are more highly educated than other senior officials in Ottawa. That is, academics most often possess the high levels of expertise in a particular field demanded of central agents.

Although most central agents who entered the federal public service in mid-career had worked in the private sector, several had held posts either in Crown corporations (11 per cent) or in

provincial governments (9 per cent). An additional 8 per cent of
our respondents had served in the armed forces and 5 per cent in
international organizations. Only one central agent had held an
elective office before joining the federal service. Thus, our
officials had moved about in the public sector a great deal.
Several, for instance, had belonged to the famous "Saskatchewan
mafia" of bureaucrats which came to Ottawa in considerable
numbers from Regina in the early 1960s. It is surprising, however, that only one of our respondents had served in elective
office, since Porter found in his 1953 study that almost as many
senior officials had been in politics as in business.[16] The virtual
absence of former politicians among our central agents perhaps
indicates the degree to which the merit system determines
advancement to senior positions in these departments.

Chapter 4 noted that, except for the Maritimes, Canada's
various regions are adequately represented among central
agency personnel. And central agents' jobs just prior to their
entry into the federal bureaucracy also seem to have covered a
fair cross-section of the country. Alberta is the only western
province none had worked in. The greatest number came at mid-
career from Ontario (20 per cent) and Quebec (16). Almost 9
per cent of our respondents had worked outside the country just
before coming to Ottawa. Only 4 per cent came from the
Atlantic provinces, however, and all of them from Nova Scotia. In
view of what Campbell reports about MPs and Senators, the
figures show just how hard it is for individuals from the Atlantic
provinces to break into significant roles in Ottawa.[17]

As might be expected from what we have seen, our central
agents had been in the public service a relatively short time
when we interviewed them. The average respondent had been
there only eleven years. This figure falls considerably short of
Chartrand and Pond's 1967 figure of seventeen years.[18] The six-
year gap may be attributed to two main factors. First, the public
service has recruited intensely from outside government in the
last ten years. Second, central agencies have offered "high fliers"
abundant opportunities to rise quickly to important posts. Comparable data from other countries highlight this point. While

only 3 per cent of our central agents had started their bureau-cratic careers by 1950, Putnam in 1971 found that most of his senior officials from other countries had done so. The percent-ages are: 99 (Italy), 85 (England), 41 (U.S.A.), and 31 (Ger-many).[19] Furthermore, only 32 per cent of our respondents currently hold positions in their initial departments, whereas Putnam found much greater stability in his officials' career routes. His percentages are: 82 (Italy), 49 (England), 80 (U.S.A.), and 69 (Germany). Not only are our respondents relative new-comers to the bureaucracy, but they are often recent arrivals in their department as well. They moved to their present agency an average of five years before our interviews (1976), and assumed their present posts, on average, two years before the interviews.

To learn just how varied their experiences had been in other departments, we asked respondents to detail the steps of their careers through the federal bureaucracy. We wanted especially to see whether or not some departments send considerably more people to central agencies than others. First, our findings indi-cate that a sizeable number of our respondents have served in central agencies at some earlier point in their careers (see Table 5.1). Yet, National Defence, External Affairs, and Industry, Trade, and Commerce sent considerably more individuals to central agencies than other non-central-agency departments. These departments offer prestige to officials by virtue of their importance to national security and foreign relations. Next, several general-service departments and agencies sent three or more individuals to central agencies. These general-service units are the Economic Council, Statistics Canada, Supply and Ser-vices, Bureau of Management Consultants, Public Works, the Secretary of State Department, and the Public Service Commis-sion. Senior officials in these units provide services for other departments; apparently, they find it relatively easy to make the move to central-agency work.

Individuals from many operational departments in the domes-tic-policy field must have found it very difficult to break into central agencies. A large cluster of such departments contri-buted only one former member to our group of central agents;

these include Consumer and Corporate Affairs, Manpower and Immigration, Transport, Urban Affairs, and Regional Economic Expansion, all of which administer actual social, economic, and/ or public-service programs. Other departments in the field failed even to produce a single central agent among our respondents: these include such departments as Veterans' Affairs, Labour, the Ministry of [the] Solicitor General, Science and Technology, and the Post Office. The data thus suggest a pecking order of recruitment sources. Listed in descending order, these sources are: central agencies, prestigious international portfolios, general service-oriented departments and agencies, and, finally, operational departments in the domestic-policy field.

TABLE 5.1
PREVIOUS DEPARTMENTS/AGENCIES
OF CENTRAL AGENTS

DEPARTMENT/AGENCY	NUMBER OF OFFICIALS
Auditor General of Canada, Consumer and Corporate Affairs,° Chief Electoral Officer, Central Mortgage and Housing, Canadian Pension Commission, Defence Research Board, Federal-Provincial Relations Office,° Health and Welfare,° Manpower and Immigration,° Transport,° Urban Affairs,° National Capital Commission, Regional Economic Expansion,° Science Council, Unemployment Insurance Commission, Prices and Incomes Commission	1 each
Agriculture,° Canadian Radio-Television Commission, Environment Canada,° Justice,° Revenue Canada,° Government Language Schools, Prime Minister's Office°	2 each
Economic Council, Finance,° Statistics Canada, Supply and Services,° Bureau of Management Consultants	3 each
Communications,° Public Works,° Energy, Mines, and Resources,° Indian and Northern Affairs°	4 each
Secretary of State°	5
National Defence,° Public Service Commission, Privy Council Office°	6 each
External Affairs,° Treasury Board Secretariat°	9 each
Industry, Trade, and Commerce°	10

° Denotes Cabinet portfolio.

How do central agents perceive the role of expertise in their work? We have found so far that our central agents do not follow the classic bureaucratic career route whereby officials enter the public service at a young age and stay in one department so as to deepen their special knowledge and skills. We might ask then whether their experience in a particular field takes a back seat to their desire for advancement and proximity to power.

Somewhat to our surprise, three-quarters of our central agents told us that they had some type of expertise; 64 per cent apply it in their present jobs. Most of those who mentioned an issue-area speciality named expertise in some aspect of economics or finance (38 per cent of all respondents). Each of the following areas of expertise was mentioned by only one or two respondents: security and defence, foreign affairs, official languages, native peoples, broadcasting and culture, social and manpower policy. A fairly large proportion of the central agents believe that they are specialists by virtue of providing some general skill required by government operations, such as knowledge of machinery of government (5 per cent), the details of federal-provincial relations (4 per cent), data processing (1 per cent), information services (4 per cent), constitutional law (1 per cent), social psychology (2 per cent), decision-making methods (2 per cent), law (1 per cent), or accounting (1 per cent). But, more than all of these combined, officials cited skill in management *per se* (26 per cent). Thus, the distinctive nature of the bureaucratic career, as perceived by our central agents, is brought into focus; the specialist-generalist dichotomy which we discussed in Chapter 4 comes especially to mind. Clearly, some of our officials — primarily the economists — do see themselves as specialists. On the other hand, a very sizeable proportion of our officials are generalists, that is, they pursue expertise in management or some other skill which is important to over-all government operations. These generalists move from department to department, capitalizing on their talent for government administration rather than a detailed knowledge of a specific policy field. Our respondents' answers to questions about how they developed their skill support the specialist-generalist hypothesis. Twenty-five per cent cited academic experience. Thirty-eight per cent of the officials attributed their speciality to experience in government. Thus, both types, the specialist and the generalist, exist among central agents.

The existence of the two modes of thought becomes even clearer when we analyse what officials say they have specifically tried to accomplish during their government careers. The officials frequently cite more than one personal goal; 49 per cent mention two and 13 per cent discuss three goals. Nine types of goals receive at least some mention from respondents. The highest proportion of officials (33 per cent) say that they have tried to accomplish some specific policy goals during their careers. The second-greatest proportion (29 per cent) state that they want to bring better planning and co-ordination to government. A Finance official's and PMO respondent's answers reflect this type of individual goal:

I try to bring out more rationality in decision making. This is a real problem for any government. We try to have the gradual influence on the economy that provides planning instead of spectacular action which gets us nowhere. Let's take an example from your line of work. Governments over-invested in post-secondary education during the sixties because that's what the public wanted. In the process they totally distorted social conditions. Priorities were shifted without a plan and the system was set up for disaster, i.e., the emergence of the current glut of university-trained people. The thing I want to accomplish more than anything else is to help the government avoid that type of disaster in the economic sphere.

You really don't become conscious of trying to accomplish specific things. Rather, it's the over-all picture that you begin to take note of. I started thinking along these lines in my first job in government. It struck me that my job was to help mould the political will into a respectable public policy. That is, a policy that will work and fit the general conditions at that particular moment. I guess I've been lucky. I've chosen jobs which stress that aspect.

Consistent with our earlier finding that many central agents got into government partly for career advancement, a high proportion (21 per cent) report that they have sought goals related to personal development and advancement. An economist and a lawyer, respectively, dwell on this aspect of their goals:

One thing that makes my job interesting here is that it relates to my main research interest. I have found out a lot of things by seeing what is done in Ottawa. In fact, the experience has given me the basis for development of a model in my area of economics.

When I first came to Ottawa I was offered a few jobs in government. But I thought government lawyers were dull and incompetent. Since I've entered the public service my ideas have changed. I've met a lot of extremely interesting people and I get a lot of challenging work. I get into legal work which I wouldn't be able to get into elsewhere.

Equal proportions of officials (16 per cent) cite, respectively, bringing greater humanity to government and development of personnel in their unit or within the public service at large as key goals. One respondent expressed his desire for greater humanity in government in vivid language:

I came from a public-oriented family. In retrospect, my dad was screwed because he was a francophone. This always bothered me. Mom had tremendous dedication to doing something for the underprivileged, even though we were not that well off ourselves. This dedication rubbed off on all of us. Combine it with Dad's sense that the people, particularly the francophones, are getting screwed and you have a pretty strong commitment on my part to do something to make government more human. That has really been a driving force for me. I've always viewed my job as an opportunity to help make government more responsive, particularly to the little guy.

Another respondent typifies those who highlight development of personnel as a key goal:

The most important accomplishment for me has been to infuse a different style of management. I really believe that every person under me is an asset and capable of making a significant contribution, irrespective of rank. I personally cannot change the whole world, but I can affect how we function here, and how the people I work with feel about it. What we are trying to do here is to depart as far as possible from the traditional and prevailing style of bureaucratic management, which is hierarchic and autocratic.

In addition, many of our respondents concerned with personnel emphasize recruitment of the best professionals and maintenance of conditions which will encourage these individuals to stay in government.

Four types of goals attract mention from relatively small proportions of respondents. Overarching humanitarian goals not related to specific policies and the desire to have a sense of efficacy each received mention from 12 per cent of all respondents. Ten per cent of the central agents focus part of their attention on giving the best possible advice to political figures; 9 per cent perceive themselves to a degree as statesmen who are trying to encourage consensus on various policy issues.

In sum, large proportions of our respondents stress the importance of their contribution to policy making and to government planning. Many, however, place some emphasis on individual goals such as personal development and efficacy. Clearly, goals other than simply imparting substantive expertise motivate our officials to work in government; we have found strong evidence of both self- and other-centred goals which go beyond the mere contribution of particular skills.

Officials' responses to our question on what they would miss if they left government suggest, indeed, that personal development and a general sense of efficacy are crucial to many central agents' sense of satisfaction. Influencing a specific policy field, improving management, serving government, and serving the public all failed to receive mention from more than 10 per cent of respondents (these types of satisfaction were mentioned by 5, 3, 8, and 10 per cent of officials, respectively). Thirty-four per cent of the officials would miss most a general sense of efficacy in the policy arena if they left government. A TBS official's and a PMO respondent's answers reflect this sense of efficacy:

I see the future of the country unfolding and I have a hand in it. This is something I just would not be able to experience in other sectors.

I would miss most the distinctiveness and importance of government, the intimacy and knowledge that I have by being here. The loss would be in the feeling that I would no longer be part of the process.

Yet the vast majority of responses that we received contained elements of satisfaction more related to basic physical and psychological needs than to a desire either for a specific or general impact on government or for public service. Twenty-one per cent of our respondents say they would miss the high quality of their colleagues; 16 per cent would miss the great variety of problems that come their way; 7 per cent would miss the excellent facilities they have for research; 5 per cent would miss the life-style which their job and/or Ottawa sustains for themselves and their families; 2 per cent believe that they would not be able to find a comparable position in the private sector. But, by far the greatest proportion of the basic-needs aspect of their job satisfaction falls under the category "atmosphere and challenge". Sixty-two per cent of our officials simply would miss the excitement of being at the centre of activity. The following three responses, from the PMO, the PCO, and again the PMO, respectively, convey the importance of atmosphere and challenge as key aspects of their jobs which central agents would miss:

Sometimes I wonder if there are other jobs which are as much fun and as absorbing as this one. Some people must wonder what would happen if they got shoved out and had to get work that isn't fun. The idea appalls me! I find my work very fulfilling. By the nature of the process you have to promote yourself. The first guy on high ground wins the day. You have to get in and fight. I like a good scrap. Plus, if you end up on top, people have to respond to you.

In government work you are close to the pulse. You know the way
things are being done. On the outside, you're a slave.

I almost wept when I left my profession. I always wanted to be a ___ .
I've come a hell of a long way since. This work has been ten times more
fascinating and challenging. There's tremendous excitement involved
in working directly with the PM. I have immense respect for him.

We have seen in this section that central agents' career paths
and orientations break most stereotypes of the bureaucrat. Large
proportions of our respondents came to government after careers elsewhere, entered for advancement and challenge, have
since moved frequently from department to department, stress
management-oriented specialties not necessarily linked to substantive-policy expertise, and register political and/or self-
centred goals. However, officials' responses to our question
about what they would miss most if they left government reveal
orientations which suggest that many of our respondents prize
proximity to power and the importance of the game they play
rather than public service *per se*, the opportunity to impart
expertise, or even the ability to have an impact on policy.

Pitching Tents on the Mountain

Our respondents, as we have seen, generally register a great deal
of enthusiasm about their work as central agents. In fact, they
stressed so often that central agencies are "where the action is"
that we were reminded of the apostle Peter, who once proclaimed to Jesus while he stood with him and two other disciples
on a high mountain: " . . . Lord, how good it is for us to be here!
With your permission I will erect three tents. . . . "[20] Many of our
central agents believe that they stand at the apex of power and
authority, albeit temporal, in the Canadian policy process. Many
of them actively sought their current position. Human nature
would seem to dictate that, now that they are at or close to the
top, they too want to erect "tents" and stay.

Is this so agency by agency? If not, which officials are able to
retain their positions the longest? We already know that many

PMO officials have served in that agency since Pierre Elliott Trudeau became Prime Minister in 1968. But what about the other agencies? Because Finance officials (as noted in Chapter 4) are largely specialists — that is, they bring rare and valued economic expertise to Ottawa — we might expect that Finance would recruit them relatively early and keep them long. Because many PCO, FPRO, and TBS officials are more often generalists, on the other hand, we might expect that other agencies would also vie for their talents; they probably served in other agencies before entering their present one, and will probably move on to other departments in the relatively near future. We conjecture that PMO officials pin their hopes on the political fate of the Prime Minister; that Finance officials use their prized skills to gain virtual tenure in their department; and that PCO, FPRO, and TBS officials move from department to department because they are generalists, and thus many departments require their skills as facilitators and policy analysts in key posts. To test these predictions this section will look, agency by agency, at when our officials entered government, what their initial career motives were, what experiences they had outside of government, what routes their careers have followed within the public service, and what their current expertise is.

We expected Finance's officials to enter the public service along Weber's classic vocational lines because it is the most hierarchical of central agencies and, until the mid-sixties, was in large part an operational department. However, we found only modest evidence that Finance officials decided upon their careers before the others (Appendix II). They cited idealistic motives for entering government more than other officials, but the difference falls short of statistical significance. Their academic studies, apparently, influenced their choices no more than academic background affected the choices of officials in other central agencies. Surprisingly, Finance officials indicate slightly more than others that they came to government because an opportunity arose which they could not find elsewhere. Two other findings deserve comment. First, TBS officials more than others believe that a government career offers greater chal-

lenges than a career in the private sector. Of course, the heavy
TBS work load, especially in the Program branch, might intensify
its officials' consciousness of challenge as a motive. Second, PMO
officials state somewhat more than PCO/FPRO respondents that
they entered government at mid-career because they were
offered the opportunity. These perceptions among PMO officials
stand to reason because, as discussed in Chapter 3, they often see
themselves more as political operatives than bureaucrats.

We thought that Finance officials, more than others, would
have taught university before coming to government, because
Finance requires the type of knowledge most often found in
academe. Although Finance officials more frequently held posts
in universities than our other respondents, the difference falls far
short of statistical significance; former academicians appear to
be almost as numerous in other agencies as they are in Finance.
In fact, none of the five central agencies seem to hire individuals
who have had more experience in any one part of the private
sector than another.

The data underscore dramatic agency differences — such as,
that Finance officials generally assume high posts through seniority. With an average age of 47, they have a two-year edge on
TBS officials and almost a five-year spread over PMO/PCO/FPRO
officials. Their average tenure in the public service (13.8 years)
exceeds that of TBS officials by three years and of PMO/PCO/FPRO
officials by four years. More important, our respondents in
Finance have experienced much more stable careers than the
others. Whereas PMO/PCO/FPRO and TBS central agents, on the
average, have spent about half of their careers in their departments, Finance officials have served 76 per cent of their careers
in their department. Moreover, they have spent more than twice
as many of their years in the public service in their present
department and longer in their posts than other central agents.
We thus see considerable evidence that Finance provides opportunities for officials to pitch their tents and enjoy lengthy tenure
close to the seat of power.

Curiously, officials in the other agencies have not changed
departments as often as we expected. Conventional wisdom has

held that the PCO, the FPRO, and the TBS turn over officials at a very rapid rate.[21] The rapid turnover would accomplish three things: it would assure that officials would not burn out from the gruelling pace of the central agencies; it would prevent the development of a caste of superbureaucrats who never leave central agencies; and it would circulate into the programmatic departments officials with first-hand experience of central-agency and cabinet operations. However, our respondents' career paths indicate a trend towards stability within these three central agencies.

On the average, TBS officials have served just over half of their careers in their current department; PMO/PCO/FPRO officials have spent 42 per cent of their careers in their current agency. Since many of our central agents in the PMO/PCO/FPRO/TBS have held more than one post in their agency, a pattern has probably developed in these departments. Officials who take up senior positions in the four central agencies are often those from within who have demonstrated exceptional talent. Thus, rather than circulate out of the agencies, the more talented move up the hierarchy of their central agency. The continual expansion of the agencies, illustrated in Chapter 3, assures a reasonable supply of new and more senior positions through which the chosen few may advance their careers while remaining close to the centre. If the central agencies continue to expand as rapidly as they have and to serve as niches for those with superbureaucratic inclinations, careers within them might begin very soon to approach the stability of tenure found in Finance.

The PMO differs considerably from the PCO and the FPRO with respect to the career routes of its officials. PMO officials' average age of 38.6 years is almost six years less than that of PCO/FPRO officials. Yet, PMO officials have served, on the average, almost a year and a half longer in their agency than PCO/FPRO officials have in theirs (3.91 *vs.* 2.57 years). The limited turnover in the PMO results, as we saw in Chapter 3, from the Prime Minister's tendency to keep staff as long as possible.

Are there "typical" career routes for central agents? Do officials in certain central agencies tend to come directly from one or two specific departments? During the interviews it occurred to us that Finance officials frequently come from Industry, Trade, and Commerce. That department, we believed, serves as a point of entry for economists who fail to find a position in Finance as soon as they enter the public service. The data indicate, however, that a slightly greater proportion of TBS than Finance officials come from Industry, Trade, and Commerce. In fact, we found that only veterans of Defence and of Indian Affairs and Northern Development went on to particular central agencies in any appreciable numbers. Of the six former Defence officials, four currently serve in the PCO/FPRO; of the four former Indian Affairs and Northern Development officials, three hold posts in the PCO/FPRO. The fact that William Teschke, deputy secretary to the Cabinet for Plans, came to the PCO from Defence perhaps explains the former finding; Gordon Robertson's move to the PCO from Indian Affairs and Northern Development in 1962 perhaps explains the latter. Thus, we cannot find a clear and consistent outline of officials' movement from programmatic departments to central agencies. The specialist-generalist differences between the PMO, the PCO, the FPRO, and the TBS on the one hand and Finance on the other cannot be explained by previous experiences in specific departments.

While officials in the PMO, the PCO, the FPRO, and the TBS stressed management as an area of their expertise, Finance officials did not; they mainly focused on economics. Not surprisingly, fully 36 per cent of them said that economics alone was their forte; at least 77 per cent mentioned economics or some branch of it — taxation, banking, or financial law. A significantly greater proportion of Finance officials than others said they specialized in policy questions related to external affairs; these officials, of course, serve in the department's International Trade and Finance branch.

We also wanted to know whether different career experiences help explain the specialist-generalist dichotomy between Finance and the other agencies. We tested to see if respondents in the respective agencies gave different reasons for their particular expertise. As we have already seen, the largest proportion of officials say they acquired their expertise from experience in government. A more detailed breakdown indicates that PMO/PCO/FPRO and Finance officials place almost equal emphasis on the importance of experience in government while TBS officials tend somewhat less to stress this aspect of the development of their expertise. The differences, however, fall short of statistical significance.

It appears, then, that our central agents, whether primarily specialists (as in Finance) or generalists (as in the other central agencies), learn on the job. Private-sector experiences are not thought crucial to their present work, while public-service experience is granted considerable importance. Finance officials, of course, follow almost tenure-track careers based on the preference of Ottawa's "Department of Economics" for home-grown economists.

With regard to our respondents' views of their goals since entering public service, we again find Finance officials fitting the specialist mould better than others. An overwhelming majority of them (64 per cent *vs.* 16 per cent in the PMO, the PCO, and the FPRO, and 29 per cent in the TBS) report that they have attempted to affect specific fields of policy during their careers. Finance officials speak most often of their efforts to influence governmental planning, but almost as many TBS officials mention this (34 *vs.* 36 per cent); only 19 per cent of PMO/PCO/FPRO officials give the same response. And, more Finance officials (18 per cent) register facilitation of the policy process as a career goal than do either PMO/PCO/FPRO officials (9 per cent) or TBS officials (3 per cent). It is notable that PMO/PCO/FPRO officials cite contributing a human dimension to government and aiding personal development somewhat more than other officials (28 *vs.* 5 and 13 per cent, and 31 *vs.* 14 and 16 per cent for Finance and the TBS, respectively). The officials' interest in contributing a human dimension derives mainly from the very large proportion of PMO officials who mentioned this goal (55 *vs.* 14 per cent in the PCO and FPRO). Indeed, PCO/FPRO officials view their work as promoting personal development slightly more than PMO officials do (33 *vs.* 27 per cent) and somewhat more than Finance and TBS officials do (14 and 16 per cent, respectively). Although disparities in the kinds of individual goals of officials in various central agencies emerge, this is not the case regarding what they would miss if they left government. Most officials would miss the same things, probably because their jobs fulfil basic psychological needs.

Conclusion

The literature on career routes in the Canadian bureaucracy suggests that senior public servants in this country do not follow Weber's classic bureaucratic career routes. First, Canadian senior officials, in the public service generally, enter government much later in life than top bureaucrats in other countries. Second, rather than staying in one department, they tend to move from ministry to ministry, receiving promotions as they go along.

Our study supports this thesis; Canadian central agents rarely view their career choice as a vocation. Instead, they usually chose a career in public service after working outside government. Most also reported that they came to government for advancement and challenge rather than to serve the public or to contribute their knowledge and skills. Once in government, a very large proportion of the respondents have developed expertise in management. Just as Chartrand and Pond found among senior Canadian officials in 1967, many of our central agents have moved from department to department, instead of staying in any one through most of their careers. The comparison of career routes among the agencies, however, reveals some signs of stratification. Finance clearly differs from the others in that officials there may attain virtual tenure, because their department tends to rely as much as possible on "home-grown" economic expertise. In recent years, expansion of the other four agencies has meant that many officials could obtain promotions without leaving their central agency.

The evidence that career stability is taken almost as a matter of course in Finance and is at least incipient in the other agencies suggests the possibility that power in Ottawa is coming more and more to be held by an inner circle. A coterie, composed mostly of central agents, the theory goes, interacts in interdepartmental and cabinet meetings to usurp much of the policy-making authority from cabinet ministers. Suspicions that such inner circles actually exist intensify considerably when we remember that many of our central agents are, by their own admission, not indifferent to power.

Interactions:
One Inner Circle or Many?

The life of Ottawa is dominated by one huge industry: government. Unlike many other national capitals, it does not offer major alternative places of employment or competing arenas for enterprise. Government mobilizes practically all human talent available, all professional and intellectual skills. Very few corporate headquarters, industrial plants, and major service institutions are located in the city. During working days, most professional men and women think, feel, and breathe government. The one-dimensional nature of this milieu has not changed over the years, but its size has grown dramatically. Nearly all the growth can be directly related to the tremendous expansion of the bureaucracy.

The pervasiveness of government in Ottawa sets the tone of daily bureaucratic interactions, and the rather insular atmosphere influences public servants' behaviour. Twenty-five years ago a small group of key deputy ministers could meet for a leisurely lunch at the Château Laurier (at that time Ottawa's only elegant hotel) and resolve major policy differences between the departments and agencies they served. Today, the decision-making process is immensely more complex and cumbersome: several departmental committees, several interdepartmental committees, and at least one and often two cabinet committees will become involved before any measure of consensus or compromise is reached. These committees are, in a way, as protected from public view as the deputy ministers' table at the Château Laurier was in the past. But there have been changes. If it can be claimed that, today, all significant decisions in government are reached in committees, it is also important to note that, as never before, central agents play crucial — though varying — roles in the process.

This chapter takes a close look at the daily activities of the superbureaucrats, and the contexts in which they occur. It examines how committees serve as the principal means of interaction and decision making. It identifies various types and levels of committees, their authority and relationships, their membership and who has access to them, and, finally, the style of interaction which characterizes committee decision making by ministers and officials. Our respondents have been more than generous in providing us with examples and illustrations of committee behaviour.

Types and Levels of Committee

Government committees in Ottawa normally share the following distinguishing features:

1. They are relatively small, usually consisting of up to fifteen members, and there is often some restriction on membership and access. Members are expected to be of approximately equal rank, that is, either cabinet ministers, deputy ministers, or officials below DM level.

2. The chairmanship of each committee (and often also the vice-chairmanship) is entrusted to an individual designated by someone in higher authority; thus, the Prime Minister names the chairmen of cabinet committees and committees composed of deputy ministers, while DMs designate the chairmen of interdepartmental and departmental committees composed of officials. A chairman is normally expected to continue in office throughout a committee's mandate.

3. The authority granted to each committee is specific but permits some flexibility; it is usually given informally, often in writing, and never by way of a statutory or other legal instrument. This informality of authority distinguishes committees from task forces and commissions which are normally established by orders-in-council.

4. Committee membership properly includes representatives of each major contending interest relative to its authority. Thus, for example, the Social Policy cabinet-committee members

are drawn from such areas as Health and Welfare, Justice, Labour, Urban Affairs, and Employment and Immigration.

5. Each committee meets regularly, but the frequency may vary considerably depending on the nature of the mandate. Some record of proceedings and decisions or recommendations is usually kept. Unlike task forces and commissions, committees conduct their proceedings out of the public eye.

These distinguishing features are not rigid, and exceptions and modifications occur quite often in the name of flexibility or convenience.

There exists an implicit three-tiered hierarchy among governmental committees. At the bottom of the ladder are departmental committees whose memberships and authority are usually confined to one department or agency. Each department and agency has an internal management committee chaired by a deputy minister (or secretary) and composed of all ADMs and sometimes directors general; it must resolve internal conflicts and issues, and fashion the department's strategy or position on specific policy issues or problems. Such committees constitute the first level of input into the decision-making process.

Next on the ladder are interdepartmental committees. Since 1968 they have become the principal means of communication and deliberation in the federal bureaucratic establishment. We do not know precisely how many of them exist and operate at any given time. From the responses of our central agents, however, we have been able to compile a list of almost a hundred interdepartmental committees. Some of these have continued for two or three years or longer; others have lasted only a few months; many have set up sub-committees. It is not entirely clear how these committees are created. Undoubtedly, many of them have been formed on express instructions of cabinet committees, or the Prime Minister, and given a mandate to report back. Probably, however, a good number have been created by departments and agencies themselves in order to resolve interdepartmental conflicts and policy differences. Many of our central agents have shown great interest in the work of particular committees which they perceive as quasi-institutional links between Cabinet and programmatic departments, and a very important second level in the decision-making process.

At the top of the ladder are the eight standing cabinet committees. A hierarchy and specialization exists even among these. First is Priorities and Planning, which now includes Federal-Provincial Relations, and is the only standing committee chaired by the Prime Minister; its membership is rigidly restricted to designated ministers, and it alone issues guidelines (to be distinguished from mere decisions) which the remaining standing committees are expected to take into account. Next come two additional "co-ordinating" committees: Legislation and House Planning, and the Treasury Board. And finally come the five "subject matter" committees intended to encompass within their mandates all substantive-policy areas: Economic Policy, Social Policy, External Policy and Defence, Cultural and Native Affairs, and the omnibus committee called Government Operations. In addition to these standing committees, Cabinet is divided into special, ad hoc committees which meet only when the necessity arises. They include Security and Intelligence, Public Service, and Labour Relations. Finally, there exists a committee of council which meets regularly and passes formal orders and regulations. The distinction between standing committees and special ad hoc committees is not always clear, but in theory the former provide an on-going structure for top-level policy formation, while the latter take care of special issues which require resolution outside of the regular decision-making process. Thus, during the prolonged postal strike in 1970, for example, the Labour Relations committee met frequently and finally forced a settlement of the dispute. We must add that Cabinet itself is a committee of the Privy Council and, pursuant to constitutional principle, it assumes responsibility for all actions and decisions taken by any of its organizational sub-units.

These three levels of committee — departmental, interdepartmental, and cabinet — complete the structure for decision making in Ottawa. Of course, the equally complex intergovernmental domain of federal-provincial relations, involving countless meetings between ministers and officials on both levels, has a highly significant impact on federal decision making. But to some extent this impact is channelled through FPRO and the Federal-Provincial unit of the Finance department.

The Authority and Relationships of Committees

This section deals with a few selected interdepartmental committees, and then focuses more fully on cabinet committees which are of immediate concern to central agents. The purpose here is to illustrate the variety of problems and issues which have been assigned to bureaucratic committees for resolution, and the interdependence between the interdepartmental level and the cabinet level of decision making — so characteristic of contemporary executive/bureaucratic behaviour. For a large number of central agents, committees have become their lifeblood; they identify themselves with them almost to the same extent as they do with their "home" agencies. In the words of a TBS official:

I perform the role of a trouble-shooter or a problem solver, and I am often called upon to sit on a committee which may have been set up to solve a particular burning issue. Sometimes this issue is unrelated to my work here at TBS. For example, not long ago there was an ad hoc committee with a mandate to rationalize the government's approach to a specific policy issue. I was asked to chair this committee even though most of the other members on it were from two departments. So, you can see, I can move in and out of a committee where TBS is not directly involved whenever the situation demands.

Yet, senior officials in Ottawa must face up to one unpleasant aspect of interdepartmental committee work. Mandates notwithstanding, the length of the gestation period for most policies is so long that it makes for extremely arduous negotiations. Early in the summer of 1976 an interdepartmental committee was established to look into the possibility of integrating federal welfare expenditures with the income-tax system and of developing a unified welfare/tax system. A respondent who sat on this committee described its work as "the path for the future . . . the most creative and intellectually challenging" of tasks. In November 1977, the newly appointed Minister of National Health and Welfare, Monique Begin, announced only a partial adoption of the new integrated approach which had so inspired our respondent, and she promised to introduce shortly the necessary legislative measure. The interdepartmental process, in other words, was only getting off the ground more than a year after the initial discussions. Finally, in August 1978, a faint echo of our respondent's words was heard when Jean Chrétien, Minister of Finance, announced a very modest system of tax credits to the poor.

Another important aspect of interdepartmental committee work is the fact that, inevitably, there will be more than one group working in any general policy sector. For instance, in the area of personnel policy, three committees were singled out by our respondents as being very important: COSO (Committee on Senior Officials), whose mandate we have already described in Chapter 2; a committee on post-employment regulations, which was formed in reaction to the growing market for early retired senior officials in the consulting and corporate fields; and a committee reviewing levels of compensation paid to government economists — the so-called ES category — which, according to fellow-economist Douglas Hartle, has become one of the best-paid groups in the federal public service. In Hartle's view "the annual salaries paid in Ottawa to some professional groups (not to mention overtime pay and perquisites) is nothing short of outrageous. While I hesitate to name the names, the economist-statistician group immediately comes to mind...."[1] The ES-category committee took on the task of looking into the grounds for such criticism.

In December 1976, during our final set of interviews in Ottawa, officials representing central agencies took active part in the proceedings and deliberations of numerous interdepartmental committees. Their authority included: the post-Anti-Inflation-Program regulation strategy (the so-called DM-10 committee which was recently reconstituted into DM-5 under the chairmanship of Deputy Minister Shoyama), nuclear energy, security, commercial policy, demographic policy, native policy, employment strategy, technological forecasting, royal visits, law of the sea, and government organization. We emphasize that this list names only a few committees and serves chiefly to illustrate the variety and heterogeneity of issues and problems which cross the institutional boundaries of bureaucratic departments. If there is one conclusion to be drawn, it is this: no department in Ottawa today enjoys a monopoly of a policy domain, no matter what may be the terms of its statutory authority; and officials agree that the exercise of bureaucratic power takes place in interdepartmental and cabinet committees, largely because issues usually overlap and affect the interests of many departments.

Full Cabinet no longer serves as the exclusive decision-making apparatus for ministers. Nevertheless, its work is still very significant. Cabinet must give formal approval to all decisions taken by its committees; it acts as a court of last appeal whenever contending interests have failed to reach agreement at the committee level; it offers a forum for highly political, controversial issues — often unrelated to the on-going policy process — wherein ministers can register their greatest concerns about the direction of the government. Since most policy issues receive much threshing out before reaching the agenda, the full Cabinet usually gives only a formal stamp of approval. In cases of disagreement on a matter of policy, it prefers to refer the issue back to committee rather than make a substantive decision. However, the process does break down in some instances, forcing Cabinet to make the final decision. Only two to three issues in a week require this type of treatment. As a collective body for political leadership, the Cabinet plays a creative role when it freely deliberates issues which fall outside of the systematic decision-making process.

We have already named the three co-ordinating standing committees of Cabinet. Their specific authority may be briefly described as follows:

Committee on Priorities and Planning, which now includes federal-provincial relations, acts as the executive management board for the cabinet-committee system. It is clearly the senior decision-making body; however, its role is kept flexible and currently it includes the following functions:

a) articulation of broad policy objectives and priorities for the longer term and initiation of major policy reviews consistent with these priorities;

b) formulation of priorities for the annual budgetary expenditures and policy guidelines consistent with the fiscal framework;

c) determination of macro-economic policy;

d) overseeing personnel policy with respect to key executive appointments and promotions;

e) formulation of the federal government's strategy *vis-à-vis* the provincial governments and overseeing federal-provincial relations, including the issue of Quebec's role in Confederation.

Committee on Legislation and House Planning scrutinizes draft legislation to make sure that the language used truly expresses the intention of the decision makers. It fashions the government's strategy against the opposition parties in the House of Commons and establishes priorities for the passage of government bills. *Treasury Board* reviews departmental program forecasts and renders final decisions on the allocation of expenditure budgets. In addition, it hears submissions from departments and agencies with respect to specific expenditures and acquisitions, and issues regulations and guidelines about the management of physical and human resources.

Substantive policy is made in the so-called subject-matter committees. In the insiders' terminology, a substantive policy field is referred to as "a sector"; the minister designated to chair the committee is called "the lead minister in the sector"; the head of the PCO secretariat supporting the committee becomes "the sector manager". In Figure 6.1 all departments and agencies are arranged within the five policy sectors and the lead minister is identified in each sector.

Access and Membership

A cabinet-committee meeting was once rescheduled on short

FIGURE 6.1
POLICY SECTORS, LEAD MINISTERS, DEPARTMENTS WITHIN SECTORS

POLICY SECTOR	LEAD MINISTER(S)[1] THE SECTOR	DEPARTMENTS WITHIN SECTORS
Economic[2]	Minister of Finance	Finance; Regional Economic Expansion; Industry, Trade, & Commerce; National Revenue; Energy, Mines, & Resources; Agriculture;[3] Consumer & Corporate Affairs; Fisheries; Small Business
Social	Minister of National Health & Welfare or Minister of Justice (depending on the issue)	Health & Welfare; Justice; Labour; Urban Affairs; Employment & Immigration; Solicitor General; Veterans' Affairs
External & Defence	Secretary of State for External Affairs or Minister of National Defence (depending on the issue)	External Affairs; Defence; CIDA; Industry, Trade, & Commerce (international trade); Labour (ILO); Finance (IMF, GATT, OECD)
Culture & Native Affairs	Secretary of State or Minister of Indian Affairs and Northern Development (depending on the issue)	Secretary of State; Indian Affairs & Northern Development; Communications; Fitness & Amateur Sport Multiculturalism

notice from its usual afternoon hour to the morning of the same day. All regular members and participants — with the exception of one deputy minister who was out of town and could not be reached — were advised by telephone of the change. The deputy minister had planned to return to Ottawa and attend the meeting in the afternoon as originally scheduled. The meeting took place in the morning and an ADM substituted for the absent

POLICY SECTOR	LEAD MINISTER(S)[1] THE SECTOR	DEPARTMENTS WITHIN SECTORS
Government Operations[4]	Minister of Transport	Transport; Environment; Public Works; Supply & Services; Science & Technology; Post Office; Agriculture[3]

Notes

[1] According to some well-placed respondents, there is no necessary relationship between "lead ministry" and membership on the Priorities and Planning committee. However, it is an acknowledged fact that all chairmen of the "subject matter" committees also sit on the P&P committee. Because the latter acts as an "executive management board" for the entire cabinet system, membership on it implies not only ministerial seniority but also a special favour of the Prime Minister. For these reasons, the PCO still continues to insist that the names of committee chairmen (and members) are confidential information.

[2] Due to the importance of economic policy in recent years, the cabinet committee on Priorities and Planning devotes much of its time to macro-economic issues. On those occasions it is supported by the Economic Policy secretariat instead of the P&P secretariat in the PCO.

[3] The non-economic aspects of agricultural policy fall within the omnibus sector called Government Operations.

[4] This is not a "true" policy sector but a grouping of several mandates under an omnibus heading, the largest of which is Transport.

deputy minister. When the deputy minister returned he discovered that one item on the agenda had been resolved in a manner with which he strongly disagreed. He wasted no time and dispatched a terse and unequivocal memo to the minister who chaired the meeting. It read: "During my absence and without my knowledge a cabinet-committee meeting was held and a decision taken against which I had no opportunity to speak. This must not happen again."

On-going access to meetings of cabinet committees is probably the most valued privilege of Ottawa officials. In theory, any minister may attend a meeting of any committee he wishes —

with the exception of Priorities and Planning. In fact, most ministers cannot even find the time to attend all the meetings of the two or three committees to which they have been assigned. Increasingly, they choose to delegate their attendance to officials. This may be a disturbing development to those who draw a sharp line between the elected political leaders and the appointed career bureaucrats. Central agents in particular have developed "ministerial" abilities — that is, they can perform on behalf of ministers with ease and effectiveness. When we questioned one of our respondents about the role senior officials play at cabinet-committee meetings, he recounted the following episode:

A group of ministers circulated a proposal which they wanted to present at the next regular meeting of the cabinet committee on federal-provincial relations. I knew that my minister (who was a member of the committee) was opposed to the proposal, and he knew that I shared his view. He asked me to attend the meeting in his place. When we reached the item on the agenda, the Prime Minister asked one of the sponsors for a short summary of the proposal. He later turned to me and said "Do you have any objections?" I replied, "No, Prime Minister, I do not have any objection, but the minister I represent does. And if I may I would like to speak, on his behalf, against the proposal." I then meticulously and point by point destroyed the proposal. The PM looked around the table, noticing that the sponsoring ministers were disturbed and eager to get even. He asked them to elaborate further and make sure that everybody fully understood the substance of the proposal and its implications. For over half an hour I listened to their arguments which, in reality, did not contain anything new and made no more sense then than they did before. When they finished, the PM turned to me again and said: "Are you satisfied now? Did the additional explanation clear up the matter for you?" I replied: "Prime Minister, I must repeat that my own satisfaction is irrelevant. I am here only to represent my minister, but I can say on his behalf without any hesitation that he would not be satisfied with the explanation given, for the following reasons. . . ." And here I presented an even more formidable critique of the proposal and of its inadequate defence. I had the facts on my side and my analysis was clear, precise, and again devastating. When I finished, the PM turned to the sponsoring ministers and said simply: "I think you should get back to the drawing board with this. . . . Next item on the agenda. . . ."

The participation of officials in cabinet-committee delibera-tions was introduced by Prime Minister Trudeau in 1968–69. This innovation departs from the British practice. It is held in theory that participation by officials in cabinet committees increases ministers' influence over officials and, thus, strengthens the Cabinet — the political executive — against the bureau-cracy. Our own analysis does not support this hypothesis. Ten years of continued active participation has produced officials highly sensitive to political considerations. They have learned this sensitivity from their new colleagues — the ministers — after sharing countless hours of education and socialization with them at the committee table. Given their intellect, their profes-sional or academic training, and their knowledge of government acquired over the years of service, their new standing simply provides a forum in which their great potential for collegial relations is brought into play. Their positions as top political administrators are fully tenured, their status is guaranteed. To suggest that their influence has not increased is unrealistic.

The average or below-average minister, we believe, has, on the other hand, stood to lose a great deal of power from the new arrangement. His intellectual shortcomings are now known to cabinet colleagues and officials alike. His standing with the PM and senior cabinet colleagues is equally revealed. He must constantly worry about his seat in the House and cater to his constituents. As soon as he begins to understand how his depart-ment operates, he is shifted to another portfolio. Lucky for him, because he could have been dropped from Cabinet altogether. Gordon Robertson wrote in 1971 that the participation of ministers and officials in cabinet-committee meetings leads to "a blending of the roles that requires mutual confidence and an awareness of their differences".[2] We agree. Bureaucrats have become politicized and ministers tight-lipped as never before. As

for differences in influence, we believe these are greater between Allan MacEachen (Deputy Prime Minister and President
of the Privy Council) and Norman Cafik (Minister of State for
Multiculturalism) than between Jean Chrétien (Minister of
Finance) and Maurice LeClair (Secretary of the Treasury
Board). The admission of officials to cabinet-committee meetings
has upgraded the art of political administration. Some ministers
cannot keep up with the league; many officials have found
themselves in their element.

A particular style of interaction is determined by the authority
of a cabinet committee as well as by the preferences and
personalities of the chairman and the key participants. However,
each style emerges only within the context of basic uniformities
which apply to all cabinet committees. A *formal agenda* pre-
scribes the order of business and excludes surprises. Opposing
and supporting positions adopted by the participating actors are
circulated in advance to all members in secret *cabinet papers
and memoranda*; these may include analytic work prepared in
the PCO or the TBS. *Meetings* normally take place once every
week, or every second week, and last three hours on the average.
The *chairman* is in charge of the proceedings and responsible for
the results. Decisions taken are recorded in the *minutes*. Reports
of decisions are distributed to all cabinet ministers, all deputy
ministers, and to selected senior officials, especially key people
in central agencies.

One hard-nosed official with considerable experience in government highlighted the degree to which committee styles differ
by comparing the ways in which the Treasury Board and
Priorities and Planning function:

Treasury Board is a true decision-making committee. It resolves issues
once and for all. In fact, it works not unlike a court of law. . . . On the
other hand, the Committee on Priorities and Planning is not really a
decision-making body; rather, it's a deliberating body. It resolves
nothing.

This opinion reflects one respondent's bias in favour of the more clear-cut and down-to-earth problems which the Treasury Board considers and resolves. We recognize that the work of Priorities and Planning in reality is not as ethereal as this respondent indicates.

A meeting of Priorities and Planning (when it does not concern federal-provincial relations) is not unlike a lengthy quasi-academic seminar with several, often diverse, subjects on the agenda (Figure 6.2). The Prime Minister and ten senior ministers chosen by him occupy places around the table. Next to them sit the deputy ministers or other key departmental and agency officials. Officials from the PCO Priorities and Planning secretariat are seated at a separate table. Mr. Pitfield, who is usually present, moves freely around the room but takes his place most frequently by the Prime Minister. When Priorities and Planning discusses federal-provincial matters, officials from the FPRO are also present. In either case, there is no voting and the decisions are arrived at by a form of consensus or compromise extracted by the Prime Minister.

A typical Treasury Board meeting presents a different picture (Figure 6.3). The President and four members of the board sit at one side of the table facing a group of TBS officials headed by the secretary. They have previously read a submission prepared by a particular department requesting either an approval of a substantial expenditure from the allocated budget or an increase in the proposed budget level. The minister and the officials representing the department are asked to join the meeting and to address the board. When they do, the board members, as well as the secretary, interrupt frequently with questions and observations. When the discussion is over, the departmental delegation — including the minister — leaves the meeting room. The board then deliberates under the direction of its president with active participation of the secretary and his staff. If unanimity is not obtained, the president may ask for a vote. Once the decision is made, it is communicated to the department, immediately and in person, after the minister and his officials have been invited back into the room, and later in writing.

Not all meetings of the Treasury Board, however, follow the

FIGURE 6.2
POSSIBLE "FIRST STRING" FOR THE PRIORITIES AND PLANNING COMMITTEE (NOVEMBER 1977)

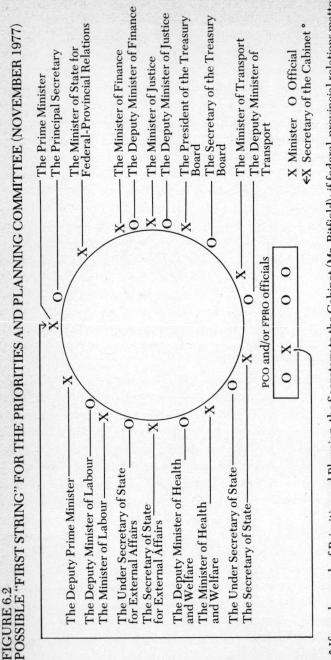

* If regular work of Priorities and Planning, the Secretary to the Cabinet (Mr. Pitfield); if federal-provincial relations matter, the Secretary to the Cabinet for Federal-Provincial Relations (Mr. Robertson)

FIGURE 6.3
ACTUAL TREASURY BOARD (NOVEMBER 1977)

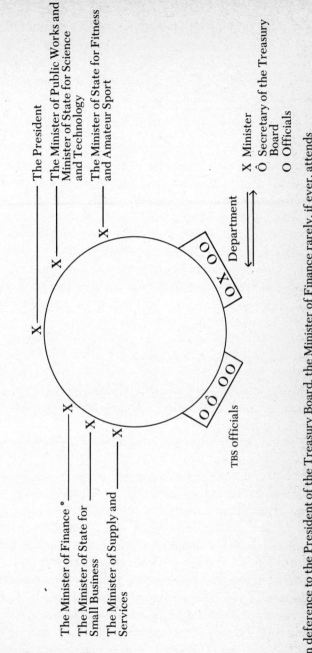

The President

The Minister of Public Works and Minister of State for Science and Technology

The Minister of State for Fitness and Amateur Sport

Department

The Minister of Finance *

The Minister of State for Small Business

The Minister of Supply and Services

TBS officials

X Minister
Ô Secretary of the Treasury Board
O Officials

* In deference to the President of the Treasury Board, the Minister of Finance rarely, if ever, attends

described pattern. In addition to its adjudicative role, the board meets to discuss issues relating to the management of human and physical resources of the government. In the course of such meetings the style of interaction is like that in cabinet committees responsible for specific policy sectors.

Using the Network: How Central Agents Interact

So far this chapter has indicated the many points of contact available to senior officials in central agencies. Besides being able to participate in a myriad of interdepartmental committees, they may attend cabinet committees and interact with ministers and officials from other departments. The preceding pages concerned structure more than behaviour. While looking at the complete array of our bureaucrats' interactions, we shall, in this section, first try to ascertain how our officials utilize the various channels of communication in Ottawa, and then try to discover whether central agents consider the policy process to be opened or closed to broad official participation.

During our interviews we tried to obtain as comprehensive a picture as possible of our respondents' interactions with various people in Ottawa. So we asked them whether they normally worked personally with the Prime Minister; ministers of their own department and others; deputy ministers of their own department and others; and MPs and Senators. In addition, we wanted to know what the usual context of such exchanges was, i.e., telephone, personal visits to offices, letters and memos, official meetings, and informal encounters in hallways or at social gatherings, and whether such exchanges concerned matters of policy rather than administration. (See Table 6.1.)

We expected that our central agents would encounter the greatest difficulty in obtaining opportunities to interact with the Prime Minister. Certainly, officials close to the PM spend a good portion of their time making sure that needless contacts with colleagues, or anyone for that matter, are deflected. Yet, fully 39 per cent of our respondents report personal contacts with the PM (Table 6.1). Indeed, 35 per cent say that they come in contact with him personally at least once a month and 23 per cent

TABLE 6.1
PERSONAL INTERACTIONS OF CENTRAL AGENTS (IN PERCENTAGES, N=92)

TYPE OF CONTACT	WITH WHOM						
	PM	Own Minister	Other Ministers	Own Deputy Minister/Secretary	Other Deputy Ministers/Secretaries	MPs	Senators
Personal							
Any Kind	39.1	59.8	72.8	88.0	84.8	62.0	29.3
Frequency							
once a month	34.8	66.7	67.4	75.0	79.3	44.6	23.9
twice a month	22.8	56.7	56.5	67.4	65.2	34.8	16.3
Telephone	7.6	15.2	20.7	42.4	48.9	32.6	10.9
Personal Visit	21.7	41.3	22.8	68.5	41.3	15.2	10.9
Letters/Memos	18.5	17.4	12.0	32.6	25.0	13.0	8.7
Official Meetings	30.4	40.2	64.0	72.8	66.3	23.9	13.0
Hallway	0.0	0.0	0.0	2.2	1.1	0.0	0.0
Social	1.1	0.0	2.2	1.1	3.3	7.6	4.3
About Policy	37.0	48.9	62.0	69.6	67.4	37.0	15.2

estimate that they do so at least twice a month. Such contacts take place in several settings. Most mention official meetings such as cabinet committees (30 per cent); visits to the PM's office and letters or memos prove to be good channels as well (mentioned by 22 and 19 per cent, respectively). Mr. Trudeau, however, must have an aversion to the telephone as only 8 per cent of our respondents use this means for contact. Informal contacts, in hallways or at social occasions, are extremely rare. Finally, 37 per cent of our officials say they interact with the PM about policy questions, rather than administration.

Our officials report even greater access to cabinet ministers. Sixty per cent of the respondents interact with their minister; an even larger proportion, 73 per cent, come into contact with ministers of other departments. Further, these interactions appear to occur relatively frequently, usually in meetings. A relatively large 44 per cent meet their ministers in their offices, no doubt because this is where briefing sessions appropriately take place. Forty-nine per cent of our respondents contact their own ministers about policy, while 62 per cent interact with ministers of other departments about policy. Thus, officials have several opportunities to discuss policy issues with cabinet ministers. The data in Table 6.1 indicate that officials very frequently interact personally with deputy ministers of their own and other departments. These interactions also overwhelmingly concern policy matters.

We might expect that senior officials in operational departments come into frequent contact with their own minister or deputy minister. But, the central agents have at least as much contact with other ministers and deputies in town as they do with their own (and in many cases more). Unfortunately, we lack comparable data about the interactions of officials in operational departments with ministers. Yet the data in Table 6.1 suggest that central agents occupy a favoured position in the policy process. This position stems from their responsibility for various co-ordinative functions between departments.

Table 6.1 also contains data on our officials' interactions with MPs and Senators. Although respondents in other surveys have played down legislators' roles in the policy process,[3] we wanted to discover if our central agents work with legislators, at least to some degree. Sixty per cent of our respondents say they do come into contact with MPs, while 29 per cent say that they are in touch with Senators. Many respondents contact MPs by telephone or in official meetings, primarily committee hearings; few do so by personal visits to offices or through letters and memos. These findings make sense, as MPs frequently must call officials in Ottawa about constituents' inquiries, while House of Commons committees rely heavily on testimony by officials.

As we saw earlier, senior officials in Ottawa employ inter-departmental committees as a key vehicle for developing policy proposals and legislation. We asked our respondents to state their involvement in these committees, their roles on them, and the benefits that they derive from this involvement. Seventy-four per cent of our respondents regularly attend at least one committee; 32 per cent work on more than one. Further, 13 per cent of our officials serve as chairman of at least one committee.

Previously we noted that the committees mentioned by our respondents number close to a hundred. They range from the very important DM-10, the committee of the top ten deputy ministers which advised the government through much of the Anti-Inflation-Program period, to the relatively unimportant committee which co-ordinates planning for royal visits. Most of the committees on our list were attended regularly by only one or two of our respondents, with, however, notable exceptions. Five or more officials claim that they regularly attended: a committee on tax policy; DM-10 (officials who are not deputy ministers were often invited to attend and participate in this committee); a committee on inflation which antedated DM-10; and an advisory committee to the Unemployment Insurance Commission.

For purposes of clarification, we have grouped committees according to six types, which enables us to see the kinds of issue committee work centres on. The groups distinguish among committees concerned with general aspects of economic policy; economic development, including technology, resources, and commerce; the rights and benefits of individuals and groups (e.g., native rights, unemployment insurance); foreign affairs and defence; bureaucratic management, including machinery of government, administration, and personnel; and, finally, umbrella committees with over-arching responsibilities for co-ordination of policies, including DM-10 and the PCO committee for policy development. Respondents participate most often in bureaucratic-management committees (34 per cent). Twenty-six and 23 per cent of our officials serve on economic policy and umbrella committees, respectively. They are less involved in economic development, rights and benefits, and foreign affairs and defence committees (19, 17, and 14 per cent, respectively). It thus appears that central agents stress work on committees concerned with questions of general importance to government (the state of the economy included), rather than with narrower issues within various policy sectors.

With so many committee obligations, our respondents must be selective about which committees they personally attend. Indeed, 26 per cent delegate many of their committee obligations to less-senior officials in their units. One assistant deputy minister who at least keeps track of the committee obligations of officials in his branch asserts that colleagues at his level rarely know from day to day what the committees to which they nominally belong are doing.

Officials say that they derive four types of benefits from their interdepartmental committee work. First, 20 per cent find that committees provide useful information on what is happening in other departments, e.g., responses to proposed policies, or how a policy is being administered and received by the public. Second, 11 per cent see committee work as an opportunity to bring expertise to bear on a problem more effectively than is usually possible. For instance, one respondent who worked on a committee studying inflation asserts that this body became somewhat more than an advisory panel during the development of the Anti-Inflation Program in 1975; he thereby was able actually to formulate policy. A TBS official recounts that a committee chaired by a PCO official gave him a sufficient base of operations to study a question which he had been interested in for some time. Third, 16 per cent of the officials emphasized that committee work greatly facilitates the policy process. A PCO official states that it is essential for him to work closely with interdepartmental panels whose proposals he must steer through Cabinet. A Finance department official points out that he was one of four young officials placed on a committee to assure that certain policy ideas ultimately won acceptance. Finally, 14 per cent of our respondents maintain that in interdepartmental committees they can see if their policy ideas are working out as intended, and iron out any problems.

Turning to cabinet committees, 72 per cent of respondents (practically the same proportion which reported interdepartmental committee work) attend cabinet committees on a fairly regular basis, an average of nineteen cabinet-committee meetings per year. Further, 32 per cent frequently become full-fledged discussants in such meetings, whereas 30 per cent speak only in an advisory capacity when asked questions, and 7 per cent simply observe the proceedings. The 32 per cent are discussants largely because ministers, as Chapter 3 mentions, are often unable to attend committee meetings. Two respondents from the Finance department explain their participation:

I would characterize my participation as either speaking only when called for advice, and that is in cases when my minister is present, or, in the event that he is not present, actively involving myself in the discussion. My minister is not present at the cabinet committee about 50 per cent of the time; this is roughly how often I become a discussant.

If my own minister is present at the meeting, then I will speak only when called upon for advice. If my minister is not present, then I become the representative of the department and involve myself fully in the discussion.

The data in Table 6.2 indicate that officials gain access to all cabinet committees. Twelve per cent or more, however, regularly attend Economic Policy, Priorities and Planning, Federal-

Provincial Relations (now merged with Priorities and Planning), and the Treasury Board; this suggests that our officials gravitate to the more important committees. More officials join in the discussions of the Treasury Board than do so in Priorities and Planning (27 *vs.* 20 per cent). We saw earlier in this chapter that the tribunal-like proceedings of the Treasury Board allow for especially collegial relations between board members and the TBS officials who give advice on departments' submissions.

TABLE 6.2
CENTRAL AGENTS' PARTICIPATION IN CABINET
COMMITTEES (N=92)

COMMITTEE	ATTENDS COMMITTEE %	PARTICIPATION %	
		Advisor	Discussant
1 Co-ordinating			
Priorities and Planning	20.0	9.8	6.5
Legislation and House Planning	7.6	1.1	5.4
Treasury Board	27.2	9.8	15.2
Federal-Provincial Relations	12.0	6.5	5.4
2 Subject Matter			
Government Operations	7.6	2.2	5.4
Economic Policy	12.0	4.3	4.3
External Policy and Defence	8.7	5.4	2.2
Social Policy	8.7	4.3	3.3
Culture and Native Affairs	7.6	4.3	2.2

As with interdepartmental committees, officials benefit from attending and participating in cabinet committees. Twenty-eight per cent believe that they gain immense insight into the policy process by attending committees. Such knowledge, our officials point out, can prove to be especially useful in future dealings with cabinet committees:

Attendance at these committees makes one more sensitive to the political issues and problems faced by the government. You come to realize that you have to suggest solutions which are politically realistic. I don't mean in a partisan sense. I mean realistic in terms of solving a problem given the current mood in the country.

If I am going to do my work properly, I must attend cabinet committees. I have to have an accurate feel for what's going on. I have to know what the concerns and expectations of ministers are.

In a somewhat different vein, 13 per cent of our officials garner information about what other departments are pressing and about the state of current issues by attending committee meetings. Fully 25 per cent of respondents believe they can influence policy through committee work. As one Finance official said:

I'm the one in the department on top of issues which come up before that committee. If I go, it's because Finance has something specific to say about a matter. I'm not there as an observer. I'm there because I have a viewpoint and something to say.

For 11 per cent of our officials, their involvement in cabinet committees relates even more directly to policy-making roles. An official in the FPRO and one in the TBS brought this point out particularly well:

Our relations with ministers are conditioned very much by our exposure on this level. They take note of our presence and role in the process. If we haven't reached agreement with a minister on something, he knows that he can expect a follow-up because we will register our concerns with the PM.

I'm known in the community as someone who will disagree with ministers, i.e., to make sure that my point gets across to them. There is a limit to how much you can hold things up and get away with it. But, I can do a fair amount of this by working within cabinet committees.

Finally, 7 per cent of our central agents believe committees actually resolve issues and, therefore, merit attention.

Despite their contribution and involvement, most of our officials (56 per cent) maintain that an inner circle of ministers and/or officials makes the really important decisions in Ottawa.

For example:

When I started here in TBS I was told that if I didn't win the approval of some top deputy ministers connected with the policies I'm responsible for I wouldn't get anywhere. So I appointed these key people to my advisory committee. Two of them have proved to be especially important to take into consideration. I would put them in the inner circle.

The big decisions these days are economic. So it's pretty well coming down to the PM, Pitfield [Secretary of the Cabinet], Ian Stewart [Economic Adviser, the PCO], and Gordon Osbaldeston [then Secretary of the Treasury Board] as the group which is making the really tough decisions. There is an aura to all this. Just because it's believed that there is an inner circle the group can have a tremendous impact. The rumour that you are a close friend of the PM can be a terribly potent instrument. For instance, the fact that Ian Stewart is seen as Trudeau's closest economic adviser makes him an awfully important person in town.

A further 28 per cent believe that there are several inner circles which make key decisions:

I guess you mean the mandarins. At any given time they'll be senior officials who have considerably more influence than others because of personality and position. But their influence depends in part on whether the issues for which they have responsibility are the ones that grab ministers at a particular time. A few years ago government and the issues were small enough [the latter in number] so that you could identify four or five mandarins who were knowledgeable about everything. Things aren't that simple any more.

Only 12 per cent of our officials flatly denied the existence of any inner circle:

Definitely not. The system is just too big for an inner circle. If I had a viewpoint on a specific policy and thought that a mistake was going to be made, I would simply contact fifty people. Each of these would be equally important. An sx-1 [the lowest senior-executive rank] can have as much impact as a deputy minister in some cases. This is why Pitfield has no effect. He introduces all sorts of changes in structure and form, but it's hard to say he has changed outcomes at all. For example, take atomic-energy policy. Eight deputy ministers get together and discuss an issue. The actual decision was taken long before. Their discussion is pedestrian. It reflects how they were briefed by officials in their departments. There is no vote. The guy who records the sense of the meeting has more influence than they do. I try to influence the guys who do the briefings and write up the minutes. This whole mandarin thing is garbage. Deputy ministers are simply conduits of information.

Those who believe in an inner circle or circles find it hard to agree on who belongs. Only 20 per cent of all respondents mention the Prime Minister, perhaps because they take his involvement for granted. Seventeen per cent mention the cabinet or one of its committees. A relatively large 34 per cent mention ministers with specific portfolios, for example, Finance and External Affairs. Most of our respondents (64 per cent) state that central agents are clearly best situated for membership in the inner circle(s), or mention specific colleagues who belong. The central agencies named most often as good bases for aspirants to the inner circle(s) were: Finance, 12 per cent; the PCO, 11 per cent; and the TBS, 8 per cent. That only 3 per cent named the PMO supports our contention made in Chapter 3 that the PMO performs best in a switchboard rather than policy-making role. A final 19 per cent mention deputy ministers of operational departments (no officials, however, below this level) as participants in the inner circle(s).

Telling us why they chose certain individuals or groups, our respondents throw light on the make-up of the possible inner circle(s). Eighty-two per cent named individuals or groups on the strength of their formal positions. In the words of two respondents:

It really depends on a person's position. The Minister of Finance and the government leader in the House are at the core of most questions. There are certain officials as well who fit in the group, especially the Clerk of the Privy Council and the deputy secretary to the Cabinet for Operations.

Trudeau is a great process man. He, unlike Diefenbaker, is very much aware of the organizational questions. He tends to use his Cabinet more like King than Diefenbaker. He relies heavily on a few ministers like the Minister of Finance and the President of the Treasury Board. He also will try to set up an independent source of advice for crucial questions. For instance, he uses Ian Stewart, his economic advisor in PCO, to counter the control of Finance in that field. To a degree, deputy ministers of programmatic departments have lost ground as a result of Trudeau's use of the Cabinet and its committees. They could regain their status, however, if they develop a system of DM committees which parallels cabinet committees. I see a drift toward this in the formation of the committee on inflation and DM-10.

Several of our respondents named individuals on the basis of their personal qualities. One PMO official had worked out quite exact criteria:

Both senior officials and ministers are candidates for the inner circle. With respect to officials, there are three important elements. First, the person has to have an excellent knowledge of governmental procedure, the "rules of the game". Second, he has to be persuasive, the logical force of his arguments has to come across. Third, he has to be a team player, willing to help his colleagues. With respect to cabinet ministers, I first rank the person's formal position in the government; second, his knowledge of practical politics; and third, his feel for public opinion.

A Finance department official discussed individuals and thus revealed the qualities he thinks are important for entrance to the inner circle(s):

The Finance minister always belongs, but some are stronger than others. John Turner grasped issues with amazing quickness and usually was in command; Donald MacDonald demonstrates intelligence but he's too reluctant to indicate his judgment. Tommy Shoyama [the deputy minister] is tremendously impressive from the standpoint of his ability to chair difficult meetings. Simon Reisman [Shoyama's predecessor] was too intuitive — he used to browbeat people, too. Mickey Cohen [then assistant deputy minister of the Tax Policy branch; now deputy minister of Energy, Mines, and Resources] is brilliant, fast, and very pleasant. Bill Hood [the associate deputy minister] has an outstanding mind and has everyone's respect, but he's difficult to work with. I've seen a lot of Gordon Osbaldeston [secretary of the Treasury Board] and he strikes me as very able. He's tough, but very rational. These are the fellows whom I've seen in operation. Their positions might have helped them get into the inner circle. Their personal qualities have determined their success.

The old adage "it's not what you know but whom you know" that makes the difference in one's power and influence finds only very modest support among our central agents when they name individuals as part of the inner circle(s). Fourteen per cent do believe that friendships and trust may move one into the inner circle(s). One TBS official elaborates:

Take the case of Mr. Pitfield. The contacts he has with the government party are very important. I don't think he has all that much experience, but his advantage lies in the fact that he knows personally all the ministers and is on a first-name basis with every one of them.

A Finance official links the role of personal relationships to Trudeau's style:

The Prime Minister is a unique being. He's very much his own man. Pitfield, along with several people at PCO, has tremendous influence on how the PM thinks, and how the PM thinks in a personalized system has a tremendous influence on what the country does. We're fortunate to have a member of the group here in Finance. Mickey Cohen, of course. The PM took note of his work on the resource problem, the social-

security review, and the Anti-Inflation Program. So, Mickey has been in
contact constantly. He's unassuming, he handles DMs superbly, he has
an uncanny ability to avoid reacting before figuring out what stance he
should take, he's already excelled in one career — tax law in Toronto —
so he's not trying to impress anyone. In a word, he's Trudeau's type of
guy. He fits in.

Interagency Differences

As Chapter 3 explained, the five central agencies fulfil quite
different roles. The PMO serves as a switchboard, keeping the
lines of communication open between the Liberal party, cabinet
ministers, bureaucrats, the media, and the general public. It
attempts to maximize the Prime Minister's political effectiveness
with these various elements mainly by assuring that he controls
the way in which what he does is communicated to the public.
The PCO and the FPRO help the Prime Minister and the Cabinet
search out the common ground between bureaucratic departments and/or governments, expediting decisions and assuring
that these are implemented. The Finance department, as the
repository of economic expertise, serves as the principal source
of economic advice for the government and oversees a number of
economic policies which other departments administer or must
adhere to. The TBS performs essentially two functions. It scrutinizes how departmental estimates fit into the over-all fiscal
framework; and it develops and monitors administrative, personnel, and financial-management policy.

Chapter 3 also explained that officials in the various central
agencies have different job statuses in the policy process. PMO
officials, as the Prime Minister's agents, may monitor cabinet and
interdepartmental committees but they are not tied down to
specific bureaucratic responsibilities related to policy development and implementation. PCO and FPRO officials, in addition to
frequently providing advice to the Prime Minister, serve also as
staff for the Cabinet and its committees. Finance officials participate widely in interdepartmental and cabinet committees without having to shoulder staff duties. However, they work in one of
the most hierarchical departments in Ottawa, and this imposes

certain constraints on the type of advice they give and the policies which they pursue. TBS officials employ the Treasury Board as a touchstone for an immense caseload of regulatory work on departments' estimates, and administrative, personnel, and financial-management policies.

In view of their various roles and statuses, we expect our respondents' personal and committee interactions and views of the inner circle(s) to differ. If positioning is essential to participation in the inner circle(s), then we expect our respondents to show group differences in both these areas according to which central agency they belong to.

First, with respect to interactions, PMO/PCO/FPRO officials come in direct contact with the Prime Minister much more often than those in Finance and the TBS. Whereas 53 per cent of our respondents in the PMO, PCO, and FPRO interact directly with the PM at least twice a month, only 9 and 5 per cent in Finance and the TBS, respectively, do so. (See Appendix II.) Further, of the three agencies, PMO officials contact the PM the most frequently (91 per cent, at least twice a month). This interaction exceeds considerably that of PCO/FPRO officials (33 per cent, at least twice a month). The PMO, PCO, and FPRO make contacts via all media: phone, visits, memos, and meetings; the content of these contacts, moreover, is policy oriented. However, the 46 per cent of PMO officials who regularly speak to the PM on the telephone or intercom far exceeds the figures for other officials. Only 5 per cent of officials in both the PCO and the FPRO and in Finance and none in the TBS interact with the PM this way. Many PCO/FPRO officials also report contacts with the PM in other settings; 43 per cent make visits, and 62 per cent attend meetings where the PM is present. Thirty-three per cent send briefing notes to and receive memos from him, whereas 82 per cent of PMO officials do so. PMO respondents have a higher percentage here, probably because they receive direct assignments from the PM, so long as the principal secretary knows generally the nature and results of such interactions, whereas PCO/FPRO respondents normally work for the PM only indirectly — even their briefing notes are channelled through the secretaries of their respective agencies.

Although this distinction is technical in many cases, it under-scores the unique status of PMO officials: they often do not have to deal with the bureaucratic hierarchy in their relations with the PM. Thus, they are given an opportunity for a special kind of effectiveness. One PMO official put it succinctly: "If I left PMO, I would miss above all people senior to me, cabinet ministers and deputy ministers, coming on the line quickly when I tell their secretaries that it's ＿＿ from PMO."

While officials in the Finance department and the TBS indicate less direct contact with the Prime Minister, we expected them to report frequent direct contact with their own ministers, namely the Minister of Finance and the President of the Treasury Board. Their estimates of interactions with these respective political heads of agencies bear out our expectations. They indicate as well, however, that while 73 per cent of Finance officials personally contact their minister at least twice a month, only 47 per cent of TBS officials contact theirs that often. Finance officials also meet their minister in more varied settings and more often discuss policy than do TBS officials. Perhaps because TBS officials serve, strictly speaking, a board rather than a single minister, perceptions of personal contact with the President of the Treasury Board are less clear.

More PMO/PCO/FPRO officials contact ministers of other de-partments at least twice a month than do Finance and TBS officials (81 *vs.* 50 and 40 per cent). PMO/PCO/FPRO officials, moreover, phone, visit, and send memos and letters to other ministers much more frequently than Finance and TBS officials do. Finance and TBS officials do, however, interact personally with other ministers at meetings almost as much as do PMO/PCO/FPRO officials. When comparing the responses of PMO and PCO/FPRO officials we find that the latter visit other ministers' offices almost as often as the former do and interact with them at meetings considerably more. PMO officials, however, come in touch with ministers by phone much more than PCO/FPRO officials do. It appears that even regarding contacts with ministers of other departments, an aura exists whereby PMO and PCO/FPRO officials, by virtue of their proximity to the PM and the Cabinet, move in relatively prestigious company.

Looking at our officials' contacts with their deputy minister, we find that while over 80 per cent of officials in the PMO, PCO, and FPRO, and in Finance, interact personally with their deputy minister at least twice a month, only 45 per cent of TBS officials claim the same amount of contact. In each possible context, a greater proportion of PMO/PCO/FPRO officials report having contacts than do officials in Finance and TBS. PMO/PCO/FPRO officials use various means of communication more frequently, especially memos (59 *vs.* 23 and 16 per cent for Finance and the TBS, respectively), and meetings (84 *vs.* 77 and 61 per cent). The relatively large and complex organizational structure of the TBS no doubt limits somewhat the ability of officials there to interact personally with their Secretary.

TBS officials, nevertheless, quite frequently say that they interact with deputy ministers of other departments at least twice a month (63 per cent). Of all central agencies, Finance reports the least monthly contact (50 per cent) with deputy ministers. (The PMO, PCO, and FPRO report 78 per cent.) Consistent with previous responses, PMO/PCO/FPRO officials report the greatest use of the telephone and memos in contacts with deputy ministers.

Because PMO officials perform many party-related functions, such as maintaining peace with caucus, responding to legislators' political requests and grievances, and assuring that the party machinery is in good order, we fully expected that they would report more contact with MPs and Senators than other central agents did. Our findings bear out this expectation. Whereas all PMO officials interact personally with MPs at least twice a month, only 14, 32, and 29 per cent of PCO/FPRO, Finance, and TBS officials, respectively, do so; and whereas 82 per cent of PMO officials interact personally with Senators at least twice a month, only 14, 9, and 3 per cent of PCO/FPRO, Finance, and TBS officials, respectively, do so. The low percentages for non-PMO officials here probably reflect the fact that legislators in Ottawa generally work at the periphery of the policy process *per se*.[4] It is interesting that officials in Finance and the TBS do interact with MPs a fair amount in meetings. Presumably, these contacts occur mainly when parliamentary committees review either Finance department legislation or Main or Supplementary Estimates of the Government. Indeed, many fewer TBS than Finance officials interact personally with Senators at meetings (5 *vs*. 32 per cent). Whereas both the Banking, Trade, and Commerce committee in the Senate and the Finance committee of the House of Commons often submit Finance department legislation to relatively intense study, National Finance, the Senate committee responsible for the estimates, scrutinizes these much less comprehensively than the various Commons committees do.[5]

So far this section has indicated that an official's central agency in part determines how he interacts with others in Ottawa. PMO officials appear to have the greatest amount of personal contact with the other players in the system, from the Prime Minister to Senators. Further, they report that such interactions take place in practically all the possible settings. By comparison, the career bureaucrats in the PCO, the FPRO, Finance, and the TBS find that interactions most frequently occur in formal and group sessions such as presentations of briefs in individuals' offices or meetings. We found evidence as well that TBS officials interact considerably less through these formal means than do bureaucrats in the PCO, the FPRO, and Finance. These findings raise the question: are some agencies' officials more involved than others in interdepartmental- and cabinet-committee work? Does exposure vary according to the nature and breadth of the subject matter of committees? In other words, do officials in some central agencies have more involvement than others in committees concerned with problems which relate to the very survival and direction of the political system? Do officials from various agencies have different views of the benefits they can derive from committee work?

First, although officials in all of the central agencies generally do interdepartmental-committee work, 46 per cent of Finance officials and 34 per cent of TBS officials report regularly attending three or more of these committees, while only 19 per cent of PMO/PCO/FPRO officials do. Indeed, 46 per cent of Finance officials state that they have so many committee obligations that they must frequently delegate attendance to less-senior officials in their unit. The data suggest as well that officials in various central agencies regularly attend different types of committee. Clearly, Finance officials attend most those committees which consider economic policies (55 per cent *vs.* 28 and 8 per cent for the PMO, PCO, and FPRO and the TBS, respectively), and, although the differences are not dramatic, they attend most regularly committees considering economic development (including technology, resources, and commerce); the rights and benefits of individuals and groups; and external affairs and defence. These data underscore how Finance is involved in virtually all sectors of the policy process. TBS officials, on the other hand, most frequently attend committees concerning bureaucratic management (including machinery of government, administration, personnel, and financial administration). In fact, we find under each of the other five committee categories that fewer than 20 per cent of TBS officials regularly participate. No doubt the orientation towards practical detail of much of the TBS's work contributes greatly to its relatively high participation rate in bureaucratic-management committees. Finally, we looked at our officials' attendance in umbrella committees (such as those concerning the state of the economy, or the development of government policy priorities). Here PMO/PCO/FPRO officials are most involved. The PMO's officials more often say they attend than the PCO/FPRO's do (46 *vs.* 24 per cent). In addition, although the small number of cases rules out statistical tests, we find that, whereas 19 and 24 per cent of PCO/FPRO officials attend economic development, and rights and benefits committees, respectively, our PMO respondents did not attend committees in these categories. From the data, we can conclude that: PMO officials, because their small numbers dictate that they avoid spreading themselves too thinly, mostly attend umbrella committees; PCO/FPRO officials, because they head secretariats for cabinet committees, distribute their attendance much more evenly; Finance officials, because their advice and consent on economic matters is indispensable, participate the most in four of the six committee categories; and TBS officials, because of their responsibility for bureaucratic management in government, overwhelmingly favour management-oriented committees.

Along with these differences in committee attendance, officials in the various agencies view the benefits that they derive from such work somewhat differently. PMO/PCO/FPRO officials were relatively reticent about these benefits. TBS officials, again revealing their practicality, most often said that they gain useful information and help implement policies through such committee work. Finance officials, on the other hand, maintained considerably more than the others that they influence policy through committees (32 vs. 13 and 11 per cent for the PMO, PCO, and FPRO and the TBS, respectively). Given their omnipresence, Finance officials perhaps develop relatively strong feelings of efficacy about their work on committees.

Our data on cabinet-committee attendance, on the other hand, suggest many fewer differences among agencies. Fewer Finance officials go to cabinet-committee meetings twice a month or more. But the difference falls short of statistical significance. More PMO/PCO/FPRO and TBS officials than Finance officials attend co-ordinating committees, obviously because their departments house the secretariats for Priorities and Planning, Legislation and House Planning, and the Treasury Board. PMO officials, however, have little time for subject-matter committees. None of them reports attending these committees at least once a month. On the other hand, a slightly greater proportion of PMO than PCO/FPRO officials (27 vs. 24 per cent) attend Priorities and Planning at least once every two months. Interestingly, 40 per cent of PMO/PCO/FPRO officials participate in committees only as advisors; that is, they speak up only when asked to comment on specific matters. Only 13 per cent usually become involved as full participants in discussions. Nearly the same proportion of TBS officials are advisors (32 per cent) as are full discussants (34 per cent). Most Finance officials, on the other hand, are discussants (55 per cent); only 14 per cent are advisors. Fittingly, Finance officials, more than others, derive from cabinet-committee work the satisfaction of lending their expertise (46 per cent *vs.* 22 and 16 per cent for the PMO, PCO, and FPRO and the TBS, respectively) and of influencing policy (23 per cent *vs.* 3 and 11 per cent). Finance officials do not enjoy access to the PM and cabinet ministers as other central agents do. PMO's officials find such access through staff work for the PM, while PCO/FPRO officials find it through their staff work for the Cabinet and its commit- tees. Finance's officials apparently compensate for this lack of access by trading on their expertise at cabinet-committee meet- ings.

It appears that central agents try to have an influence in the policy process and apparently employ those media that best serve their purposes. This finding sheds light on why our respon- dents do not all agree that inner circles dominate the policy process. Looking at the responses of those who do perceive inner circles, we find that officials within various central agencies tend to agree on who belongs.

Conclusion

Early in this chapter we asserted that the process of making decisions in government has undergone an immense transforma- tion in the past twenty-five years. One very significant change has been in the extent to which senior officials in central agencies have come to participate in decision making through interactions both among themselves and with cabinet ministers. Whereas, in the early 1950s, one small cadre of senior officials was able to remain knowledgeable about and to influence all important policy issues, in the late 1970s groups have tended to form around specific pressing issues and to disband when they have been resolved. Twenty-five years ago senior officials worked through a network of relatively informal contacts; now they work through formal and quasi-formal networks of inter- departmental and cabinet committees. This situation argues against the existence of one central group or inner circle of all- powerful political administrators. And while it suggests the existence of inner circles which centre on issues, it gives no clear indication that holding a certain post or membership in a certain central agency automatically lifts one into such a circle.

We recognize, none the less, that officials play a strong role in the policy process. Central agents, at least, indicate to us that their policy roles are flourishing. Many have particularly easy access to the Prime Minister and/or to cabinet ministers. PMO/PCO/FPRO officials enjoy such access through the myriad of staff functions performed in the agencies for the PM, the Cabinet, and cabinet committees. TBS officials work, often on a collegial basis, with the ministers on the Treasury Board. Finance officials obtain access through their participation in cabinet-committee meetings; there they become fully involved in discussions and believe that they influence policy.

The collegiality between senior officials and cabinet ministers raises important questions about accountability. It is an old saw that the Cabinet is accountable to Parliament because ministers feel both an individual and a collective responsibility to that body. But to whom are central agents accountable? This question has particular importance since we know that they frequently sit in for their ministers at cabinet-committee meetings, that they draft policy proposals in interdepartmental panels, that they report to the Prime Minister, that they approach ministers on his behalf, and that they facilitate, record, and report Cabinet and cabinet-committee proceedings.

Accountability:
To Whom and for What?

In the Fall of 1975 Michael Pitfield stated publicly that:

... the question of the lines and standards of accountability that should apply to senior officials in a system which also requires the interplay of ministerial and collective responsibilities in a parliamentary forum ... [creates] a technical problem of enormous practical impact upon government. . . .[1]

A year later, Gordon Osbaldeston, at that time secretary of the Treasury Board, reviewed some technical aspects of the accountability problem and concluded that:

What is needed is an evaluation of the quality of judgment ... [as] the key to accountability for management performance within the Public Service organization. . . .[2]

On November 22, 1976, the president of the Treasury Board, Robert Andras, announced that Allen T. Lambert would chair the new Royal Commission on Financial Management and Accountability. Lambert was then the chairman of the Toronto-Dominion Bank. His personal success in bridging the gap between private enterprise and public service had been remarkable. In a June 1977 press release, he identified a number of issues and areas of concern. He listed among them:

— the nature of the accountability within government of deputy
  ministers to ministers, to the Prime Minister and to the central
  agencies ... and their reporting relationship to Parliament; and
— the functions and responsibilities of the central agencies in the
  framework of accountability.[3]

There is little doubt that the commission intends "to consider how the central agencies themselves can best be held accountable for the exercise of their own responsibilities."[4] Chapter 2 discussed how certain conventional and structural features keep Parliament and the public from looking closely at much of central agents' activities. One conventional feature is the fluid and undefined authority which the Cabinet and the Prime Minister may delegate to central agencies. Another feature is central agents' growing role in policy formulation and in the continuing process of integration and mediation between career bureaucracy and elected political leadership.

This chapter carefully analyses how our respondents perceive their own accountability. Before we proceed with the examination of the data, however, let us first consider the main constitutional, political, and technical issues involved with accountability. First we will discuss the relationship between ministerial responsibility and bureaucratic accountability; then the distinction between objective and subjective accountability; and finally the unique circumstances of accountability in central agencies.

Ministerial Responsibility and Bureaucratic Accountability

At best, ministerial responsibility amounts to this: the cumulative impact of questions, allegations, and attacks in the House of Commons may produce a ministerial scalp or even bring down the government, and that possibility alone is taken to be a sufficient guarantee of responsibility. This theory rests on several dated and not very believable assumptions: that the Crown is the master, the ministry its sole constitutional representative and executor, and the bureaucracy its faithful and humble servant. Closer inspection, however, compels us to modify this view.

In Canadian practice, a minister is rarely required to resign as a penalty for wrongdoing. As long as the Prime Minister and his cabinet colleagues are behind him, a minister will survive the worst. If a repugnant act or omission is not his own but originates in a department or agency for which he is theoretically responsible, he is expected to shield and protect all bureaucratic officials from public exposure. If disciplinary action is taken, it is done quietly and with the least possible damage to the department and the person concerned. The top official in a department, the deputy minister, cannot be held publicly responsible, even though he — not the minister — is expected to run the bureaucratic organization and know in detail its programs and activities, as well as the people engaged in them.

We do not attack the present system of political accountability in its entirety. Those who are in favour of radical reforms must also realize that *very* much stricter checks on government could lead to unstable governments or short-lived ministers, or both, and to the weakening of prime-ministerial leadership and control. We are here primarily concerned with the "lines and standards" of bureaucratic accountability in general, and the accountability of central agents in particular. From this perspective, we question only those aspects of the traditional responsibility theory which stand in the way of a more complete and effective accountability of senior and central-agency officials. The key issue is clearly this: purely internal accountability even of the highest standard does not suffice whenever officials perform executive acts either by actually representing ministers or by implicitly acting like ministers in the course of their normal duties. In these instances, they are shaping policy decisions which are intended to have a profound effect on the political and economic system as a whole. They should, therefore, share political responsibility for these decisions with ministers. However, the present theory of political responsibility makes this impossible.

Ministers' public responsibility may be political or legal. Individually, each minister is politically responsible to Parliament for all his own acts, and for the acts of his officials, within the scope of his cabinet portfolio. There is no individual responsibility for decisions or actions taken in Cabinet or its committees. The ultimate sanction for a breach of individual responsibility is resignation. Collectively, ministers are publicly responsible to Parliament for all announced policy decisions including the national budget. The ultimate sanction is a defeat in the House of Commons on a clear issue of non-confidence. Each minister may be legally responsible to anyone having the right to sue him for wrongful acts committed beyond his ministerial jurisdiction. In such a case, a court may compel the minister to pay personal damages.

Officials, on the other hand, cannot be held publicly responsible. Instead, they are accountable internally according to lines and standards applicable in their department. Deputy ministers are accountable to the Prime Minister and, to a lesser extent, to their own ministers for the administration of their departments or agencies and for any other duties they may be assigned to perform. Central agents are accountable to their hierarchic superiors for all their acts and decisions. In the PMO, the PCO, and the FPRO, where the Prime Minister is the responsible minister, they are also ultimately accountable to him. In the TBS and Finance, the final links of internal accountability end with the President of the Treasury Board and the Minister of Finance, respectively. Dismissal, demotion, or transfer are in theory the ultimate sanctions for the breach of internal accountability.

Objective and Subjective Accountability

Political scientists have struggled with the theory of bureaucratic accountability for some time. They have made a distinction between *objective* accountability, which relies on an external standard of performance, and *subjective* accountability, where the standard is developed by the individual himself.[5] Formally, bureaucracy has always operated on the basis of an external standard of performance. It was and, in some circles, still is believed that highly detailed rules limit discretionary behaviour and increase accountability. However, Victor Thompson argues persuasively that formal rules guarantee very little because bureaucratic organizations develop "natural" latent forms of behaviour which provide them with a sort of autonomy — effectively counteracting the rigidity of formalism and protecting the members from external sanctions.[6] It would appear that the answer lies in subjective accountability. If the personal values and objectives of bureaucrats merge with organizational objectives, the result is often positive — accountability becomes a matter of conscience and loyalty, providing the strongest and most demanding standard of performance. Kenneth Kernaghan contrasted the two kinds of accountability:

The objectively responsible bureaucrat feels responsible primarily to the legal or formal locus of authority and takes a passive approach to the determination of the public interest. His most prominent characteristic is accountability to those who have the power to promote, displace, or replace him. In making and recommending decisions, he anticipates and reflects the desires of his superiors. . . . He does not take initiatives or risks which may get him or his superior into trouble. . . .

The subjectively responsible bureaucrat is a striking contrast. He feels responsible to a broad range of policy participants and is active in the pursuit of the public interest. His most outstanding characteristic and value is commitment to what he perceives to be the goals of his department or program. . . . Tension and conflict between him and his superiors are frequent, but he is minimally concerned by the threat of negative sanctions. . . . He is innovative, takes risks, and bends the rules to achieve his objectives. . . . [7]

In our view, MBO (management by objectives), a close relative of subjective accountability, is a welcome innovation in the world of bureaucratic behaviour. But we strongly doubt that the reliance on conscience and personal values is sufficient. Moreover, the problem of accountability of central agents takes on an added and special dimension.

Accountability in Central Agencies: A Special Case

We wrote earlier that according to existing theory central agents are formally accountable to their hierarchic superiors, just as all other bureaucrats are. What sanctions are actually available to extract such accountability? Superiors cannot dismiss, demote, or transfer without the risk of involving themselves, and others, in a lengthy and unpalatable process of adjudication. They can, however, resort to less direct penalties such as barring the agent from participation on committees, excluding him from staff meetings, and cutting him off from the flow of information, thereby forcing a resignation. Personal ostracism by peers may effectively lead to a similar result. In cases of minor import, a verbal tongue-lashing in private or in the course of a meeting with others will normally put the individual back on track. Instead of punishment, a scaled system of rewards for effective work, culminating with rapid and repeated promotions, might be a better means of ensuring accountability. This approach received the endorsement of many of our respondents who believe that a form of positive reinforcement might be the best guarantee of internal accountability.

We believe that the advocates of positive reinforcement come close to revealing the special nature of work relationships in central agencies. These relationships are characterized by competitive collegiality — that is, an intense absorption in one subject or issue continuously tested against shared mutual interests and strongly held individual opinions. It is a confident and creative approach to a particular problem originating from the desire to live up to powerful peer expectations. Formal, bureaucratic lines of accountability exist, but little attention is paid to them. Everyone, regardless of rank, is considered a peer, provided that the challenge of on-going intellectual competition is met and one "delivers the goods" when expected. In such an intense inward-oriented environment, the quality of judgments exercised by participants is always open to criticism, provided the criticism is levied according to the accepted norms of collegial professionalism. This inward orientation makes accountability towards external objects very difficult, as is clearly illustrated in this statement: "I cannot see myself being accountable to the people of Canada. They don't even know I exist."

The climate of competitive collegiality is sustained and supported by the following circumstances which, taken together, are unique in government:

1. in relative terms, a very high level of educational and professional achievement by central agents;
2. again in relative terms, the youthfulness of central agents confident of success and upper mobility;
3. strong motivation and feelings of personal satisfaction and efficacy, with high incomes and security of tenure in public service, if not in a specific central agency;
4. small size of organizational units in central agencies;
5. access to information unavailable to many others in government;
6. close and frequent interaction with cabinet ministers;
7. assumption of executive roles with ease and effectiveness and the authority to act and speak on behalf of the Cabinet and the Prime Minister;
8. collegiality with ministers;
9. a particular kind of sensitivity and discretion intrinsic to the highest level of policy making;
10. freedom to exert influence in any area of government activity and on any segment of the bureaucratic establishment.

These unique circumstances create a serious dilemma of accountability in central agencies. From one perspective, as political administrators who engage in executive tasks, central agents, like ministers, perhaps should be answerable to Parliament. From another perspective, it is clear that the exigencies of public accountability often impair efficiency and would very likely destroy the climate of competitive collegiality which — at its best — can extract from participants their highest quality of judgment. We are convinced that the introduction of a very formal and strict system of internal accountability in central agencies is unnecessary; if introduced, it could well prove to be counterproductive. We are not convinced, however, that public or external accountability should be dismissed outright as unworkable. The dilemma is how to preserve and protect competitive collegiality and, at the same time, encourage central agents to be more sensitive to the public interest. The concluding chapter will discuss this point in greater detail. For the time being let us see how central agents regard two aspects of the accountability issue: (1) styles, objects, and priorities, and (2) agents' interactions with people and organizations which are not part of government.

Central Agents and Accountability

EXPECTATIONS

The last section discussed why bureaucratic accountability has become a major issue *vis-à-vis* central agencies in Canada. If senior officials long ago have evolved from faithful and humble servants of the Crown to full-fledged political administrators who participate collegially in executive functions, central agents should represent *par excellence* these new bureaucrats, because they possess the background and all the requisite institutional and personal characteristics. As we have seen, they assume critical integrative and mediative roles in the policy process; they largely come from relatively non-elite families and, relatedly, generally register very ambitious career orientations and experience rapid advancement in a system which considers educational attainment at least as important as socio-economic origin; they usually interact very freely with cabinet ministers and with senior-agency and extra-agency officials; they often derive a tremendous sense of efficacy from their interactions.

Let us look at the literature on political administrators abroad and in Canada to predict how our central agents might view their accountability. Studies by Ezra Suleiman, Robert Putnam, and Aberbach and Rockman supply some interesting findings. Suleiman discussed how France changed from an administrative state — in which bureaucrats eschew politics and trade on their mastery of the details of implementation — into a political-administrative state in which bureaucrats, especially by joining the advisory staffs of ministers, have become more and more involved in policy making.[8] Suleiman finds that senior officials in *departmental* positions still believe there is a dichotomy between the political and administrative sectors, and that their (the officials') job is to assume almost total monopoly over the technical details of policy.[9] Ministerial *cabinet* officials, on the other hand, believe that politics and administration cannot be divided, so that they must be constantly aware of the alternatives to particular policies and their political implications. They also maintain that any political-administrative dichotomy is mere illusion.[10] Robert Putnam addresses specifically this possibility. Citing Richard Rose[11] and Michael R. Gordon,[12] Putnam suggests that while the classic view holds that bureaucrats must leave political questions to the politicians, nevertheless in practice it allows the bureaucrats to monopolize the policy process, especially through control of the flow of information, technical expertise, and agenda-setting powers.[13] Civil servants in Germany and Britain also minimize the political-administrative distinction. Moreover, three out of five say that they enjoy the political aspects of their jobs.[14] Aberbach and Rockman made similar findings in a comparative study of U.S. federal executives (including career officials) and Congressmen in Washington. Their respondents shared similar orientations towards interest groups, ideology, and partisan beliefs.[15] Indeed, the Washington respondents' lack of support for the dichotomy leads the authors to observe: "... we want to emphasize the notion that American legislative politicians *and* top federal executives must be well schooled in the arts of politics in a system that provides ample opportunities for both politicians and bureaucrats of an entrepreneurial spirit."[16] Their reference to an "entrepreneurial spirit" acknowledges the importance, both in political and bureaucratic work, of mobilizing group support for proposals in addition to adjudicating differences between groups.

Canadian scholars have only very recently paid attention to the question of bureaucratic accountability. Robert Presthus's major work on interest-group accommodation in Canada says that members of the economic, bureaucratic, and political elite groups share technical and political perspectives; such communality provides a foundation for mutual problem solving.[17] However, in a study which touches more directly on the question of accountability — at least to legislators — Robert Presthus and

William Monopoli report that Canadian bureaucrats tend considerably less than their U.S. counterparts to believe that legislators are competent players in the policy arena and provide lobbyists useful access to decision making.[18] They also find that Canadian bureaucrats are somewhat more receptive to lobbyists than the American officials. Lee Sigelman and William G. Vanderbok, however, report, on the basis of comparison of the public policy preferences of Ottawa senior officials and MPs whom Presthus interviewed, that the bureaucrats indicate less sensitivity to social issues than do the legislators.[19] Canadian bureaucrats' relatively high-profile image of their role in the policy process and their openness to groups might conceal a selectivity in the publics to which they actually respond.

CONFLICTING OBLIGATIONS

We thus see that accountability is not a straightforward matter. Very few, if any, bureaucrats or legislators believe that bureaucrats could maintain accountability by concentrating on the technical details of their domains. Indeed, many bureaucrats today believe that their work encompasses much more than mere administration. They see themselves as political administrators, for whom the concept of a dichotomy between the political and administrative spheres of activity is fraught with ambiguity.

Our interviews dwelt at length on the question of accountability. We asked our central agents whether they believe that they are at all accountable to any or all of the following: their immediate superior, their minister, the Cabinet, Parliament, the people of Canada, and/or their consciences; to which of these they feel the *most* accountable; and in what sense. Respondents described their accountability in four different ways: staff, line, democratic, and personal. Several officials named more than one type.

The largest proportion of our respondents (53 per cent) view accountability at least partially in terms of staff responsibilities. That is, they say that they must provide the best possible information and policy advice to the political head of their agency. As a respondent from the Finance department put it, staff accountability transcends immediate relationships within the agency hierarchy:

I'm most accountable to my minister. I must assist him in the discharge of his mandate. I work, of course, most closely with my ADM. In my view, however, even if the minister knows only 2 per cent of all that is going on in the department, he still is responsible and accountable for the whole 100 per cent. I must hold up my per cent of the whole by giving the best possible advice, from a professional point of view.

A PMO official speaks more directly of the need to look beyond obligations to one's immediate superior:

My ultimate accountability to the Prime Minister is tempered only by the constraints of time. When I feel that Jim Coutts is not giving the PM good advice on a specific matter, I'm morally obliged to go directly to the PM and register my view. But, time constraints dictate that I don't run off to the the PM whenever I disagree with Jim.

Forty-four per cent of our respondents view accountability as involving, to a degree, classic line-bureaucratic obligations to their immediate superior. That is, they see themselves as directly accountable to the official to whom they report rather than the political head of their agency. As a corollary to this, these officials often speak of how important it is to maintain the integrity of that aspect of the policy process or program which they manage. In the words of a TBS official:

I have the normal line-type responsibility. For most of the operation of my division I have a lot of individual responsibility and scope for initiative. You'll find that generally the deputy secretary doesn't run this branch, he oversees it. That is, the individual directors have a fair amount of latitude so long as they work within the mandate of their division. The deputy secretary becomes involved when a question arises as to whether something belongs here or elsewhere, or when political questions come into play.

Fully 26 per cent of our respondents maintain that account-ability involves more than simply one's staff or line obligations. These respondents believe that they must hold themselves ultimately accountable to the public. None see this as a respon-sibility to a specific segment of the public or an interest group. An official in the TBS, after pointing out the various ways in which he is accountable to others in the policy arena, tells us how the public interest influences his work: "Ultimately, though, I feel responsible to the taxpayer. Everything I do affects the expenditures of the public service. I have to be especially careful about precedents which are going to end up costing too much in the long haul." Finally, almost 10 per cent of our central agents base their accountability on the personal qualities of a specific individual, usually the Prime Minister.

When we look specifically at the various objects of our central agents' accountability, we see even more clearly the degree to which they view their obligations as being multi-dimensional. Although 58 per cent report that they are accountable at least in part to their immediate superior, large proportions of respon-dents believe that they have obligations to others. Thirty-three per cent register accountability to the Prime Minister; 29 per cent to the minister of their department; and 30 per cent to the Cabinet generally. In addition, fully 35 per cent report some sense of obligation to the public. Thus, our officials' sense of ac-countability is distributed pretty evenly between these objects. The pattern is broken, however, in two important respects. Only 10 per cent say they are accountable to Parliament and indi-vidual conscience. This low proportion mentioning Parliament underscores the peripheral role of the House of Commons and the Senate in the policy process. The low proportion mentioning conscience probably indicates that bureaucrats prefer not to act on their own authority; we hope it does not mean they believe that their conscience should not come into play.

To clarify our respondents' priorities we asked them to choose the one or two objects to which they feel most accountable. Thirty-eight per cent named their immediate superior and 20 per cent named the PM. Only 7 per cent named the minister of their department; 11 per cent, the Cabinet; 5 per cent, Parliament; 12 per cent, the people of Canada; and a mere 1 per cent, their personal conscience. Thus, our officials' responses hardly break with the classic view of accountability. The classic-view studies show that, while bureaucrats may report more than one object of accountability, they will attend first to their superior (for PMO officials, this means the Prime Minister).

How do our respondents resolve conflicts among their various obligations? The vast majority (82 per cent) say no conflicts arise because they always yield to a hierarchy of objects of accountability. Accordingly, even if an official believes that he is accountable in part to his own conscience and to the Canadian people, if he also feels ultimately accountable to his immediate superior, he will attend first to this commitment. Eighteen per cent, on the other hand, report that conflicts arise fairly frequently as they wrestle with various obligations. Most of these officials, however, believe that they yield to their superior after all avenues of representation have been exhausted. Only four respondents say that they probably would leave the public service on a question of principle. Even in serious conflict situations, our respondents believe that it is better to work within the system than outside.

INTERAGENCY DIFFERENCES

Previous findings suggest that officials in different central agencies follow different lines of accountability. PMO/PCO/FPRO officials, for instance, receive many assignments directly or indirectly from the Prime Minister and, therefore, we expect these officials to view themselves as ultimately accountable to him. Finance officials work within the most hierarchical department in terms of career routes and, therefore, we might expect their accountability to centre on their immediate superior. Since TBS officials administer the mandate of a cabinet committee — the Treasury Board — we expect them to focus their accountability on the Cabinet. Within the PMO/PCO/FPRO block of agencies, we expect that PCO/FPRO officials' sense of obligation will be divided between the Prime Minister and their immediate superior, because these officials must channel their interactions with the PM through the heads of their respective agencies much more often than PMO officials must pass their contacts through the principal secretary. With respect to Parliament and the people of Canada, two features of the tax-and-tariff policy process suggest that Finance officials might register account-ability most often to these two objects.[20] Finance officials monitor and respond to complaints about tax and tariff structures from individuals and corporations; they also must shepherd the budget and tax bills through Parliament. Many TBS officials might, because they have to testify about estimates before its committees, believe that they are accountable to Parliament and, because review of expenditures involves the interests of the taxpayer, might register more often a sense of obligation to the people of Canada.

We tested these expectations by making certain comparisons. First, we asked whether different central agencies evidenced different styles of accountability. The hierarchical career routes of Finance notwithstanding, we find that officials there tend no more than those in the PMO, PCO, and FPRO and the TBS to describe their accountability in classic bureaucratic terms of line responsibilities to their superior. (See Appendix II.) Indeed, slightly more PMO/PCO/FPRO officials give this type of description than Finance officials (47 vs. 41 per cent). Paradoxically, in terms of our expectations, Finance officials mention that they perform staff functions for the political head of their department slightly more often than PMO/PCO/FPRO officials mention them (59 vs. 53 per cent). Further, we find that relatively few PMO officials (18 per cent) employ line-like descriptions of accountability while fully 62 per cent of the PCO/FPRO officials do. Yet, in terms of style, the greatest differences concern officials' use of descriptions which involve the people of Canada and personal loyalties. Forty-one and 29 per cent of Finance and TBS officials, respectively, say they are somewhat accountable to the public while only nine per cent of PMO/PCO/FPRO officials do. On the other hand, 25 per cent of respondents in PMO/PCO/FPRO say they have some personal loyalty to the PM, while only 5 per cent of Finance and none of the TBS officials say they do. PMO accounts for most of the personal loyalty, as only 14 per cent of PCO/FPRO mention it. The findings regarding style thus suggest that, although officials in the various agencies employ much the same staff or line-like language about accountability, Finance and TBS officials reveal a relatively great awareness of their obligations to the public and PMO officials disclose considerable loyalty to the Prime Minister as a political figure.

When we asked our respondents to choose one or two main objects of accountability, some interesting interdepartmental differences appeared before and after winnowing. For example, before winnowing, respondents in various departments listed some objects almost as a matter of course. Thus, 82 per cent of PMO/PCO/FPRO officials say that they are at least partially accountable to the PM (*vs.* 14 and 3 per cent, respectively, in Finance and the TBS). Seventy-three per cent of Finance officials say that they are accountable to their minister (*vs.* 29 per cent in the TBS). Both Finance and TBS officials (46 and 45 per cent, respectively) indicate very often that they are partially accountable to the people of Canada. TBS officials cite accountability to the Cabinet more than the others do. As well, between 55 and 59 per cent of officials in all five agencies mention their superior as an object of accountability. Although the main objects of accountability differ from agency to agency, many officials in each indicate that they take several obligations into consideration.

After winnowing, we gain a somewhat clearer picture of agency priorities. A much greater proportion of PMO/PCO/FPRO than Finance and TBS officials say they are accountable primarily to the Prime Minister (53 *vs.* 5 and 3 per cent, respectively). Yet, PMO officials account for much of this large proportion. All of our respondents in PMO indicate ultimate accountability to the PM, but only 29 per cent of PCO/FPRO respondents do. The largest proportion of PCO/FPRO officials (48 per cent) say that they are primarily accountable to their immediate superior. Finance officials, much more than other respondents, believe their strongest obligation rests with their superior (59 *vs.* 31 and 32 per cent in the PMO, PCO, and FPRO and the TBS, respectively).

This supports our prediction that Finance officials would register relatively classic views of bureaucratic accountability. In fact, the Minister of Finance comes a distant second as the primary object of his officials' accountability (18 per cent). TBS officials indicate little consensus after winnowing. Thirty-two per cent select their immediate superior; 24 per cent, the people of Canada; 18 per cent, the Cabinet; 5 per cent, the president of the Treasury Board; and 3 per cent, the Prime Minister.

In sum, officials believe that they have obligations to a variety of objects. PMO officials feel especially accountable to the Prime Minister and the principal secretary; PCO/FPRO officials to their superior, the Cabinet, and the Prime Minister; Finance officials to their superior, the minister, and the people of Canada; and TBS officials to their superior, the president, the Cabinet, and the people of Canada. PMO officials apparently resolve this ambivalence by giving priority to the Prime Minister, and PCO/FPRO and Finance officials do so mostly by deferring to their immediate superior. TBS officials, on the other hand, produce less consensus on the ultimate object of their accountability. The next section will show the degree to which these departmental differences are reflected in officials' views of communication with the public and interest groups.

Contacts with Outsiders

EXPECTATIONS

If we acknowledge the degree to which our central agents have changed from classic bureaucrats to political administrators, then we might expect that the central agents interact quite frequently with people and groups outside government. Putnam reports that politically oriented bureaucrats in Italy, Germany, and Britain report significantly greater interaction with "others" than classic bureaucrats do.[21] Suleiman finds that senior officials in France are more receptive to interest groups than to legislators.[22] They generally indicate, however, that discussions with interest groups concern the application more than the formulation of policy. The tightly knit group which actually formulates decrees and laws in each ministry usually tries to isolate itself from outside influence when developing policy.[23] George B. H. Cruickshank and his colleagues note that Canadian Finance department officials follow a similar turtle syndrome in the process of developing the budget.[24] Finance officials will spend a great deal of time with individuals and groups who point out features of existing tax laws that they consider undesirable. After policy gestation has begun (i.e., approximately six months before the budget), however, the officials seclude themselves. This section will discuss the degree to which our officials are ambivalent towards those outside government.

Robert Presthus's research suggests another characteristic of bureaucratic interactions with outsiders which we might find among our respondents. He notes that, although interest-group leaders in Canada view senior Ottawa officials rather than legislators as the prime targets of their substantive claims, a pecking order exists whereby bureaucrats perceive some business and industry groups to have greater influence on their department.[25] We will examine the degree to which central agents prefer to interact with some groups more than with others.

VIEWS OF INTERACTION WITH THE PUBLIC:
KEEPING AT ARM'S LENGTH

We asked a number of questions to find what extra-governmental sources our respondents contact to learn how the public views specific issues, and how our respondents view interactions with interest groups. We find that our respondents tap several different sources of information. The most-mentioned source is the media (55 per cent). This means more than simply reading the (Ottawa) *Citizen* or watching CBC's "The National". Most of our officials receive résumés of media information and opinion compiled within either their unit or agency. Business leaders are next (49 per cent). Then come provincial officials (46 per cent); this high percentage reflects the importance of federal-provincial diplomacy in our system. Following closely are friends and acquaintances, usually former colleagues in academe, the professions, or business (42 per cent). Next our respondents contact political and party leaders (25 per cent). Union leaders received 23 per cent of the citations and public-information polls 22 per cent. Next come leaders of citizens' groups which cut across economic, religious, and ethnic lines (19 per cent). Only 16 and 17 per cent approach local-government officials and farm leaders, respectively. A fairly large proportion utilize outside expertise — academics (15 per cent), and consulting firms, research institutes, and professional associations (14 per cent). Only 10 per cent contact religious and ethnic leaders.

As with accountability, respondents were quite specific when asked to name the sources which give them the most accurate and reliable information. Sixteen per cent each state that they find business leaders and provincial-government officials the most reliable. Twelve per cent cite the media and just under 10 per cent mention friends and acquaintances. Other sources suffer much more from the winnowing process. Officials did not put any farm, religious, and ethnic leaders or academics and consultants in the "most reliable" category. Respondents' primary sources do not come as a surprise. Both business leaders and provincial officials play key roles in the policy process. Media and friends, however, draw a bit more attention than we might expect. We surmise that the in-house résumés increase the media's usefulness, and that queries among friends procure the perspective of outsiders, without the lobbying of interest groups.

Our officials' responses do not indicate strong consensus about whether interest groups play a significant role in the policy process. Only 9 per cent say that groups play a highly significant role; that, in particular, to do their job adequately they must take groups into account. One respondent in Finance reveals very strong beliefs along these lines:

Groups are a major source of information for me. I find out from them where the anomalies are in the law and what the temperature — the mood in the business community — is concerning these. It's endemic to the tax system that people don't agree with it and want to change it, or resist change.

Thirty-seven per cent of our respondents indicate that interest-group appeals should be regarded sceptically. As one PMO official tells us, a group's approach often reduces its effectiveness:

This all depends on the issue. Some have an effect on me. However, if they are narrowly self-serving, I will write them off. If it's a wider group, I will listen and determine whether they reveal a concern for the general public interest. After all, it's important that I get all viewpoints.

Many of our respondents simply do not believe that interest groups play a significant role in the policy arena, possibly because groups do not come to them or they avoid the groups. A TBS and an FPRO official explain:

Groups concentrate their efforts on Parliament. Or, they will go to the department responsible for whatever they are concerned about. That's part of the department's job, to advocate the case of the groups it works with.

I try, because of my position, to disassociate myself as much as possible from these groups. They just try to get information out of you on what is happening with their issue.

The response of the FPRO official raises the question of whether central agents should have contacts with interest groups at all. Only 9 per cent of our respondents, however, go so far as to say that they should have no relations with interest groups. Such respondents reflect the view of a TBS official who says:

We have to draw the line at central agencies. Not long ago some of these groups wised up to the role we play on certain issues and they started to want to see us. I said, "Hold the goddamned fort, we're not having those guys come in here."

Another 14 per cent of our officials say they believe such

contacts are proper. Yet groups seldom contact these officials because they do not know what role central agencies have in the policy-making process. So the 14 per cent say that they are seldom contacted. As one Finance official remarked:

Most interest-group people don't even know that I exist. They will contact the minister and I'll see this correspondence. Take the ___ decision in Cabinet this morning. I've been quite involved in that whole thing. I've kept abreast of the representations made to the minister. But, interest groups don't know anything about my involvement.

INTERAGENCY DIFFERENCES

As we might expect, officials in various central agencies indicate that they rely on different sources of information and have different views of interest groups. For instance, PMO officials keep a close check on party workers' views and public-opinion polls; Finance officials closely monitor the business community's attitudes, especially those related to taxes and tariffs.

PMO officials report that they consult party leaders — 91 per cent vs. 14 (the PCO/FPRO), 18 (Finance), and 16 (the TBS) — and polls — 64 per cent vs. 19 (the PCO/FPRO), 14 (Finance), and 16 (the TBS) — much more than officials in other agencies. Within the PMO/PCO/FPRO block of agencies, PMO officials appear to account for the lion's share of all types of outside consultation. These findings underscore the degree to which the switchboard role dominates PMO activity. The data suggest as well that PCO/FPRO officials tend to avoid outside consultation. Indeed, only the media attract the attention of a large proportion of PCO/FPRO officials (57 per cent).

Finance officials far exceed officials elsewhere in consultations with business leaders. In addition, they most often say that they approach provincial-government officials and union, farm, religious, academic, and citizens'-group leaders as well. Thus, notwithstanding the PMO's consultation with party leaders and polls, Finance officials report the most extensive consultation of all of our central agents. Under all headings, TBS officials report a moderate amount of consultation, that is, somewhere between

PMO and Finance on one hand, and PCO/FPRO on the other. However, TBS respondents more than any others report that they contact consulting firms, research institutes, and professional associations for information — 24 per cent *vs.* 3 (the PMO, PCO, and FPRO) and 14 (Finance), respectively. The technical nature of much of the work in the Planning, Administrative Policy, Personnel Policy, and Financial Administration branches probably accounted for much of this consultation. Winnowing in various agencies amplifies what we have just noted. PMO officials are the only respondents who frequently choose party leaders as the most reliable sources of advice. Finance officials more often than others give the greatest credence to business leaders. TBS officials reveal no consensus about the most reliable sources of advice and information.

When asked how they view interactions with interest groups our respondents reinforced what we have found so far. PMO and Finance officials tend to be open to such interaction; PCO officials tend to be self-sufficient and, therefore, somewhat closed to such interactions; and TBS officials fall somewhere in between the two. PMO and Finance officials come relatively neck-and-neck in saying that interaction with interest groups is important to their work (54 *vs.* 68 per cent), that they are contacted frequently by groups (64 *vs.* 46 per cent), that groups share information and attempt to influence policy (46 *vs.* 55 and 64 *vs.* 59 per cent, respectively), that contact from groups is proper (55 *vs.* 50 per cent), and that business groups in particular contact them (46 *vs.* 41 per cent).

Conclusion

The first sections of this chapter touched upon the accountability crisis in bureaucracy. Modern senior officials have made, in the last two decades at least, a transition from classic bureaucrat to political administrator, from objective to subjective accountability. Thus, these public servants have assumed, often by default, executive roles in the policy process, which allow them a tremendous amount of discretionary judgment. Can we still look upon bureaucratic discretion benignly? Does it not entail more than freedom from rules and much more than acting on better managerial instincts? In the 1960s, the question was: since bureaucrats' personal values and objectives are founded in conscience and loyalty and are, therefore, congruent with the authority of their organizations, why not let them be expressed fully? Or, as the Glassco Commission Report[26] suggested, why not let the managers manage?

We have seen that central agencies' mandates are not all that clear. Indeed, these agencies are virtually unrestrained by statutory limits, particularly in the case of the PMO, the PCO, and the FPRO. Moreover, precious few mechanisms exist whereby Parliament may review the work of central agencies and it is altogether unable to scrutinize the roles of officials in the PMO, PCO, and FPRO. No parliamentary committee may call Finance officials to testify in support of the budget. The entire document receives consideration only in debates of the House and the Senate; ways-and-means motions undergo review in the House only by the Committee of the Whole which is not able to call for or receive testimony from officials or any other interested parties. The federal government's lack of success in controlling expenditures, annually publicized by the Auditor General, supports our case for the TBS's inadequacies in maintaining financial and managerial accountability in government. In addition, the government has not come to terms with a major side-effect of the "let-the-managers-manage" mentality. The framework of political administration has spawned a new breed of bureaucrat. We have found that this new official, at least the central-agency hybrid, very often describes his role in terms of critical policy-making functions; is upwardly mobile and extremely ambitious; eschews classic bureaucratic vocational motives and ideals in describing his choice of career; and operates collegially with superiors, officials from other departments with higher rank, and ministers on the interdepartmental and cabinet committees which make key policy decisions. We are not saying this new species of bureaucrat is necessarily a threat to the system. In a system, however, where even common bureaucratic discretion comes under only the most cursory scrutiny of Parliament, we ask whether the competitive collegiality which serves as the new breed's main nutriment meets its needs for career fulfilment too well. Does the delicate ecological balance between elected politicians and career bureaucrats in the once-placid pond called Ottawa face a possible threat? Considering the terms of reference of the Royal Commission on Financial Management and Accountability, which include accountability in central agencies, we believe that our question is clearly compelling.

The data provide grounds for both optimism and pessimism. If we are looking for congruence among how officials view accountability, how frequently they consult with outsiders, and what the roles of various central agencies are, we find that responses in the PMO and Finance best fit our expectations. PMO officials, in keeping with the switchboard perceptions of their roles, consult very frequently with outsiders even though they are unanimously loyal to the Prime Minister and hold themselves accountable to him above all else. Because the PM needs to keep in contact with the public in order to survive politically, his officials in the PMO are not in real danger of losing their public responsiveness in exchange for this loyalty; as extensions of the Prime Minister they work continually to keep him responsive enough at least to win elections. Thus the switchboard role as it relates to political survival keeps a check on PMO officials.

Finance officials' responses indicate the turtle syndrome. In several respects, they appear to be political administrators *par excellence*. Probably because they provide advice on the economy and develop and oversee a number of economic policies they often employ staff-like terminology to describe their accountability and register the belief that they are accountable to the public. Indeed, Finance officials report the most extensive consultation with outsiders among central agents. Yet, two tendencies in their responses temper somewhat the degree to which we can say Finance officials have become political administrators. First, they indicate that when there is any kind of conflict, they feel accountable to their immediate superiors. Further, they see the business community as their most reliable source of information.

PCO/FPRO and TBS officials' responses to the accountability and consultation items fit less well with what we know about their roles. If we recall that PCO/FPRO officials mainly search out the common ground between departments, expedite cabinet decisions, and assure that these are implemented, their responses strike us as perplexing. More officials in the PCO/FPRO than any other agency employ line-like language in describing their accountability. In addition, they focus their accountability on their immediate superior, the Prime Minister, and the Cabinet, and practically exclude Parliament, the people of Canada, and their consciences. PCO/FPRO officials report the least amount of consultation with almost every outside source of advice and information; they also indicate the least frequent contact with interest groups. PCO/FPRO officials, we stress, do not confine their roles to the administrative details of programs. If they did, we might have concluded from their views of accountability and consultation that they give a time-capsule glimpse of the stereotypical nineteenth-century bureaucrat who stayed away from conflict and consultation. In fact, PCO officials channel their considerable skill and energy primarily into husbanding, facilitating, and monitoring the policy process for the entire government. Our finding that they rarely consult outside government perhaps may be explained by the fact that departments, more than the public or groups, are their clients. Yet, because PCO/FPRO officials feel practically no obligation to Parliament, to the people of Canada, and to their own consciences, these central agents probably rely too much on competitive collegiality as a device for maintaining accountability. It is one thing to cut oneself off from contact with outsiders for fear of being unduly influenced; but the dangers of too-great insularity should not be ignored. We noted in Chapter 3 that respondents in other central agencies believe that sometimes PCO and FPRO officials manifest excessive superbureaucratic attitudes, especially by second-guessing, delaying, and even obstructing policy decisions which already have involved considerable reconciliation and integration. If PCO/FPRO officials truly have compartmentalized their world view and believe that outside accountability and consultation are superfluous, our findings offer a clue as to why officials in other central agencies become critical and annoyed. The PCO/ FPRO officials should at least ponder the words of the Glassco Commission on the managerial lacunae that central agencies are supposed to fill:

Although the departments are the primary operating units, each, as has just been noted, is only a segment of a single entity — the Government of Canada. The policies and programs of each must be balanced against and harmonized with those of other departments and agencies; they must justify themselves, in the last analysis, in terms of the contribution, not to the department itself or its particular interests, but to the general interests of the Canadian people. . . . Thus, the authority of each department, however much it should be strengthened, must be subject to the overriding needs of the government for unity, coherence and *a proper regard for the general interests of the Canadian public.* (Authors' emphasis.)[27]

One further point. The Treasury Board Secretariat, as Chapter 3 explained, mainly reviews departmental budgetary submissions, and develops and monitors administrative and personnel policy. The data on their perceptions of accountability and consultation suggest that TBS officials' roles provide considerable latitude for accountability to people inside and outside government, and fairly wide consultation with outsiders. If anything, TBS officials feel accountable to several sources. Since no clear priorities emerged in their perceived obligations, it is possible that the TBS might suffer from a lack of the consensus needed for true competitive collegiality. As reported in Chapter 3, TBS officials said that since departments were not accountable to them they could not easily fulfil their agency's mandate. If, however, they are confused about accountability in their own agency, the prospect appears remote that they can help improve the level of accountability throughout government. We stated in Chapter 3 that separating central financial administration and its ancillary services from TBS and placing them under the new Office of the Comptroller General will probably exacerbate rather than re-

solve the current accountability problem in government. This
attempt at reform really adds to the confusion by creating the
unsatisfactory arrangement whereby two deputy ministers of
equal rank lead two competing organizations and report to a
single minister — the President of the Treasury Board.

TABLE 7.1
CONSULTATION FOR ADVICE AND INFORMATION (N=92)

SOURCE	CONSULTS %	MOST RELIABLE %
Media	54.5	12.0
Political Leaders/Party Workers	25.0	6.5
Business Leaders	48.9	16.3
Union Leaders	22.9	2.2
Farm Leaders	16.3	0.0
Local Government Officials	17.4	2.2
Provincial Government Officials	45.7	16.3
Religious Leaders	8.7	0.0
Ethnic Leaders	9.8	0.0
Friends	42.4	9.8
Citizen Groups	18.5	2.2
Polls	21.7	5.4
Academics	15.2	0.0
Consulting Firms/Research Institutes/ Professional Associations	14.1	0.0

Evaluation of Central Agencies:
                         Summary and Proposals
                                    for Reform

This book has attempted the most detailed analysis to date of
central agencies and their officials. It presents a great deal
of what has, hitherto, been regarded as inside information.
However, it was never our intention to stop at mere description.
Throughout the book we have tried to evaluate the roles of
central agencies and their officials. We believe the findings of
this study point out weaknesses in central agencies which require
a fair amount of remedial attention, perhaps even radical surgery. We have found gaps between the performance and the
design of central agencies. Some units within central agencies fail
to live up to their mandates; others appear to exceed their
jurisdictions. With respect to recruitment, the evidence presents
a dilemma. On the one hand, current recruitment patterns show
an influx of officials with socio-economic backgrounds perhaps as
representative of the general populace as officials' backgrounds
in any other advanced liberal democracy. On the other hand,
such open recruitment has produced officials with relatively
little experience in public service; their career perceptions are
more akin to those of businessmen than of bureaucrats. Regarding inner-circle theories of the policy process, we do not find
evidence that a small clique of ministers and senior officials in
Ottawa makes all the important decisions. Yet the way our
officials interact and how they speak of these interactions
suggest that the distinction between political and bureaucratic
participants in the policy process simply does not exist in many
crucial decision-making settings, even in cabinet committees.
Finally, our findings speak to the accountability problem in
central agencies which the Lambert Commission has already

marked out as a special concern. The findings indicate further that central agents, although full-fledged political administrators, have not yet sorted out the degree to which they are responsive to the public interest, nor how they should tap and utilize various sources of information on public opinion.

This chapter first summarizes the findings of our research and presents profiles of the strengths and weaknesses in each central agency. We then propose reforms in personnel development, organizational structure, and mechanisms for accountability, which we believe are vital to improve central-agency performance.

Summary of Findings

Our research stemmed initially from two developments in the way scholars study executive and bureaucratic institutions in government. First, the public administration sub-field within political science has all but abandoned the concept of politics and administration as two separate vocations. Today, scholars prefer to think in terms of political administration — political leaders and senior bureaucrats integrate political and administrative goals and maintain a community of interest to sustain such integration.[1] Scholars have shown renewed interest in de-mythologizing the images of bureaucrats' roles. We have tried to do this by penetrating the secrecy which has protected public servants from scholarly scrutiny and by assuming at the outset that even officials who claim total administrative detachment in fact play politically significant roles.

The second development which sparked our research is the increasingly important role of central agencies in advanced liberal democracies. By the early 1960s, executives in, for example, Britain, France, and Italy were turning more and more to specialized agencies to perform various integrative functions. Canada has both adopted institutional structures developed elsewhere and seen some of its innovations copied by other countries. The increased importance in Canada of the Prime Minister's Office and the Privy Council Office and the creation of the Treasury Board Secretariat, the Federal-Provincial Relations Office, and now the Office of the Comptroller General illustrate the dramatic degree to which our country has come to rely on executive-bureaucratic institutions. This book has examined where such developments have led. It has focused, in particular, on central agencies' responsibilities for strategic planning and formulation of substantive policy, development of integrative economic and fiscal policy, allocation of funds and management of resources, management of senior personnel, and conduct of federal-provincial relations.

Chapter 2 set out to describe the genesis, the content of authority and its limits, and the formal organizational structure of each central agency. The genesis of each central agency can be traced on a continuum from "evolution" to "formal legislative creation". The birth of Finance and the TBS both fall on the "creation" end of the continuum because Acts of Parliament were directly involved in their genesis (Finance in 1869 and the TBS in 1966). In addition, these two agencies exercise considerable conventional authority delegated to them by the Cabinet. The PCO and the FPRO, on the other hand, fall on the "evolution" side of the continuum. Although they evolved from positions which claim some statutory base — Clerk of the Privy Council and Secretary to the Cabinet, and Secretary to the Cabinet for Federal-Provincial Relations — the major share of their present mandate has emerged from conventional authority. The PMO originated entirely from constitutional convention and thus falls at the "evolution" end of the continuum. Its annual budget allocation is included in PCO estimates and its principal secretary lacks legal status. Chapter 2 noted that the heavy reliance of central agencies on conventional as opposed to statutory authority fits within the framework of British constitutional theory. Nevertheless, one must question the extent to which this theory allows for institutional extensions of the Prime Minister and Cabinet without Acts of Parliament and the creation of powerful and largely non-accountable organizations which assist the political executive in fulfilling its obligation and commitment to govern.

Thus, in many respects, one may view central agencies as

multi-functional organizations, rather than as air-tight compartments with strictly defined jurisdictions. In support of this view,
we were able to determine from the evidence that, first, strategic planning and formulation of substantive policy involve six
crucial functions: annual expenditure budgeting; forecast of revenues; design of the legislative program; consideration of policy
issues and the timing for their resolution; evaluation of performance of senior government personnel; and evaluation of the
adequacy of governmental machinery. All five of our central
agencies assist the government in these functions, although PCO
(in particular its Plans division) is the chief agency to do so.

Second, Finance shoulders most of the responsibility for developing integrated economic and fiscal policies including tax
policy, economic development and government finance, fiscal
policy and analysis, and international trade and finance.
However, the principle of countervaillance prevails when, for
example, the economics secretariats of the PCO and the Program
and Planning branches of the TBS participate in this field of
policy development.

Third, the TBS assumes the lead-agency role for allocating and
managing physical resources and expenditure budgets. Within
this sector, however, both Finance and the PCO make major
contributions; Finance develops the fiscal framework and the
PCO assists the Cabinet in making policy guidelines for the
budgetary cycle. All central agencies, insofar as they have
policy- and program-review staffs, have a say in whether existing
and proposed programs are useful and effective.

Fourth, two agencies share the lead role in managing senior
personnel. The TBS advises the Treasury Board regarding policy
governing the classification of positions and employees, and the
determination of compensation rates and scales; the PCO contains
the shop which develops the rules regulating the selection of
senior personnel and which advises the PM and the Cabinet on
actual appointments. The PMO advises, as well, on political
appointments and the political dimensions of senior bureaucratic
assignments, although Gordon Robertson, the secretary to the

Cabinet for Federal-Provincial Relations, exercises the ultimate advisory authority for actual appointments to senior posts.

Fifth, the FPRO fills an undisputed lead-agency role in federal-provincial diplomacy and the national unity crisis. In addition to FPRO, only the Finance department, through its responsibility for tax and fiscal policies, continues to contribute significantly to federal-provincial relations.

Thus, although each central agency except the PMO assumes greater responsibilities in one or more of the five control roles, none enjoys a monopoly even if its mandate is based on statute. The degree to which a central agency exercises even its statutory authority depends upon what the Prime Minister and Cabinet have been prepared to entrust to it by way of conventional authority. Rather than permit agencies to develop monopolies of control, political leaders have preferred to encourage counter-vaillance.

Chapter 3 examined central agents' views of exactly how they and the departments within which they work fulfil their conventional and statutory mandates. In the PMO, officials centre their roles on the switchboard functions which they must perform for the Prime Minister. Previous attempts notwithstanding, officials in the PMO generally do not believe that they should exercise more fully their conventional authority to monitor comprehensively policy development. PCO and FPRO officials gave us vivid descriptions of how their agencies perform integrative functions on behalf of the Cabinet and attempt to maintain a sense of urgency within programmatic departments about the over-arching requirements of government policy. Two tendencies among these officials, however, seem to get in the way of their performing their mandates effectively. First, they lack sufficient staff to handle day-to-day firefighting and simultaneously to conduct medium- and long-range planning. Second, they tend from time to time to assume gatekeeper roles, i.e., they second-guess departments' proposals even when accords have been struck which are acceptable to the interested parties, and, presumably, to the Cabinet. Second-guessing is a risky business for the PCO and the FPRO, again, because of their lean staffs and resources.

Finance officials clearly view their agency as the economics powerhouse. As advisors, they trade on their expertise to bring economic considerations to bear on policy and program development by other central agencies and by programmatic departments. In fulfilment of the department's responsibility for the budget and related legislation, Finance officials also believe that they must safeguard the integrity of such economic instruments as taxation and tariffs. TBS officials have a twofold task as well. On the one hand, they review departmental submissions from the standpoint of the fiscal framework and advise the Treasury Board accordingly. On the other hand, they are the guardians of probity and prudence in the administrative and personnel-policy fields throughout the bureaucracy. Generally, our respondents in the Program branch, the unit most vitally engaged in review of expenditures, say they are very effective in performing their share of TBS responsibilities. Officials in other branches indicate various shades of concern about their ability to hold deputy ministers accountable for what happens in their departments. This was found to be the case even among officials in Financial Administration, a branch of the newly evolved Office of the Comptroller General, which theoretically is rectifying the perceived malaise. We thus have seen evidence of a considerable shortcoming in the TBS's ability to live up to its mandate by maintaining probity and prudence throughout the public service.

Judging from the literature, both Canadian and comparative, we had every reason to believe that the individuals who man the stations of various central agencies would report origins in Canada's socio-economic elite. That is, they would come mainly from families which resided in an urban centre either in Ontario or Quebec, which traced their ancestry to Protestants from the British Isles, and in which the breadwinner had a university degree and a professional or managerial occupation. We believed that many of our respondents would have benefited from education in Canada's elite universities. Since our respondents hold many of the most prestigious and influential posts within the

Canadian public service, we expected that they would represent correspondingly the socio-economic elite of Canadian society.

Our actual findings give a substantially different picture. In comparison to senior bureaucrats in other countries, our central agents are relatively young and representative of the various regions and ethnic and religious groups of the country, and come very frequently from families in which the breadwinner had both received a low level of education and held a clerical or blue-collar job. Thus, many of our central agents are upwardly mobile. They have used education as their principal vehicle for advancement. Practically all have a bachelor's degree, and a much higher proportion of them than of other senior officials have a graduate or professional degree.

Relatively open recruitment has led to obvious gains in representativeness. Since so many central agents are upwardly mobile, their career routes show some peculiar patterns which relate to their goals as public servants. Central agents rarely have decided upon their career routes at an early age, or spent their entire careers in government, or served in the same department since entering the public service. These findings run counter to the classic view of the bureaucratic career as a vocation whereby officials decide on careers while still youths, enter government as soon as they finish their education, and stay with one department through most of their lives. We do not assert *a priori* that central agents' departure from the classic career route poses a danger. Indeed, judging from what we know about their socio-economic backgrounds, we expected that when senior officialdom became open to individuals who have not followed classic career routes, central agencies would recruit not only the best and the brightest but those who are dedicated as well to the idea of public service. These optimistic expectations, however, were not borne out. From comments concerning their motives for entering public service, their expertise, and their current career goals, we learn that, although they do place some value on developing expertise and attempting to improve policy and/or the policy process, central agents emerge most clearly as personally ambitious individuals. Their responses suggest that a strong motive for entering government was that of advancing careers in management and of experiencing the exhilaration of being close to the centre of power. When asked what they have tried to accomplish while in government, they very frequently cite personal development and maintaining a sense of efficacy as major goals. They say as well that if they left government they would most miss, first, the exciting atmosphere within which they work and, second, their top-quality colleagues. We suggest that such orientations indicate that central agents have not adequately adopted modern bureaucratic values.

Chapter 6 turned to a detailed analysis of the interactions among central agents. It looked at "inner-circle" theories of the policy process and re-appraised them in the light of two developments, namely, the increased importance of interdepartmental committees to the development of policy proposals and the wide participation of senior officials in cabinet committees. We found that very little credence today, if any, is given to the view that one inner circle dominates the policy process. In the minds of most officials, the ways and means of decision making are simply too diffuse. Central agents frequently make personal contacts with higher-ranking officials and cabinet ministers, and attend interdepartmental and cabinet committees, which extends their sphere of influence. Spheres of influence tend to revolve around issue areas rather than one decision-making centre. Those who find themselves less strategically placed in relation to key people compensate for their disadvantage by utilizing more fully the positions that they do have. For instance, Finance officials, who lack informal channels for contact with the Prime Minister, with cabinet ministers, and with deputy ministers, participate most often in interdepartmental meetings and most often become full discussants in cabinet committees.

The accountability of political administrators poses one of the greatest problems faced by advanced liberal democracies. Chapter 7 points out that senior officials have publicly recognized this problem in the Canadian federal government. The chapter also notes that the accountability of central agents constitutes one of the major concerns of the Lambert Commission. The chapter finds a considerable shift in the scholarly understanding of the term "accountability". Traditional theories argue that bureaucrats maintain accountability by virtue of their posture as faithful and humble servants of the political leaders. Revisionist scholars who believe that the classic view is too simplistic point out that accountable officials are not only committed to anonymous service of political leaders, but also take on personal values and obligations congruent with the norms of the organization within which they work. They immerse themselves sufficiently in departmental goals and programs so that they can be trusted to make discretionary decisions of considerable importance. Today, however, the mandate of the Lambert Commission suggests (see Chapter 7) that not even the revisionist concept of accountability is adequate for the new type of political administrator, especially for the central agent.

Central agents do not immerse themselves in programs. Instead, they attempt, through integration and mediation, to help synchronize the resource demands, the administrative practices, and the programmatic goals of officials and political leaders throughout government. Two checks exist on the central agents' behaviour, both of which come from the community of politicians and administrators which sustains the collective action of central agencies. First, political leaders and/or public-service superiors can decide whether or not a central agent may win promotions. Second, the principle of countervaillance dictates that officials be able to work harmoniously in a community where resolution of differences is more important than any one programmatic commitment. Thus "competitive collegiality" may to some extent keep the central agent accountable.

To what degree are central agents actually influenced by competitive collegiality? To answer this question we examined our respondents' views of accountability and their interactions with individuals and groups outside government. We found that competitive collegiality affects them to a large degree. With respect to views of accountability, we found that most central agents do not hold to classic lines of accountability. They most often describe their accountability in terms of advisory responsibilities to political leaders and relatively frequently in terms of the general public and/or personal loyalty to a particular political leader. Their objects of accountability are often multiple; these most often include the Prime Minister, ministers, the Cabinet, and the public. Almost all of them say, moreover, that multiple loyalties rarely place them in conflict situations. With respect to contacts with people outside of the federal government, we found that many central agents consult various sources of advice and information, although most believe such outsiders hardly influence their work. Further, they give much more credence to business leaders and provincial-government officials than to other sources. Chapter 7 tells us two things about accountability in central agencies: competitive collegiality among central agents considerably affects their views of accountability; and many officials make at least some effort to consult with individuals and groups outside government. The views of many central agents display characteristics of the political-administrator type of bureaucrat.

Central Agency Profiles

Comparisons of various central agencies and their officials' role perceptions, backgrounds, career orientations, interactions, and views of accountability have formed an integral part of this book. How then are our central agencies set off from one another? To answer this question we will look at what, specifically, we have found about each central agency. Does the authority and role of each agency fit well with its officials' characteristics and responses?

The fact that the PMO lacks statutory authority conceals a potential advantage in its position *vis-à-vis* other central agencies, namely, that the Prime Minister may delegate to the principal secretary or to other officials any tasks for which he is constitutionally responsible. Thus, from 1968 to 1972, Marc Lalonde, Pierre Elliott Trudeau's first principal secretary, served essentially as the PM's chief political administrator, in many respects eclipsing the role of the secretary of the Cabinet. Through many of the Trudeau years, Ivan Head, senior advisor

(International Relations), served as a non-flamboyant Henry-Kissinger type, essentially pre-empting the foreign-affairs advisory roles of three successive Secretaries of State for External Affairs. In addition to these outstanding performances, units within the PMO have had a very great impact from time to time. For instance, Chapter 3 told us that officials in Michael Kirby's policy-analysis shop contributed a great deal to ending the bureaucratic deadlock in 1975 over whether the government should introduce a mandatory anti-inflation program. Yet, on the whole, the PMO's performance has been uneven. Coutts currently runs an excellent political switchboard, but he is not a chancellor type. The policy-analysis group has suffered loss of key personnel and has dissipated its attention to brushfire functions, including the manning of unofficial regional desks. The correspondence and communications units seem to be operating reasonably well at present; their performance through most of the 1970s, however, was marginal. The responsibility for all this flux rests directly with the current Prime Minister. At times Trudeau will allow such units as policy analysis to atrophy when he can get what he wants elsewhere. If he stops worrying about his public image (as some of his people claim he does from time to time), only an heroic commitment on the part of aides can maintain morale and direction in such units as correspondence and communications. Finally, the PM seems to have been incapable of dismissing staff members who have been with him since 1968. Even some of the long-tenured officials in the PMO recognize that the staff lacks the vitality and flexibility of the office during the Lalonde days.

The attitudes and backgrounds of respondents in the PMO shed some light on its mixed performance. The officials whom we interviewed performed switchboard functions and did their part to keep the machinery of government going much more often than they developed policies and monitored programs. PMO officials more frequently than others bring formal training in administration to the switchboard and machinery tasks. They also most frequently entered government at mid-career in another sector, and most frequently saw their work as an opportunity to bring greater humanity to government. PMO officials interacted directly with the Prime Minister much more often than others, and they contacted other top political leaders and officials in Ottawa quite freely in the course of fulfilling direct assignments from him. On the other hand, they generally attend only the most comprehensive interdepartmental and cabinet committees because they do not want to overextend themselves. Considerably more PMO officials than others interpret accountability as personal loyalty to the Prime Minister. The officials temper this singular commitment to the Prime Minister by consulting heavily all possible sources of advice and information. The backgrounds and responses of PMO officials fit perfectly the switchboard function. We will discuss in a later section whether the PMO should go beyond this function.

The statutory origins of the PCO and the FPRO can be traced to parliamentary acts establishing two offices: Clerk of the Privy Council and Secretary to the Cabinet, and Secretary to the Cabinet for Federal-Provincial Relations. Primarily, however, the PM and Cabinet assign authority to the PCO and the FPRO in the course of fulfilling their executive obligations and responsibility to govern. Thus, the PCO has become the lead agency in cabinet strategic planning and substantive policy making. In addition, it makes important contributions to Cabinet's integration of economic and fiscal policy, allocation of budgets and management of resources, and management of senior personnel. The FPRO serves as the Cabinet's lead agency for federal-provincial relations. Both PCO and FPRO officials have eclipsed PMO officials' briefing responsibilities towards the PM in their respective executive fields. The PCO and FPRO as well shoulder tremendous responsibilities for helping the PM and the Cabinet plan for, decide upon, and implement the government's legislative program. Both the PCO and the FPRO perform best when they are called upon to facilitate the integration of departmental objectives and programs, and to ensure the smooth and effective operation of government.

Not unexpectedly, PCO and FPRO officials tended to describe their roles in terms of improving the structure and operation of government, facilitating actual decisions, and performing independent analyses of departments' proposals. PCO and FPRO officials represent practically every academic discipline, although lawyers are clearly more numerous proportionately in the two offices than elsewhere. We find among them relatively large proportions of former Montrealers, individuals whose fathers at least completed high school, Catholics, and graduates of elite universities. Despite the conventional wisdom that officials circulate through the PCO and the FPRO rapidly, we found that the average tenure is fairly long, undoubtedly because the constant expansion of these offices has provided many promotions. Despite their current involvement in the policy process, PCO and FPRO officials minimize policy roles in their statements of career objectives. Interestingly, these officials more than any others believe bureaucratic careers provide opportunities for personal development. Officials in the PCO and the FPRO, much like those in the PMO, interact quite readily with the PM, ministers, and top officials of other departments. They frequently participate on interdepartmental and cabinet panels concerned with broad issues. Unlike PMO officials, they tend to channel briefing notes to the PM through their respective secretaries. This suggests that PCO and FPRO officials generally do not receive assignments directly from the PM as often as PMO officials do. PCO and FPRO officials, moreover, clearly keep outsiders at a distance. Generally, they do not believe that they are even partly accountable to the public and they rarely consult outsiders. In view of these officials' strategic positions as political administrators, we find it distressing that they do not at least try, as Finance and TBS officials told us they do, to think of the public as they perform their tasks. This lack of a sense of public accountability among PCO and FPRO officials suggests that they live in a detached world indeed. We will consider the implications of this in the following section.

The Finance department may claim a clear statutory base for its prime task — development and integration of economic and fiscal policies for the government. As well as being the lead agency for this function, Finance is involved in strategic planning and substantive policy making, allocation of budgets and management of resources, and federal-provincial policy making on the part of the Cabinet. Notwithstanding the statutory base of its authority, Finance's latitude in exercising its powers rests on its historic credibility both in the Cabinet and in the general bureaucratic community. This credibility is rooted in the undisputed superiority of Finance's economic expertise over that of any other agencies or departments in Ottawa. Finance officials employ such expertise when they advise other departments during the formulation of policies and programs which bear on the economy, and when they maintain the integrity of two quintessential economic instruments of government — establishing the fiscal framework, and tax and tariff policies.

Finance officials stress more than any other functions the development and monitoring of policy. They bring to their work an immense amount of formal education in economics and related fields such as tax law and accounting. Finance tends to provide its recruits with virtual tenure in the "best economics department in the country". As a result, Finance officials frequently regard economics *per se* rather than management as their specialty. Much more than officials elsewhere, they say that throughout their careers in government they have tried to influence specific policy fields. Because of this, Finance officials participate in a much greater variety of interdepartmental and cabinet committees than officials in other central agencies. Frequently, they represent superiors or the minister at such meetings. Their knowledge enables them to become full discussants in committee deliberations. Although the vast majority report that they are ultimately accountable to their bureaucratic superior, Finance officials more than those in other departments believe that they are also partially accountable to the public and to Parliament. They consult most heavily with individuals and groups outside of the federal government and with business-group representatives in particular. This bias appears to be the only sign of weakness in Finance's political-administrative role. We will suggest in the next section how the bias towards business might be tempered.

In 1966, the original statutory authority of the Finance department was divided into two mandates; the first went to Finance for the integration of economic and fiscal policy. Second, part of Finance's statutory authority was given to the TBS for intra-governmental control over allocation of expenditure budgets and management of in-house resources. Despite its youth, the TBS has attained a clear lead-agency role for government allocations. Its branches make significant contributions in three other central agency sectors, namely, strategic planning and substantive policy, integrated economic policy and fiscal policy, and management of senior personnel. The TBS is somewhat bifurcated. On the one hand, it houses the Program branch, responsible for budgetary allocations and the cyclical review of programs from the perspective of the benefits derived or expected from the distribution of two scarce government resources — money and person-years. Officials in this branch work very closely with cabinet committees and with senior officials in all departments while programs are being developed or reviewed. Planning branch, which was abolished late in 1978, maintained a similar relationship with cabinet committees, in particular with the cabinet committee on Priorities and Planning. However, the other branches' roles tend to be more post hoc; that is, they most often monitor the implementation of specific policies in the administrative, personnel, and official-languages fields. Their linkage to program proposals is less direct and vital. Therefore, officials in personnel policy, administrative policy, and official languages work less frequently with cabinet committees than do their counterparts in the Program branch. They stress above all the need for probity and prudence in departments' management of personnel and spending. Generally, however, the same officials assert that it is extremely difficult for them to assure that departments manage according to established policies and the allocations of the Treasury Board. In particular, they are seriously concerned about deputy ministers' lack of accountability to the board. We have noted that such concerns have led the government to separate two branches from the TBS — Financial Administration and Efficiency Evaluation — and place them under the newly created Office of the Comptroller General, also reporting to the president of the Treasury Board, in an attempt to improve financial administration throughout government.

The socio-economic backgrounds of our respondents in the TBS differ somewhat from those of officials in the other central agencies. TBS officials are disproportionately from Toronto, have fathers who did not complete high school, are Catholics, and are natural-science or political-science graduates. Like PCO and FPRO officials, TBS officials do not share training in a common specialty to the degree that Finance officials do. Yet, with respect to career-long goals, TBS officials fall somewhere between Finance officials, who very frequently say they have tried through their careers to influence specific policy fields, and PCO officials, who rarely say this. Further, TBS officials claim that they have tried to influence planning in government, more than respondents in any other agency. TBS officials' answers to our questions about interactions indicate that they do not informally relate to cabinet ministers and deputy ministers, including their own, to the degree that PMO, PCO, and FPRO officials do. In comparison with Finance, TBS officials participate in interdepartmental- and cabinet-committee meetings less often, but think of their responsibility to the public almost as much as Finance officials. However, they do not agree on the ultimate object of their accountability, especially whether it is the secretary, the board as a cabinet committee, or the people of Canada. Concerning consultation with individuals and groups outside government, TBS officials rank between the openness of Finance and the PMO and the aloofness of the PCO and the FPRO. These findings suggest that not only do TBS officials have difficulty making departments accountable to their policies but they also manifest considerable confusion about their own position in the public service.

Proposals for Reform of Central Agencies

We have already noted our obligation after such a detailed analysis as this to suggest ways in which the institutions that we have studied might be improved. We admit the hazards in proposing reforms. But, although we did not have the benefit of being "insiders", almost every senior official in the five central agencies talked with us for an average of one and a half hours, a total of almost 150 hours. Officials often asked us how many respondents we had interviewed up to the time of our session with them. Around the time we were able to report that we had conducted fifty interviews, they started to say: "Well, you probably know more about central agencies than I do." We cite this because we believe we have obtained the most thorough understanding possible for those outside government of the issues and problems which face central agents from day to day and over a longer term. Also, we want our recommendations to exert an impact on the insiders as well as on the outsiders.

We propose, first, that recruitment and training of central agents be improved. The intense ambition of central agents and the considerable confusion in the minds of some about accountability strongly support our appeal. Clear concepts of public-service goals and public accountability simply have not taken root in many central agencies. Since central agents represent the cream of recruits for political-administrative positions throughout the public service, we suspect that the two problems exist among senior ranks of operational departments as well.

Michael Pitfield recently touched on the causes of these two problems. He notes that graduate and professional schools simply do not provide recruits whose training fits the requirements of management in the public sector:

The law does not provide the analytic competence necessary to evaluate programmes and develop more effective alternatives. Economics teaches few political skills and little about the structure of government. Neither one nor the other provides exposure to managerial skills. . . . The business graduate came with administrative and problem-solving skills, and a smattering of economics, that made him very useful to government. What he did not have and still lacks, of course, is much of a base in the government system. . . . As regards value judgements, where the private sector manager makes his decision with a degree of privacy and according to a comparatively well-ordered set of values, the critical choices that face the public sector manager involve difficult questions of accountability, of choices among competing values, and of the ethical principles that should govern unprecedented situations.[2]

Pitfield urges universities to develop interdisciplinary schools of public administration which would cater to the requirements of government "in terms of substance, analytic and managerial techniques, and sensitivity to ethics and values".[3]

Pitfield's exhortation is well taken. Yet, today, few universities are financially able to develop such programs. Thus, the federal *and* provincial governments must be willing to offer them at least seed money. Perhaps the federal government itself should establish an institution which can provide recruits with practical knowledge of government and sensitivity to ethics and values. We do not propose that it establish an elitist institution such as France's l'École Nationale d'Administration which takes top university graduates and turns them into superbureaucrats before they are tested by actual experience in public service. Instead, we borrow our idea from Hugh Heclo who argues that the transition between middle-management and senior posts in the U.S. federal service should be institutionalized (for example, the fulfilling of some sort of formal requirements for senior posts could be instituted) so that the vocation of the political administrator might become more distinct.[4] We readily admit that Canada's management of senior personnel probably is superior to that of the United States. Yet we too might profitably seek more institutionalization.

Some central agents told us about a dozen confidential Canadian government studies (dated 1969 to 1977) which, taken together, strongly support our diagnosis. (The reports hedge somewhat on possible cures.) With respect to the diagnosis, the studies note that senior executives throughout government today are considerably younger than in previous periods. Generally these officials lack breadth and depth of government experience. At the same time, officials need, more than ever before, a sophisticated appreciation of the political process by which government decisions are achieved and agreement as to what their functions are or should be. The generally low level of appreciation of the political process has especially impaired officials' ability to implement broad socio-economic programs. In citing the malaise, the studies point out inadequacies in the training and development of senior executives which perpetuate the adverse conditions. Department managers have not shouldered their responsibilities towards senior personnel; current training and development programs serve only a small proportion of senior executives and are of uneven quality; and central agencies have not provided adequate stimulus and direction towards service-wide interests and requirements.

With respect to remedies, the most recent of the confidential reports first identifies the components of the "knowledge base" that all senior officials should have and then suggests ways in which training and development might be improved. The knowledge base includes the following:

1. public affairs, i.e., the Canadian national community, Canada's foreign stature, the parliamentary system, contemporary societal values and change, and stewardship of human resources;
2. management and organizational knowledge, i.e., leadership and decision making, administrative organization and processes, financial management, personnel management, program and project management, relationships with specialists and clientele groups, custody, dispensation and employment of information, and logic and analytic techniques;
3. functional knowledge, i.e., the responsibility to maintain a familiarity with one's discipline and other closely related disciplines;
4. personal capacities and interpersonal skills, i.e., physical and mental survival, personal enrichment and renewal, and recognition of the importance of effective interpersonal relations.

The report's most important advice, we believe, is that these components of the knowledge base be elaborated upon and made the criteria for training and development of all senior executives. In addition, the report urges the Committee on

Senior Officials (COSO), the Public Service Commission (PSC), deputy ministers (DMs), and managers and personnel advisors in departments to provide stronger links among individuals' knowledge-base needs, training and development, and departmental and service-wide needs for senior executives. The report, however, argues against the institution of a National School of Public Policy and Administration as proposed in cabinet memoranda of 1971, 1972, and 1974. Its opposition rests on two objections: such a school, while assisting thirty to seventy individuals a year, would not address the needs of all recruits to the senior levels; and selection of candidates would be centralized and, therefore, elitist — a central location of branches (probably one in Quebec and another in Ontario) would discriminate against candidates in other regions of the country. Thus, the report calls simply for the improvement of the existing programs.

We agree wholeheartedly with the report's emphasis on the knowledge base and stronger links among individual needs, training and development, and departmental and service-wide needs. We also believe that existing programs, if improved, would adequately address deficiencies in most areas of officials' knowledge base. Such innovations as executive leave and interchange programs restore and improve personal capacities; departments usually support specialists' attempts to keep abreast of their disciplines. Extracurricular courses, programs, and seminars develop senior executives' management and organizational knowledge. However, we believe the report falls short of our diagnosis when it suggests that existing government facilities and/or universities can remedy senior executives' lack of skill in public affairs. We take this position for two reasons: first, no existing government programs address public affairs in a systematic and comprehensive way; second, the current links between universities and public-service training and development are tenuous at best, especially since hiring freezes throughout government give public-administration graduates little chance of finding public-service positions. By relying on existing government and university programs, the report's proposals are inadequate for the training and development of current or future middle-management candidates for senior positions.

We propose that a federal college for those in the senior public service be established by the federal government. Each year the government would select highly promising middle-management recruits and give them a full year of advanced training in public administration. The selection procedures for the course would be as collegial and inclusive as possible. Annually, divisional committees of colleagues chaired by directors would assess personnel competence by unit in the four components of the knowledge base. In addition to making recommendations regarding the departmental or service-wide training and development programs which might benefit an individual, the committees would assess whether candidates show sufficient development and promise to be eligible for a senior-executive position within three years. Branch-level and departmental committees would annually review these assessments and would be required regularly to recommend to the Public Service Commission sufficient candidates to the federal college to supply their needs for a three-year period. A service-wide selection panel would determine whether departmental recommendations meet government's needs and choose the annual classes for the federal college. Although the college would not become a prerequisite for movement to senior-executive positions, all committees at all levels would be required to recommend the college whenever the advancement of an individual to the senior level, either in his/her own department or elsewhere in the public service, is likely and desirable within three years.

The federal college's curriculum would stress those aspects of public-service work which at present neither conventional academic training nor existing government courses examine in adequate depth and with sufficient accuracy. Specifically, the college course would improve a candidate's knowledge of the structures and processes of political administration as well as the constitutional and bureaucratic principles upon which it is based in Canada and elsewhere. This part of the curriculum would address the candidate's needs in the first two components of the knowledge base — public affairs, and management and organization — with special emphasis on government processes.

The college would augment this intense and specialized government course by exposure to a variety of critical and broader approaches to political administration in Canadian society available on one of two university campuses. Only such milieus could encourage the development of a balanced perspective on the various political, societal, ethical, and value considerations which inherently arise in the decision-making process. This part of the curriculum would address the candidate's needs in the first component of the knowledge base (public affairs), especially general societal concerns. This academic re-immersion should last at least one full term of an academic year, i.e., eight months. The government would have to carefully select and provide financial assistance to two academic institutions in the country (one English, one French), which are willing to house political-administration centres for the college.

Our next set of proposals concerns major reforms of central-agency organization and structure. Such reforms are necessary because the work of the Glassco Commission is now about a decade and a half old. The government recognized this fact by appointing the Royal Commission on Financial Management and Accountability in November 1976, known today as the Lambert Commission. The need is even more pressing in light of the considerable growth and organizational complexity of central agencies, which have developed more or less without plan since 1966. We suspect that at least some of the very recent changes in the TBS (for example, the abolition of the Planning branch) have been made in anticipation of the Lambert Commission's findings and recommendations, which are expected to be publicly revealed early in 1979.

We begin with the Prime Minister's Office. We believe that the Prime Minister is entitled to a first-class policy-advisory staff independent from the cabinet secretariat. Traditionally, many have assumed that any strengthening of the PMO's policy-advisory staff would necessarily lead to an aggrandizement of prime-ministerial power, similar to the concentration of executive authority in the White House. We reject this assumption. Instead, we contend that a strengthening could follow the contours of reforms which have been adopted and proved effective in the United Kingdom. No. 10 Downing Street houses several top career officials who monitor various sectors of the policy process for the Prime Minister, and six policy analysts led by a very senior advisor, who review the political implications of proposals.[5] As well, the British PM calls upon the very extensive Central Policy Review Staff to provide in-depth studies of especially complex, contentious, and vital issues.

We have found that the Canadian PMO's capability in policy analysis and advice is practically non-existent. Even when Michael Kirby headed the policy-analysis shop (1974–76), this capability was weak, since the officials in the unit, despite their immense native abilities, lacked experience in Ottawa, especially in dealing with bureaucracy. Thus, the Prime Minister has turned to the PCO and the FPRO to provide most of his policy briefing. His approach creates real problems. PCO and FPRO officials are too career oriented and technocratic to provide policy advice that gives adequate consideration both to the political aspects of problems and to public accountability. As a result, the Prime Minister's efforts to enlist the support of the bureaucracy have frequently lost momentum. In a broad sense, the huge discrepancies between actual policy changes and campaign promises after both the 1968 and 1974 elections have greatly undermined his credibility with the Canadian public. With regard to specific issues, Trudeau's inability to arouse in the bureaucracy as much concern for unemployment and income distribution and maintenance as for the deleterious effects of inflation on the business community casts a very dark cloud indeed over his effectiveness as a political leader.

In the social-welfare field, a process similar to the priorities exercise of 1975–76 seems to repeat itself. The PM elicits from the Cabinet some relatively bold and innovative commitments to new policy initiatives. Then the bureaucracy defuses the initiative through haggling and compromise. Since the PM's top policy advisors are mostly PCO bureaucrats, they tend to respect the results of battles that have been waged between departments and refrain from independent action. For instance, if the Finance department routs an attempt by Health and Welfare to upgrade income maintenance, PCO officials shrug and say to the PM, "C'est la guerre." Without a policy staff of his own sensitive to a much broader spectrum of political-administrative viewpoints, the PM must defer to the PCO's viewpoint. Small wonder that the title of the popular book which chronicled the failure of Trudeau's first mandate was *Shrug.*[6] One final remark on this point. If Pierre Elliott Trudeau requires a personal policy staff, this prescription applies doubly to his successor. Whether the individual is a Liberal, a Progressive Conservative, or a New Democrat, he or she will face bureaucrats who are so used to political administration according to the style and values sustained by Trudeau that re-orienting them might well occupy the entire period of the new incumbent's first mandate.

Moreover, we believe that involvement in prime-ministerial briefing has diffused much of the PCO's and the FPRO's capacity to help the Cabinet's long-range planning. For instance, officials told us that the Plans division has given so much time to brush-fire problems that it has had to cede a great deal of long-range work to operations-division secretariats. One unit in the Plans division, Planning Projects, has devoted much of its time to labour negotiations and to devising procedures for consultation of business, labour, and consumers, although it was originally designed to provide background information for the Priorities and Planning committee's long-range work. Thus, our proposal to upgrade policy advice in the PMO conceivably could improve the PCO's effectiveness as a cabinet secretariat.

The present PCO performs numerous functions which clearly fall within the domain of prime-ministerial as distinct from cabinet concern. The presence of these functions in PCO camouflages this fact and obscures the distinction. Cabinet's primary role in our system of government is the formulation of public policy. In recent years, this role has necessitated the development of a committee system and an accompanying system of secretariats. The Prime Minister, on the other hand, is the political leader of his party as well as the head of the government. His interests and concerns do not always coincide with those of the Cabinet, and in our view they need not. In the complex modern process of decision making, there is room for two independent political and policy orientations, the collective one of the Cabinet and the individual one of the Prime Minister.

We believe that the PM should have his own staff to fulfil missions related to his proper mandate. The PCO and the FPRO should adhere much more to management of the Cabinet and its committees, as does the British Cabinet Office. We rely on a specific episode in which the Prime Minister intervened to break a deadlock in the bureaucracy.

Some years ago, a labour dispute arose in the public service which the TBS negotiators could not settle. Eventually, it developed into a lengthy and tiresome strike without a solution in sight. The main obstacle appeared to be guidelines issued by the Treasury Board and strictly adhered to by its negotiators. In spite of the fact that the guidelines represented official cabinet policy at the time, a special ministerial committee decided to break the deadlock and resolve the dispute on terms clearly violating the guidelines. The President of the Treasury Board and his officials were shocked and dismayed until they learned that the Prime Minister had informally authorized the ministerial committee to settle the dispute and had condoned the violation of the guidelines.

Our point is this. Clearly, Cabinet is not bound by its earlier decisions. If a sufficient number of ministers support the Prime Minister's initiative to end a nation-wide strike at the expense of official guidelines and outside the normal channels of bargaining and negotiation, no one can or should voice an objection. However, the creation of discord and shock among some ministers and officials could have been avoided if the PMO had had an adequate staff monitoring the dispute from the beginning and advising the PM independently about the courses of action he might follow. If a dispute must be settled at the expense of existing guidelines, the responsibility for the decision should not be hidden in a group of anonymous ministers but rather should be openly assumed by the PM and his Cabinet. Only then will Parliament and the public have an opportunity to evaluate and judge such an action, and only then can we be certain that the accountability of officials will not be compromised.

We recommend that the PMO be divided into two divisions (both reporting to the principal secretary): the Political Staff and the Policy Review Staff (PRS). The Political Staff, headed by a deputy principal secretary, would subsume all switchboard functions of the current PMO, including those of the PM's private secretary, executive assistant, appointments secretary, administrative assistant and constituency liaison officer, legislative assistant, and special assistants (including official or unofficial regional desk officers), as well as the nominations, communications, and correspondence divisions. The Policy Review Staff, headed by another deputy secretary, would absorb the policy-advisory work of the current PMO, and all prime-ministerial briefing and special assignments presently carried out by the PCO and the FPRO. Recruitment of its officials would be similar to No. 10 Downing Street and the Cabinet Policy Review Staff in the United Kingdom; the personnel would include political operatives, career civil servants, and individuals from the private sector.[7] These private-sector members would include persons with experience in business, labour, and academe. The deputy secretary, preferably a senior policy advisor with a background in politics, would manage the staff and serve as the Prime Minister's chief policy briefer. Under him, one member of the senior staff would be responsible for monitoring the policy process in each cabinet committee.

Unlike the PCO and the FPRO, the rest of the professional staff would operate according to a modular system; that is, they would work in a pool rather than in separate secretariats. As well as assuring that all cabinet-committee meetings are attended when the responsible senior officials are occupied with other matters, the additional professional officers would monitor the development of particularly important policies. If an issue of particular interest to the staff merited in-depth analysis, the monitoring staff could draw upon the resources of ten or so professional officials in a special-projects section. Headed by a senior-level official, the special-projects section would house highly trained experts representing economics, management, labour, and science and technology, who would work in groups determined by the nature of the problem requiring in-depth analysis.

The organization of the PCO does not, in our view, require any major overhaul. It should remain structured along the lines of the existing cabinet-committee system but be flexible enough to incorporate changes, such as creation of additional cabinet committees or merging of existing ones. In light of our findings about accountability, we are, however, concerned about the isolation of the PCO officials from the parliamentary process, from major interest groups, and from the public. We are fully aware of the difficulties and problems which necessarily would arise from making senior officials directly accountable either to a parliamentary commissioner or to a committee of the House of Commons. We raise the question, nevertheless, whether it is appropriate and consistent with modern liberal democracy that officials attending to the business of Cabinet and its committees are not required or permitted to voice their concerns in public. We are convinced that the need for secrecy and confidentiality in policy making is much exaggerated, and that the cabinet-committee system can only benefit from increased access to its proceedings.

Some of our respondents have questioned whether the FPRO will survive the retirement of Gordon Robertson, its current secretary. Be this as it may, we seriously doubt whether the FPRO organization should remain distinct from the PCO, particularly since the cabinet committee on Federal-Provincial Relations has recently merged with the cabinet committee on Priorities and Planning. We fear also that if FPRO continues its separate existence it will follow the pattern of further growth and specialization. This may lead to an unnecessary proliferation of secretaries and deputy secretaries to the Cabinet (such as we have seen in the FPRO), with new, more specialized, and even esoteric mandates. Clearly, there must be limits to the ability to direct and co-ordinate centrally federal-provincial relations in Canada. We believe that the essence of federal-provincial co-operation in policy making lies in the horizontal and functional links between the various departments and agencies at both levels of government which share policy concerns. The example of Switzerland, with its ethnic and linguistic pluralism and strong regional and cantonal interests, comes to mind. Any attempt to establish in Bern a federal co-ordinating secretariat would be quickly dismissed on the grounds that it would only interfere with the relatively smooth federal-cantonal relations based on horizontal co-operation.

With respect to the Finance department, we heartily endorse the Canadian Tax Foundation recommendation that Finance tax bills be reviewed by a standing committee of the House of Commons.[8] The Canadian Tax Foundation believes that such a reform would benefit the business community because various factions could see the other types of representation in the sector. We maintain that this reform would bring greater public aware-ness of the traditional relationship between Finance and business interests regarding taxation. Knowledge of this relationship might stimulate other groups in society to seek comparable access and influence on the structure of our tax laws.

Finally, we have strong reservations about the business-oriented brand of economics practised in Finance. Only one division, Social Development and Manpower, concerns a branch of economics which is not, de facto, primarily a domain of corporate and industrial interests. We believe that the depart-ment should add a Labour and Consumer Economics division to the Fiscal Policy and Economics Analysis branch. Labour and consumer economics are two important sub-disciplines which could introduce greater balance to Finance's attempts to inte-grate the economy and preserve economic stability.

We now come to the Treasury Board Secretariat. This central agency recently underwent major organizational surgery (described in detail in Chapter 3). These internal reforms arose from the increasing concern about the adequacy of controls over expenditures and the effectiveness of financial administration in operational departments, and, in particular, Crown agencies. The origin of the problem dates to the Glassco Commission hearings and recommendations in the early 1960s. We believe that some very fundamental issues and questions must now be brought to light about the re-organization of financial-administration structure which followed Glassco Commission recommendations. Do the provisions of the Financial Administration Act actually give the proper legal framework for better financial administration and expenditure controls which were sought in 1966? In particular, was the creation of the Treasury Board as a statutory cabinet committee to which Parliament delegated wide authority in this field a wise solution? These questions take on particular relevance, because, after eleven years under the present structure, the government decided to establish the Royal Commission on Financial Management and Accountability, thereby clearly admitting the seriousness of obdurate problems in this field. A more general concern is whether insiders can bring about control of financial appropriations and expenditures, or whether this important role should be assigned to an independent, outside agency unfettered by the clientele mentality towards operational departments and Crown agencies that the TBS has developed over the years.

Under the scheme just put into effect, the Treasury Board has become a two-headed monster. Two senior officials at the highest deputy-minister level will administer two separate organizations both reporting to the president of the Treasury Board. It is difficult to imagine that two organizations can co-exist without skirmishes along their boundaries. Their authority, in spite of apparent distinctions, overlaps primarily because both agencies are concerned with financial administration in the public service.

We believe that the best solution to the problems of expenditure control and accountability is an *independent* Office of the Comptroller General with highly skilled staff reporting to a standing committee of the House of Commons. The precedent for this reform already exists in the relationship between the Auditor General and the Public Accounts Committee of the House of Commons. Surely it is desirable to have both financial officers report directly to Parliament — the Auditor General, whose audit is confined to making sure that government departments use proper accounting procedures and live up to the standard of probity and prudence; and the Comptroller General, who will oversee the spending of money, utilization of person-years, and other allocated resources, and who will publicly disclose departures from the purposes and objectives for which these allocations were originally made, as well as instances of ineffectiveness and inefficiency.

In reality, public accountability is closely related to authority. Central-agency officials cannot be held accountable if the authority they exercise is either unknown or unspecified. We believe that central agencies rely far too heavily on conventional authority, the scope of which is too wide and too general. The origin of this authority is buried in the murky and mystical traditions associated with the royal prerogative. Under the present constitution, this prerogative permits the Prime Minister and the Cabinet to be the absolute masters of their own organization and procedures, without the knowledge and authorization of anyone, including Parliament. It permits also the creation of executive-bureaucratic extensions to the cabinet system outside of parliamentary supervision or sanction. In our view, such unlimited scope of executive authority is undesirable and potentially dangerous. Accordingly, we welcome the "demystifying" provisions relating to federal executive authority proposed in the Constitutional Amendment Bill of 1978, but we stress at the same time that they do not go far enough. The new constitution should clearly provide that all structural and organizational changes in the public service — including the creation of new ministries, departments, agencies, or offices that perform policy analysis, co-ordination, or integration functions for the cabinet system — must be made by statute and must obtain the approval of Parliament. Once all central agencies —

including the PMO and the PCO — are established under statutory authority, they will become openly answerable, but the practical extent and effect of such accountability will depend, as it should, on the inquisitorial capabilities of the opposition parties, the media, and the general public, and on the government's determination to resist.

Given the complexity and the interdependence of governmental institutions today, effective accountability must be not only public but also multifarious. It is possible to identify at least three dimensions of administrative accountability: first, accountability for spending of the appropriated budgets, person-years, and other allocated resources; second, accountability for programs; and third, accountability for the structure and processes of decision making. We recommend that Parliament assume a much more active role with respect to all three aspects of administrative accountability. Accountability for spending is already channelled through the Office of the Auditor General and the Public Accounts Committee of the House of Commons. Additional accountability for spending would result from our proposal that the Comptroller General become an independent officer responsible to Parliament. His role in the evaluation of departmental programs and in the measurement of efficiency and effectiveness (performance) should also be linked directly to a standing committee of the House. Deputy ministers should be held directly accountable to the Comptroller General, and eventually to the committee of the House, for the administration of programs under their jurisdiction. With respect to accountability for the structure and processes of decision making, we propose the establishment of a new parliamentary commissioner with adequate staff and authority to receive from all deputy ministers and senior central-agency officials relevant information about the structure and the on-going processes of decision making at all levels in government except that of the Cabinet. The commissioner and his or her staff would analyse such information and present it annually or semi-annually to a standing committee of the House of Commons. The commissioner would have the authority to delay the presentation of information which, in his or her opinion, might prejudice the decision-making process at any particular time.

In summary, we propose the following reforms:

1. creation of a federal college for political administrators in senior positions in central agencies and program departments;
2. strengthening the PMO's policy-monitoring and advisory role in recognition of the particular needs of the Prime Minister as head of the government and the public service and as leader of the party in power;
3. restructuring the PCO as a strong policy-analysis, integration, and co-ordination secretariat catering to the cabinet system as a whole;
4. amalgamation of the FPRO with the PCO;
5. amendment of the authority of Finance in relation to the management of the national economy, making it clearer and more specific, and adding a role in the labour and consumer-economics fields;
6. confining the role of the TBS to allocation of budgets and person-years, management of the personnel in the public service (including relations with unions and the use of official languages in the public service), and management of valuable physical resources and assets used by the government;
7. transformation of the Office of the Comptroller General into an independent office that reports to a standing committee of the House of Commons and possesses statutory authority over both financial management and the systematic evaluation of programs on the basis of efficiency and effectiveness (performance);
8. adding a new provision in the constitution whereby all structural and organizational changes in the public service (including those in central agencies) must be made by statute and with the approval of Parliament;
9. establishment of a new parliamentary commissioner for accountability of the structures and processes of decision making with authority both to obtain information from depart-

ments and agencies and to present it periodically to the House
of Commons.

We hope that our readers, insiders and outsiders alike, will
give serious thought to our proposals for reform. These proposals
arise directly from our intention to examine and discover the
actual world of central agencies, and from our concern about the
gap between public knowledge and the executive-bureaucratic
reality in Ottawa. At the beginning of the book, we referred to "a
continuous process of transition and institutional innovation" in
Ottawa. We called central agencies "the best and most striking
examples of this on-going departure from the traditional bureaucratic structure" and suggested that central agencies "show most
clearly the trends of future government organization". We
welcome the process of change as a necessary result of both
evolution and creativity. Political orientation and sensitivity to
social values are essential ingredients of the policy-making
process, and those who take part in it — elected politicians and
appointed officials alike — need an organizational setting which
enhances deliberations in the spirit of competitive collegiality.
Return to classical, neutral, detached, and purely instrumental
bureaucracy is neither possible nor desirable. For today and
tomorrow, the key issues focus on the development of new
modes of effective responsibility and accountability, and on the
reshaping of fundamental relationships between policy maker,
Parliament, and public. Much of the constitutional and administrative theory derived from British tradition and still applicable
to the executive and parliamentary processes lacks relevance in
the context of Canadian federalism. We are aware that the task
of replacing it with new norms appears formidable. But we know
also that, if theory and reality are not close to and congruent with
each other, the political system as a whole is in danger of losing
its roots and its credibility. This, we firmly believe, must not
happen in Canada.

Appendix I
Methods: The Interview Data

A methodological note is in order. We will discuss briefly the execution of this research project — that is, how we gained access to respondents, the design of the interview schedule, and how we coded the data.

Access

Nearly everyone with whom we discussed this project in early 1976 said that it would be impossible to gain access to central agents. They said this would be especially so at the higher levels. In fact, all referees for our Canada Council grant proposal had serious reservations about the possibility of access, even though they thought our project would be worthwhile.

We are happy to report that we interviewed 92 of 102 officials, comprising the entire universe of those holding positions at the level of director or above in the five central agencies. An interview lasted for an average of one and one half hours. The 92 officials represent 11 out of the 14 officials whom we wished to interview in the PMO, 15 of 16 in the PCO, 6 of 7 in the FPRO, 22 of 27 in Finance, and 38 of 38 in the TBS. With respect to rank, the figure represents 3 of 5 deputy ministers, 14 of 16 associate and assistant deputy ministers, 21 of 22 assistant secretaries, and 54 of 59 directors. How did we do it? We are not too sure ourselves.

Initially, our contacts with central agents were quite tenuous. Campbell knew one official in the PMO who had previously helped with research; Szablowski had worked as an executive assistant to a cabinet minister in 1970, and knew some officials in the TBS and the PCO. Obviously, we did not obtain access because of our earlier personal contacts.

In November 1975, Campbell approached the PMO official about the possibility of interviewing in central agencies. The official suggested that we draft a proposal with an interview schedule attached. We prepared these materials and sent them off in late January 1976. The PMO official, by then sympathetic to our project, suggested how it might be strengthened, and arranged for us to see a colleague, in another agency, who might be helpful. After meeting with this official, we decided that we were prepared to write letters to the heads of the five central agencies explaining our project and asking for access.

At this point, the project began to founder. Although our letters to the principals had gone out on March 31, we had received no replies by late April. A phone call to our PMO contact informed us that no news was bad news. The principals involved had not agreed to give us formal access and the person responsible for co-ordinating the responses from all five agencies seemed unfavourable to the project. We were told, however, to expect written responses within two weeks.

We received only two letters. We quote one from a central-agency principal:

Thank you for your letter of March 31 and the enclosed material concerning your proposed study of central agencies.

I do not think it would be proper for me to authorize the use in this department of questionnaires along the lines and for the purpose proposed. I am sorry to give this negative reply.

We responded to the two letters by pointing out the rather favourable comments we had received about the project from the Canada Council referees and the fact that senior officials in other countries had already shown considerable willingness to submit to structured and systematic interviews.

By mid-June, we had received neither first responses from three agencies nor second responses from the two we had written to for the second time. We decided to telephone the three principals in the former agencies to ask whether they were planning to respond. One principal had one of his officials return our call almost immediately. This spokesman indicated that his principal was well disposed to the project but did not want to go against other principals. Given this new situation, we tried to reach by phone the superiors of a junior official in one of the agencies who had been cited by several others as opposing the project. Failing to make contact, we independently sent off rather terse telegrams stating that we were not very happy with the treatment we were receiving. (Szablowski sent his in the midst of a sleepless night, only to find, the next day, that Campbell had sent one before going to bed.) The next day, Campbell received a message that the junior official was trying to reach him about a very urgent matter. After an hour-long argument, the official agreed to see Campbell "unofficially" on the next working day, June 14, at the Chateau Laurier in Ottawa. During that meeting, it was agreed that Campbell and Szablowski would simply approach officials without the blessing of the agency's principal. In addition, the official and the colleague who accompanied him came up with some excellent suggestions as to how the interview schedule might be improved so as to evoke better responses from officials about their roles and the operations of their agencies. We communicated the tacit approval of the project from the agency in question to the other principals and interested parties, and all concerned accepted it as a green light.

Was access really as difficult as it seemed to be at the time? If we had not sought formal approval from the principals, would the process have been smoother? Some of the evidence indicates this. For instance, the second letter from the principal quoted above, which was in the mail at the time of our "unofficial" discussions, suggests that a more subtle approach to access than the one we had taken would have smoothed our path:

... While I am an enthusiastic advocate of greater knowledge of the role of central agencies, I can but repeat that as the deputy head [principal] of the ____ , it would not be proper for me to participate in a study such as you have proposed. . . .

Subsequently, after the discussions with his officials and our

written request for an interview with him, the same principal
wrote as follows:

... I know that you have been approaching on an individual basis a
number of senior people in the _____ . I understand many have agreed to
participate in your work. Hopefully this will provide you with a
sufficient data base for your analysis. . . .

If we had read between the lines, we might have interpreted the
official's first response to our request for access as saying, "Go
ahead and do the study, but I cannot use my position to gain
access for you."

Obviously, by asking for the principals' approval we brought
attention at an early stage to a project that might have been
brushed off by less-senior officials. Thus, in the long run, approaching the principals contributed to our high response rate.
However, had we not found out informally that the principals did
not want to give written acquiescence to the project, we might
have given up from sheer frustration and exhaustion.

We wish, then, to leave other researchers with some suggestions which might be helpful in comparable situations. First,
make the rounds in the capital where you intend to do your
research and discuss your project with two or three senior
officials in each of the agencies you plan to study. Second, if the
officials to whom you speak seem reasonably receptive, letters
should be written to the principals of their departments saying
very briefly who you are (attach a *c.v.*), what your project is, and
the fact that you will be in the capital during a specific period of
time and would like to see them or some other official(s) in their
agencies. Separate letters should be written to inform your
contacts of your letter to the principal. Third, the researcher
should go to the capital, get a mailing address and a telephone
number, write letters to each person whom he or she wishes to
see, and, after an appropriate interval, should start making calls.
The researcher should begin with the principals and the officials
contacted earlier. They will probably give him or her appoint-

ments. Most likely, word will spread about the researcher and
the project after these preliminary meetings with officials. The
initial letter to the principal ensures that the topic has come up
in a more formal setting, perhaps the weekly meeting of senior
staff. In such a situation, the researcher's contacts will have had
an opportunity to brief their colleagues in greater detail. If the
project is well worked out and timely, and the officials believe
that he or she is a reputable scholar who will complete the
project successfully, then they probably will agree to make
themselves available.

Interviews and Data Analysis

After resolving our difficulties with access, we found that the
interviews went remarkably smoothly. We employed a set interview schedule with twenty-eight questions, most of which were
open-ended. The questions asked respondents about the roles of
their agencies and their work within them, their views of
accountability, their interactions, their interdepartmental- and
cabinet-committee work, their views of the "inner circle", their
interactions with people outside government and interest groups,
their own careers in government, and their backgrounds before
joining the public service. We devised most of the interview
schedule ourselves, but not without consulting those of Allan
Kornberg and William Mishler,[1] Robert Presthus,[2] and Ezra
Suleiman.[3] Some officials in the PMO, the PCO, and the TBS
offered very helpful advice on how these schedules might be
adapted for use with central agents.

The coding of our central agents' responses proved to be a
formidable task, as, to our knowledge, no one had previously
used many of the open-ended items with senior officials. Thus,
many of the codes were developed especially for our project. We
proceeded as follows: Campbell, who had previous experience
with coding, sampled twenty interview schedules randomly and
used these to develop preliminary codes. Then two research
assistants independently coded each question for all ninety-two
respondents, employing Campbell's preliminary codes and
adding categories when necessary. Campbell reviewed all work
done by the research assistants and made the final decisions

when conflicts in coding arose. After the coding was completed, the data were punched on IBM cards, verified, and transcribed to an SPSS system file.

INTERVIEW SCHEDULE

Interview Number ____

PMO, PCO, FPRO, Treasury Board Secretariat, and Finance Department Study

Interviewer ____
Date ____
Office ____

This questionnaire is part of a research project funded by the Canada Council and York University to study the roles of officials in the PMO, the PCO, the FPRO, the Treasury Board Secretariat, and the Department of Finance. Your co-operation is necessary for its successful completion.

All answers to this questionnaire are absolutely confidential. Any results will be presented in an anonymous or a statistical form. *Please tell me if you prefer not to answer a question and we will go on to the next item.*

I would like to start with some questions about your present work in the PMO (PCO/FPRO/TBS/Finance department):

1) What are your responsibilities here at the PMO (PCO/FPRO/TBS/Finance department)?

2) How does what you do relate to the role of the PMO (PCO/FPRO/TBS/Finance department) as a central agency?

2a) What in your view is the role of the PMO (PCO/FPRO/TBS/Finance department) in government?

2b) Is this role being adequately performed? How so?

2c) How might the performance of your agency be improved? Please elaborate? For example?

3) How do you view accountability in your position? Do you

feel that you are accountable to your superior in this agency, to your minister, to the Cabinet, to Parliament, to the people of Canada, to your conscience, or to some combination of these?

3a) [If R says "some combination", ask him] Specifically, to which of these do you feel accountable?

3b) [For each to which R answers that he is accountable, ask] In what sense are you accountable to _____ ?

3c) [If R listed more than one, ask him] To which of these do you feel most accountable? Why is that?

I have some questions about your usual interactions with others in government in the course of your work here at the PMO (PCO/FPRO/TBS/Finance department):

4) With which of the following do you interact personally about some important matter during an average month?

List A for Question 4

Check off as mentioned		Frequency	Type of Contact	Type of Matter
( )	The Prime Minister	____	____	____
( )	Your own minister	____	____	____
( )	Ministers of other departments	____	____	____
( )	Your own deputy minister/secretary	____	____	____
( )	Deputy ministers/ secretaries of other departments	____	____	____
( )	MPs	____	____	____
( )	Senators	____	____	____

4a) How often in the average month would such interactions take place? [Register above in times/month.] ____

4b) What is the usual form of these contacts; are they by

telephone, personal visits, letters, official meetings, in the hallway or restaurant, or at social occasions?

  i   telephone
  ii personal visits
  iii letters
  iv official meetings
  v   in the hallway or restaurant
  vi social occasions
  vii some combination of the above [ask R to specify which combination]
  viii other [specify]

4c) Is the occasion for such contacts usually about an administrative governmental matter or about governmental policy?

  i   usually an administrative matter
  ii usually a policy matter
  iii both
  iv neither [record]
  v   other [record]

Please elaborate. May I have some examples?

5) Let's turn now to *interdepartmental committees* of officials. Which of these do you regularly attend?

Committee   Kind of Participation
Meetings   Frequency
Attendance

5a) Could you tell me, approximately, how often each of these met in the last year (i.e., since June 1975)?

5b) What per cent of the meetings, approximately, did you actually attend?

5c) How would you characterize your participation in these meetings? Are you simply an observer, do you speak only when called upon for advice, or do you actively involve yourself in the discussion?

  i   simply an observer

     ii speak only when called upon for advice

    iii actively involve self in discussion

    iv some combination of these [specify]

    v other

5d) For each of these committees, could you tell me, approximately, in what per cent of meetings you actively participate in the discussion?

5e) Which of these assignments interests you the most?

5f) Why is this?

6) What about *cabinet committees*? Which of these do you regularly attend?

Committee   Kind of Participation
Meetings   Frequency
Attendance

6a) Could you tell me, approximately, how often each of these met in the last year (i.e., since June 1975)?

6b) What per cent of the meetings, approximately, did you actually attend?

6c) How would you characterize your participation in these meetings? Are you simply an observer, do you speak only when called upon for advice, or do you actively involve yourself in the discussion?

    i simply an observer

    ii speak only when called upon for advice

    iii actively involve self in discussion

    iv some combination of these [specify]

    v other

6d) For each of these committees, could you tell me, approximately, in what per cent of meetings you actively participate in the discussion?

6e) Which of these committees interests you the most?

6f) Why is that?

7) No doubt you have seen the assertion, in popular literature or even in academic works, that an inner circle

of cabinet ministers and/or senior officials decides all the important policy questions here in Ottawa. What do you think about this characterization of the policy process? If there is an inner circle, what seem to be the qualities required for membership?

I would like to ask you about your interactions with people outside government:

8) Which, if any, of the following do you normally consult if you want information about the public's views on an issue? [Hand Respondent list B.]

8a) Which of these do you generally feel give you the most accurate and reliable information? (Circle 1 or 2.)

List B for Question 8	Consults	Most reliable source of information
Editorial opinions and letters to editors	1	2
Political party leaders and workers	1	2
Business leaders	1	2
Union leaders	1	2
Farm-group leaders	1	2
Public officials in local governments	1	2
MLAs and other provincial officials	1	2
Priests, ministers, or other religious-group officials	1	2
Ethnic-group leaders	1	2
Personal friends and acquaintances	1	2
Citizens' groups which cut across economic, religious, and ethnic lines [specify]	1	2
Polls	1	2
Others [list]		

Depends on the issue
  [elaborate]

8b) How about interaction with organized sub-groups and interests?

9) On the basis of your own experience, how significant a role do you feel sub-groups and interests generally play in helping you decide your recommendations on issues?

  i highly significant
  ii moderately significant
  iii insignificant

Please elaborate.

9a) How often do you come into direct personal contact with representatives of organized sub-groups and interests per month?

9b) In your experience, are you contacted more frequently by lobbyists who agree with you on a particular issue or by those who disagree?

  i agree   ii disagree

9c) Who usually initiates contact between yourself and interest-group representatives in each of the following situations?

	You		Lobbyist
Helping to write a brief	i ___	ii	_____
Getting information on a policy proposal	i ___	ii	_____
Getting the attitudes of the public	i ___	ii	_____
Massing support for a bill	i ___	ii	_____

Why is this so?

I would like to end with some questions about your own career and background. First, regarding your career:

10) Public officials in this country and in other Western democracies have given a variety of reasons to explain

why they got into government initially. How about in your case? How did you get into government?

10a) What year did you enter government service?

10b) How long have you been in this agency?

10c) How long have you held your present post?

10d) What is your present public-service category?

11) What has been your career route in government, i.e., what positions have you held at federal level?

Title   Department   Date

11a) Have you held any positions outside of government, either before coming to Ottawa or in between jobs here?

Title   Date   Firm/Organization

12) Looking at your career in government, what are the most important things you have tried to accomplish?

13) Is there a particular area of public affairs in which you feel you have become an expert?

Yes......   No......   N.A......

13a) [If "Yes", record areas.]

13b) If "Yes", how did you acquire your expertise in the(se) area(s)? [Record.]

14) If you left government service, what would you miss about your work?

With respect to your background:

15) What year were you born?

16) What is your home town and province?

17) Could you tell me your father's major occupation?

18) Could you also tell me how much formal education your father received?

   i graduate or professional work
   ii college graduate [degree obtained]
   iii one to three years of college [no degree]

    iv high-school graduate
     v ten or eleven grades of school
    vi seven to nine grades of school
   vii under seven grades of school

19) What was the original ethnic background of your family on your

    19a) father's side?

    19b) mother's side?
    Please don't answer Canadian(ien)!

20) What is your religious preference?

Catholic ....   Protestant ....
Jewish ....   None ....   Other ....

21) Could you tell me how much formal education you received?

     i graduate or professional work
    ii college graduate [degree obtained]
   iii one to three years of college [no degree]
   iv high-school graduate
     v not a high-school graduate

22) What was your major field of study at university?

23) Do you have a graduate/professional degree? If so, in what field?

     i no   v public administration
    ii law   vi business administration
   iii economics   vii engineering
   iv political science   viii other

24) Which graduate or professional degrees have you received?

     i MA   v MD
    ii MSc   vi MBA
   iii PhD   vii other
   iv LLB

25) Where did you attend high school?

26) Where were your degrees taken?
Graduate   Undergraduate

27) Please name any professional and fraternal organizations to which you belong.

28) Could you also name any social clubs to which you belong?

That's all.   Many thanks for your co-operation!

APPENDIX II
STATISTICAL SUMMARY OF DATA BY CENTRAL AGENCY (N=92)

Variable	Percentage Giving Each Response				Test Statistic for PMO/PCO/FPRO vs. Finance vs. TBS (PMO vs. PCO/FPRO in brackets)
	PMO/PCO/FPRO (PMO vs. PCO/FPRO in brackets) n=32 (11 vs. 21)	Finance n=22	TBS n=38	Total n=92	Chi-Square/Significance[1]
I. Perception of Roles (CHAPTER 3)					
1. R's perceptions of his responsibilities					
a. Policy making	65.6(54.5/71.4)	90.9	60.5	69.6	6.43/0.04(0.32/0.57)
b. Improve government	43.8(36.4/47.6)	0.0	31.6	28.3	12.66/0.00(0.05/0.81)
c. Administration and implementation of policy	12.5(0.0/19.0)	36.4	28.9	25.0	4.50/0.11(°)
d. Communication	53.1(81.8/38.1)	13.6	18.4	29.0	13.53/0.00(3.92/0.05)
2. R's style — the way in which he carries out his responsibilities					
a. Facilitator	21.9(18.2/23.8)	18.2	21.1	20.7	0.11/0.94(°)
b. Advisor	56.3(63.6/52.4)	90.9	52.6	63.0	9.73/0.01(0.05/0.81)
c. Administrator	50.0(36.4/57.1)	13.6	26.3	31.5	8.80/0.01(0.55/0.46)
d. Maintains liaison inside government	34.4(36.4/33.3)	0.0	15.8	18.5	10.54/0.01(0.05/0.83)
e. Maintains liaison with those					

3. R's views of the role of his agency					
a. Provide an independent analysis	37.5(27.3/42.9)	31.8	18.4	28.3	3.30/0.19(0.23/0.63)
b. Develop policy	37.5(36.4/38.1)	81.8	34.2	46.3	14.37/0.00(0.08/0.77)
c. Monitor implementation	28.1(9.1/38.1)	31.8	52.6	39.1	5.03/0.08(°)
d. Facilitate government business	31.3(27.3/33.3)	9.1	18.4	20.7	4.10/0.13(0.00/0.96)
e. Switchboard	18.8(45.5/4.8)	4.5	10.5	12.0	2.62/0.30(° °)
f. Forecast trouble areas	12.5(18.2/9.5)	9.1	7.9	9.8	0.43/0.81(° °)
4. Role of R's agency in relation to other departments					
a. Service	31.3(45.5/23.8)	0.0	0.0	10.9	21.04/0.00(0.73/0.39)
b. Administration	18.8(27.3/14.3)	9.1	44.7	27.2	10.71/0.00(°)
c. Policy	65.6(36.4/81.0)	95.5	71.1	75.0	6.72/0.03(4.54/0.03)
5. R describes role of his agency with reference to political leaders/bodies					
a. the PM	53.1(72.7/42.9)	4.5	0.0	19.6	35.30/0.00(1.53/0.22)
b. a minister	9.4(0.0/14.3)	27.3	7.9	13.0	5.20/0.07(°)
c. the Cabinet or a cabinet committee	25.0(9.1/33.3)	9.1	60.5	35.9	18.54/0.00(°)
6. Evaluation of Agency					
a. Changes needed	40.6(45.5/38.1)	68.2	84.2	65.2	14.66/0.00(0.00/0.98)
b. Interaction in agency should be improved	21.9(18.2/23.8)	22.7	28.9	25.0	0.54/0.76(°)
c. Improve organizational structure in agency	15.6(27.3/9.5)	13.6	36.8	23.9	5.98/0.05(°)

APPENDIX II (cont'd.)
STATISTICAL SUMMARY OF DATA BY CENTRAL AGENCY (N=92)

Variable	Percentage Giving Each Response				Test Statistic for PMO/PCO/FPRO vs. Finance vs. TBS (PMO vs. PCO/FPRO in brackets)
	PMO/PCO/FPRO (PMO vs. PCO/FPRO in brackets) n=32 (11 vs. 21)	Finance n=22	TBS n=38	Total n=92	Chi-Square/Significance[1]
d. Improve organizational structure in government	3.1(0.0/4.8)	4.5	28.9	14.1	11.74/0.00(°)
e. Improve personnel	3.1(9.1/0.0)	22.7	10.5	10.9	5.18/0.08(°)
f. Need more staff	21.9(36.4/14.3)	22.7	2.6	14.1	7.06/0.03(°)
g. Need more time to consider issues	0.0(°)	0.0	5.3	2.2	° (°)
II. Socio-economic Backgrounds (CHAPTER 4)					
1. Raised in					
a. the West	21.8(27.3/19.0)	40.9	10.5	21.8	7.56/0.02(°)
b. Ontario	37.5(18.2/47.6)	18.2	50.0	38.0	5.99/0.05(1.56/0.21)
c. Quebec	25.0(27.3/23.8)	0.0	15.8	15.2	6.33/0.04(0.05/0.83)
d. Atlantic provinces	6.3(18.2/0.0)	4.5	2.6	4.3	° (°)
e. outside Canada	9.4(9.1/9.5)	36.4	21.1	20.7	5.80/0.06(°)

f. Toronto	9.4(0.0/14.3)	18.2	18.4	15.2	1.30/0.52( )
g. Montreal	18.8(27.3/14.3)	0.0	7.9	9.8	5.45/0.07( )
2. Ethnic Origin					
a. Father					
i) British Isles	65.6(63.6/66.7)	59.1	68.4	65.2	0.54/0.76(0.05/0.83)
ii) French	25.0(36.4/19.0)	0.0	26.3	19.6	7.05/0.03(°)
iii) Other	15.6(0.0/23.8)	40.9	10.5	19.6	8.66/0.01(°)
b. Mother					
i) British Isles	62.5(54.5/66.7)	59.1	63.2	62.0	0.10/0.95(0.08/0.77)
ii) French	28.1(45.5/19.0)	0.0	31.6	22.8	8.67/0.01(°)
iii) Other	18.8(0.0/28.6)	40.9	7.9	19.6	9.67/0.01(°)
3. Religion					
a. R.C.	46.8(63.6/38.1)	18.2	42.2	38.1	5.01/0.08(1.00/0.32)
b. Protestant	37.5(36.4/38.1)	40.9	36.9	38.0	0.10/0.95(0.08/0.77)
c. Jewish	6.3(0.0/9.5)	22.7	2.6	8.7	7.46/0.02(°)
d. None	9.4(0.0/14.3)	18.2	18.3	15.2	1.30/0.52( )
4. Father's Education					
a. No high school	18.7(18.2/19.0)	40.9	31.6	29.3	3.24/0.20(°)
b. Some high school	43.8(36.4/47.7)	27.3	28.9	33.7	2.24/0.33(0.05/0.81)
c. Some college	37.5(45.4/33.3)	31.8	39.5	37.0	0.36/0.84(0.08/0.77)
5. Father's Occupation					
a. Professional/technical	28.1(18.2/33.3)	31.8	31.6	30.4	0.12/0.94(°)
b. Managers/proprietors	37.5(54.5/28.6)	31.8	36.8	35.9	0.21/0.90(1.12/0.29)
c. Other	34.4(27.3/38.1)	36.4	31.6	33.7	0.15/0.93(0.05/0.83)
6. R's Education					
a. in elite English university	31.3(9.1/42.9)	36.4	39.5	35.9	0.51/0.77(2.42/0.12)

APPENDIX II (cont'd.)
STATISTICAL SUMMARY OF DATA BY CENTRAL AGENCY (N=92)

Variable	Percentage Giving Each Response				Test Statistic for PMO/PCO/FPRO vs. Finance vs. TBS (PMO vs. PCO/FPRO in brackets)
	PMO/PCO/FPRO (PMO vs. PCO/FPRO in brackets) n=32 (11 vs. 21)	Finance n=22	TBS n=38	Total n=92	Chi-Square/Significance[1]
b. in elite French university	15.6(18.2/14.3)	9.1	7.9	10.9	1.17/0.56(°)
c. arts undergrad.	71.9(72.7/71.4)	77.3	52.6	65.2	4.69/0.10(0.11/0.74)
d. science undergrad.	12.5(0.0/19.0)	4.5	13.2	10.9	1.20/0.55(°)
e. business undergrad.	9.4(9.1/9.5)	27.3	15.8	16.3	3.07/0.22(°)
f. economics major	21.9(9.1/28.6)	54.5	15.8	27.2	11.27/0.00(°)
g. pol. sci. major	9.4(9.1/9.5)	4.5	21.1	13.0	3.93/0.14(°)
h. grad. degree from elite English school	21.9(18.2/23.8)	27.3	15.8	20.17	1.66/0.56(°)
i. grad. degree from foreign school	40.6(36.4/42.9)	50.0	18.4	33.17	7.27/0.03(0.00/0.98)
i) U.S.	28.1(18.2/33.3)	22.7	5.3	17.4	6.89/0.03(°)
ii) other	12.5(18.2/9.5)	36.4	13.2	18.5	6.15/0.05(°)
j. grad. degree — arts	25.0(9.1/33.3)	54.5	34.2	35.9	5.02/0.08(°)
i) economics	15.6(9.1/19.0)	50.0	26.3	28.3	7.72/0.02(°)

k. grad. degree — science	3.1(0.0/4.8)	0.0	7.9	4.3	° ( )
l. grad. degree — administration	12.5(27.3/4.8)	9.1	7.9	9.8	0.43/0.81(°)
m. law degree	25.0(27.3/23.8)	13.6	5.3	14.1	5.58/0.06(°)
n. PhD	15.6(9.1/19.0)	18.2	15.8	16.3	0.08/0.96(°)
o. graduate or professional degree	71.9(72.7/71.4)	72.7	65.8	69.6	0.44/0.80(0.11/0.74)
7. Memberships					
a. Social club(s)	37.5(45.5/33.3)	50.0	39.5	41.3	0.93/0.63(0.08/0.77)
b. Professional associations					
i) none	53.1(72.7/42.9)	36.4	39.5	43.5	1.91/0.38(1.53/0.22)
ii) one	34.4(9.1/47.6)	31.8	26.3	30.4	0.56/0.76(3.20/0.07)
iii) two plus	12.5(18.2/9.5)	31.8	34.2	26.1	4.74/0.09(0.02/0.89)
III. Career Routes (CHAPTER 5)					
1. Time when R decided upon career:					
a. immediately after completion of university or earlier	18.8(9.1/23.8)	36.4	28.9	27.2	2.15/0.34(°)
b. mid-career	71.9(90.9/61.9)	63.6	68.4	68.5	0.14/0.81(1.74/0.19)
2. Motivating factors in career choice					
a. idealism	15.6(9.1/19.0)	27.3	18.4	19.6	1.17/0.55(°)
b. studies	9.4(9.1/9.5)	13.6	13.2	12.0	0.31/0.85(°)
c. the challenge	15.6(18.2/14.3)	22.7	39.5	27.2	5.28/0.07(°)
d. career experiences before entering	6.3(9.1/4.8)	13.6	10.5	9.5	0.85/0.65(°)

APPENDIX II (cont'd.)
STATISTICAL SUMMARY OF DATA BY CENTRAL AGENCY (N=92)

Variable	Percentage Giving Each Response				Test Statistic for PMO/PCO/FPRO vs. Finance vs. TBS(PMO vs. PCO/FPRO in brackets)
	PMO/PCO/FPRO (PMO vs. PCO/FPRO in brackets) n=32(11 vs. 21)	Finance n=22	TBS n=38	Total n=92	Chi-Square/Significance[1]
e. a policy interest	15.6(0.0/23.8)	13.6	18.4	16.3	0.25/0.88(*)
f. the opportunity for advancement	59.4(81.8/47.6)	63.6	57.9	59.8	0.19/0.91(2.23/0.14)
3. Sector before coming to government					
a. media	9.4(27.3/0.0)	9.1	7.9	8.7	0.05/0.97(*)
b. law	9.4(9.1/9.5)	4.5	7.9	7.6	0.44/0.80(*)
c. corporate	12.5(18.2/9.5)	13.6	18.4	15.2	0.52/0.77(*)
d. Crown corporation	9.4(0.0/14.3)	9.1	13.2	10.9	0.35/0.84(*)
e. university	21.9(18.2/23.8)	27.3	21.1	22.8	0.33/0.85(*)
f. high school	9.4(9.1/9.5)	0.0	2.6	4.3	3.21/0.20(*)
g. provincial government	6.3(0.0/9.5)	13.6	7.9	8.7	0.94/0.62(*)
4. Where did he work while outside of government?					
a. Ontario	21.9(27.3/19.0)	27.3	13.2	19.2	1.93/0.38(*)

5. Age and tenure of career (means)

a. age	42.5^m(38.6/44.4)^m	47.4^m	44.7^m	44.6^m	3.08/0.05(4.65/0.04)+
b. years in government	9.8^m(5.8/11.9)^m	13.8^m	10.8^m	11.2^m	2.01/0.14(6.33/0.02)+
c. years in department	3.0^m(3.9/2.6)^m	8.8^m	4.2^m	4.9^m	15.88/0.00(2.25/0.14)+
d. years in current post	1.8^m(3.0/1.2)^m	2.9^m	2.1^m	2.2^m	1.32/0.27(5.61/0.02)+
e. proportion of time in government served in current department	0.42^m(0.67/0.29)^m	0.76^m	0.51^m	0.54^m	5.31/0.01(8.05/0.01)+
6. Departments/Agencies in which some time was spent					
a. National Defence	12.5(0.0/19.0)	0.0	5.3	6.5	3.51/0.17(°)
b. Industry, Trade, and Commerce	9.4(0.0/14.3)	9.1	13.2	10.9	0.35/0.84(°)
c. Treasury Board Secretariat	12.5(9.1/14.3)	4.5	10.5	9.8	0.98/0.61(°)
d. at least one central agency	28.1(9.1/38.1)	13.6	23.7	22.8	1.58/0.45(°)
e. most recent department was a central agency	9.4(0.0/14.3)	4.5	7.6	7.6	0.44/0.80(°)
7. R's area of expertise					
a. Economics	9.4(9.1/9.5)	36.4	13.2	17.4	7.42/0.02(°)
b. Economics and related fields	21.9(9.1/28.6)	77.3	28.9	38.0	19.25/0.00(°)
c. External Affairs and Defence	9.4(0.0/14.3)	22.7	2.6	9.8	6.38/0.04(°)
d. Management	34.4(36.4/33.3)	0.0	34.2	26.1	10.21/0.01(0.05/0.83)
8. R uses his expertise	62.5(45.5/71.4)	72.7	60.5	64.1	0.95/0.62(1.12/0.29)
9. Source of R's expertise					
a. academe	25.0(27.3/23.8)	36.4	18.4	25.0	2.39/0.30(°)
b. experience in business	9.4(9.1/9.5)	4.5	23.7	14.1	5.12/0.08(°)
c. experience in government	40.6(18.2/52.4)	45.5	31.6	38.0	1.28/0.53(2.23/0.14)

APPENDIX II (cont'd.)
STATISTICAL SUMMARY OF DATA BY CENTRAL AGENCY (N=92)

Variable	Percentage Giving Each Response				Test Statistic for PMO/PCO/FPRO vs. Finance vs. TBS (PMO vs. PCO/FPRO in brackets)
	PMO/PCO/FPRO (PMO vs. PCO/FPRO in brackets) n=32 (11 vs. 21)	Finance n=22	TBS n=38	Total n=92	Chi-Square/Significance[1]
10. R has attempted to accomplish during his career in government					
a. add human dimension	28.1(54.5/14.3)	4.5	13.2	16.3	5.78/0.06(3.97/0.05)
b. planning	18.8(27.3/14.3)	36.4	34.2	29.3	2.69/0.26(0.17/0.68)
c. influence a field of policy	15.6(0.0/23.8)	63.6	28.9	32.3	14.07/0.00(°)
d. help develop personnel	18.8(18.2/19.0)	9.1	18.4	16.3	1.10/0.58(°)
e. give good advice	15.6(9.1/19.0)	4.5	7.9	9.8	2.07/0.35(°)
f. a general policy goal	15.6(9.1/19.0)	4.5	13.2	12.0	1.61/0.45(°)
g. have an impact, generally	3.1(9.1/0.0)	13.6	18.4	12.0	3.94/0.14(°)
h. achieve personal development	31.1(27.3/33.3)	13.6	15.8	20.7	3.40/0.18(0.00/0.96)
i. facilitate in the process	9.4(0.0/14.3)	18.4	2.6	8.7	4.27/0.12(°)
11. If R left government, he would miss					
a. opportunity for impact on policy	31.3(18.2/38.1)	40.9	39.5	37.0	0.70/0.71(0.57/0.45)

b. the atmosphere	59.9(81.8/47.6)	68.2	60.5	62.0	0.49/0.78(2.23/0.14)
c. variety	18.8(9.1/23.8)	13.6	15.8	16.3	0.26/0.88(o)
d. opportunity for management	3.1(0.0/4.8)	9.1	0.0	3.3	(o)
e. facilities and colleagues	18.8(27.3/14.3)	36.4	26.3	26.1	2.10/0.35(o)
f. serve government	9.4(18.2/4.8)	0.0	10.5	7.6	(o)
g. serve public	12.5(9.1/14.3)	9.1	7.9	9.8	0.43/0.81(o)
h. lifestyle	0.0(o o)	9.1	7.9	5.4	(o)
i. opportunity (general)	0.0(o)	0.0	5.3	2.2	(o)

IV. Interactions and Committee Work
(CHAPTER 6)

1. Interactions

a. with PM — Yes	81.3(100.0/71.4)	13.6	18.4	39.1	36.68/0.00(2.20/0.14)
1/month	71.9(100.0/57.4)	18.2	13.2	34.8	29.91/0.00(4.61/0.03)
2/month	53.1(90.9/33.3)	9.1	5.3	22.8	25.69/0.00(7.44/0.01)
phone	18.8(45.5/4.8)	4.5	0.0	7.6	9.07/0.01(o)
visits	53.1(72.7/42.9)	9.1	2.6	21.7	28.75/000(1.52/0.22)
memos	50.0(81.8/33.3)	0.0	2.6	18.5	32.43/0.00(4.99/0.03)
meetings	56.3(45.5/61.9)	13.6	18.4	30.4	15.60/0.00(0.27/0.61)
policy	71.9(81.8/66.7)	18.2	18.4	37.0	25.68/0.00(0.24/0.62)
b. with own minister — Yes	NA	95.5	71.1	80.0	3.77/0.05
1/month	NA	86.4	55.3	66.7	4.75/0.03
2/month	NA	72.7	47.4	56.7	2.69/0.10
phone	NA	13.6	23.7	20.0	0.36/0.55
visits	NA	68.2	50.0	56.7	1.21/0.27
memos	NA	31.8	15.8	21.7	1.27/0.26

APPENDIX II (cont'd.)
STATISTICAL SUMMARY OF DATA BY CENTRAL AGENCY (N=92)

Variable	Percentage Giving Each Response				Test Statistic for PMO/PCO/FPRO vs. Finance vs. TBS (PMO vs. PCO/FPRO in brackets)
	PMO/PCO/FPRO (PMO vs. PCO/FPRO in brackets) n=32 (11 vs. 21)	Finance n=22	TBS n=38	Total n=92	Chi-Square/Significance[1]
meetings	NA	63.8	52.6	56.7	0.31/0.58 NA
policy	NA	86.4	60.5	70.0	3.28/0.07 NA
c. with other ministers — Yes	84.4(90.9/81.0)	77.3	60.5	72.8	5.28/0.07(0.05/0.82)
1/month	84.4(100.0/76.2)	72.7	50.0	67.4	9.72/0.01(1.56/0.21)
2/month	81.3(63.6/85.7)	50.0	39.5	56.5	12.84/0.00(0.97/0.32)
phone	43.8(72.7/28.6)	9.1	7.9	20.7	15.99/0.00(4.07/0.04)
visits	43.8(45.5/42.9)	13.6	10.5	22.8	12.27/0.00(0.05/0.81)
memos	25.0(36.4/19.0)	4.5	5.3	12.0	7.94/0.02( )
meetings	71.9(54.5/81.0)	68.2	55.3	64.1	2.29/0.32(1.36/0.24)
policy	68.8(72.7/66.7)	72.7	55.3	64.1	2.30/0.32(0.00/0.96)
d. own deputy minister — Yes	90.6(81.8/95.2)	86.4	86.8	88.0	0.31/0.85(0.36/0.55)
1/month	90.6(81.8/95.2)	86.4	55.3	75.0	13.58/0.00(0.36/0.55)
2/month	84.4(72.7/90.5)	81.8	44.7	67.4	15.16/0.00(0.64/0.42)
phone	59.4(45.5/66.7)	45.5	26.3	42.4	7.89/0.02(0.61/0.43)

visits	75.0(72.7/76.2)	68.2	63.2	68.5	1.13/0.57(1.05/0.83)
memos	59.4(36.4/71.4)	22.7	15.8	32.6	16.31/0.00(2.37/0.12)
meetings	84.4(72.7/90.5)	77.3	60.5	72.8	5.28/0.07(0.64/0.42)
policy	81.3(63.6/90.5)	81.8	71.1	77.2	1.38/0.50(1.88/0.17)
e. other DMs — Yes	90.6(72.7/100.0)	77.3	84.2	84.8	1.82/0.40(3.52/0.06)
1/month	87.5(72.7/95.2)	68.2	78.9	79.3	2.98/0.23(1.60/0.21)
2/month	78.1(63.6/85.7)	50.0	63.2	65.2	4.67/0.10(0.97/0.32)
phone	65.6(45.5/76.2)	27.3	47.4	48.9	7.74/0.02(1.81/0.18)
visits	43.8(36.4/47.6)	31.8	44.7	41.3	1.08/0.58(0.05/0.81)
memos	40.6(27.3/47.6)	22.7	13.2	25.0	7.07/0.03(0.54/0.46)
meetings	71.9(54.5/81.0)	72.7	57.9	66.3	2.05/0.36(1.36/0.24)
policy	81.3(63.6/90.5)	72.7	71.1	75.0	1.04/0.59(1.88/0.17)
f. MPs — Yes	65.6(100.0/47.6)	54.5	63.2	62.0	0.72/0.70(6.61/0.01)
1/month	56.3(100.0/33.3)	36.4	39.5	44.6	2.77/0.25(10.47/0.00)
2/month	43.8(100.0/14.3)	31.8	28.9	34.8	1.79/0.41(18.21/0.00)
phone	31.3(72.7/9.5)	27.3	36.8	32.6	0.62/0.73(10.64/0.00)
visits	31.3(72.7/9.5)	9.1	5.3	15.2	9.93/0.01(10.64/0.00)
memos	9.4(18.2/4.8)	13.6	15.8	13.0	0.64/0.73(° °)
meetings	12.5(18.2/9.5)	31.8	28.9	23.9	3.58/0.17(° °)
policy	46.9(63.6/38.1)	45.5	42.1	44.6	0.17/0.91(1.00/0.32)
g. Senators — Yes	46.9(90.9/23.8)	31.8	13.2	29.3	9.61/0.01(10.50/0.00)
1/month	43.8(90.9/19.0)	22.7	7.9	23.9	12.30/0.00(12.37/0.00)
2/month	37.5(81.8/14.3)	9.1	2.6	16.3	16.58/0.00(11.31/0.00)
phone	31.3(72.7/9.5)	13.6	7.9	17.4	6.88/0.03(10.64/0.00)
visits	21.9(54.5/4.8)	9.1	2.6	10.9	6.73/0.03(° °)
memos	12.5(18.2/9.5)	13.6	2.6	8.7	3.02/0.22(° °)
meetings	9.4(18.2/4.8)	31.8	5.3	13.0	9.24/0.01(° °)
policy	31.3(63.6/14.3)	31.8	5.3	20.7	9.36/0.01(6.05/0.01)

APPENDIX II (cont'd.)
STATISTICAL SUMMARY OF DATA BY CENTRAL AGENCY (N=92)

Variable	Percentage Giving Each Response				Test Statistic for PMO/PCO/FPRO vs. Finance vs. TBS (PMO vs. PCO/FPRO in brackets)
	PMO/PCO/FPRO (PMO vs. PCO/FPRO in brackets) n=32 (11 vs. 21)	Finance n=22	TBS n=38	Total n=92	Chi-Square/Significance[1]
2. Interdepartmental committees					
attends at least 1	62.5(54.5/66.7)	86.4	76.3	73.7	4.04/0.13(0.08/0.77)
attends 3 or more	18.8(0.0/28.6)	45.5	34.3	31.5	4.52/0.10(°)
chairman of at least 1	9.4(9.1/9.5)	9.1	18.4	13.0	1.65/0.44(° °)
delegates	21.9(9.1/28.6)	45.5	18.4	26.0	5.73/0.06(° °)
participates fully	46.9(54.5/42.6)	59.1	57.9	54.0	1.11/0.57(0.07/0.80)
economic	28.1(27.3/28.6)	54.5	7.9	26.1	15.83/0.00(°)
technology, etc.	12.5(0.0/19.0)	27.3	18.4	18.5	1.89/0.39(°)
benefits/rights	15.6(0.0/23.8)	22.7	15.8	17.4	0.57/0.75(°)
external/defence	12.5(9.1/14.3)	27.3	7.9	14.1	4.42/0.11(°)
machinery/admin./personnel	31.3(27.3/33.3)	40.9	55.3	33.5	4.15/0.13(0.00/0.96)
umbrella	31.3(45.5/23.8)	18.2	18.4	22.8	1.98/0.37(0.73/0.39)
Attends to					
get information	9.4(9.1/9.5)	13.2	31.6	19.6	6.09/0.05(°)
lend expertise	9.4(0.0/14.3)	9.1	13.2	10.9	0.35/0.84(°)

influence policy	12.5(18.2/9.5)	31.8	10.5	16.3	5.15/0.08( )
implement policy	12.5(0.0/19.0)	4.5	21.1	14.1	3.24/0.20( )

3. **Cabinet committees**

Attends

at least 1 committee	68.8(36.4/85.7)	72.7	73.7	71.7	0.22/0.89(6.04/0.01)
at least 2 committees	21.9(18.2/23.8)	27.3	23.7	23.9	0.21/0.90( )
a committee 1/month	53.1(27.2/66.7)	50.0	44.7	48.9	0.50/0.78(3.06/0.08)
a committee 2/month	46.9(18.2/61.2)	27.0	36.8	38.0	2.16/0.34(3.92/0.05)
an operations com. 1/month	18.8(0.0/28.6)	31.8	13.2	19.6	3.10/0.21( )
an operations com. 2/month	18.8(0.0/28.6)	18.2	7.9	14.1	2.08/0.35( )
a co-ord. com. 1/month	34.4(27.3/38.1)	22.7	36.8	32.6	1.33/0.51(0.05/0.83)
a co-ord. com. 2/month	25.0(18.2/28.6)	9.1	28.9	22.8	3.25/0.20( )
P&P 1 every 2 months	25.0(27.3/23.8)	13.6	2.6	13.0	7.67/0.02( )
TB 1 every 2 months	0.0( )	13.6	36.8	18.5	16.10/0.00( )
as advisor only	40.6(18.2/52.4)	13.6	31.6	30.4	4.53/0.10(2.23/0.14)
as discussant as well	12.5(9.1/14.3)	54.5	34.2	31.5	10.89/0.00( )

Attends to

get information	12.5(18.2/9.5)	13.6	13.2	13.0	0.02/0.99( )
lend expertise	21.9(9.1/28.6)	45.5	15.8	25.0	6.80/0.03( )
influence policy	3.1(0.0/4.8)	22.7	10.5	10.9	5.18/0.08( )
implement decisions	12.5(0.0/19.0)	4.5	2.6	6.5	2.96/0.23( )
learn the ropes	21.9(27.3/19.0)	27.3	34.2	28.3	1.32/0.52( )

4. **Inner Circle**

There is an inner circle	46.9(54.5/42.0)	54.3	65.8	56.3	2.57/0.28(0.07/0.80)
based on issues	34.4(36.4/33.3)	27.3	23.7	28.3	0.99/0.61(0.05/0.83)

APPENDIX II (cont'd.)
STATISTICAL SUMMARY OF DATA BY CENTRAL AGENCY (N=92)

Variable	Percentage Giving Each Response				Test Statistic for PMO/PCO/FPRO vs. Finance vs. TBS (PMO vs. PCO/FPRO in brackets)
	PMO/PCO/FPRO (PMO vs. PCO/FPRO in brackets) n=32 (11 vs. 21)	Finance n=22	TBS n=38	Total n=92	Chi-Square/Significance[1]
mentioned					
PM	28.1(54.5/14.3)	18.2	13.2	19.6	2.51/0.29(°)
the Cabinet	18.8(9.1/23.8)	18.2	15.2	17.4	0.12/0.94(°)
PCO	6.3(9.1/4.8)	13.6	13.2	10.9	1.08/0.58(°)
Finance	12.5(9.1/14.3)	13.6	10.5	12.0	0.14/0.93(°)
specific ministers	46.9(72.7/33.3)	27.3	26.3	33.7	3.82/0.15(3.06/0.08)
R's DM	12.5(9.1/14.3)	13.6	26.3	18.5	2.65/0.27(°)
central agents generally	68.8(63.6/71.4)	59.1	63.2	64.1	0.56/0.76(0.00/0.96)
central agents generally and/or mentioned specific agencies	78.1(81.8/76.2)	77.3	86.8	81.5	1.22/0.54(0.01/0.93)

V. Accountability and Interactions
with Outsiders (CHAPTER 7)

A. Accountability

his/her minister	NA	72.7	28.9	29.0	9.09/0.00	NA
the Cabinet	28.1(0.0/42.9)	13.6	42.1	30.4	5.46/0.07	( )
the PM	81.3(100.0/71.4)	13.6	2.6	32.6	53.60/0.00	(2.22/0.14)
Parliament	0.0( )	18.2	13.2	9.8	5.72/0.06	( )
the people	15.6(9.1/19.0)	45.5	44.7	34.8	7.94/0.02	( )
conscience	12.5(9.1/14.3)	4.5	10.5	9.8	0.98/0.61	( )
2. View of accountability						
staff	53.1(72.1/42.9)	59.1	50.0	53.3	0.46/0.79	(1.53/0.22)
line	46.9(18.2/61.9)	40.9	42.1	43.5	0.24/0.89	(3.92/0.05)
to the public	9.4(0.0/14.3)	40.9	28.9	25.0	7.45/0.02	( )
personal loyalty	25.0(45.5/14.3)	4.5	0.0	9.8	13.2/0.00	( )
3. Most accountable to						
superior	31.3(0.0/47.6)	59.1	31.6	38.0	5.44/0.07	(5.56/0.02)
Cabinet	6.3(0.0/9.5)	4.5	18.4	10.9	3.85/0.15	( )
the PM	53.1(100.0/28.6)	4.5	2.6	20.7	31.60/0.00	(12.06/0.001)
people	3.1(0.0/4.8)	4.5	23.7	12.0	8.48/0.01	( )
minister	NA	18.2	5.3	10.0	1.35/0.25	NA
B. Interactions with Outsiders						
1. Consults						
media	59.4(63.6/57.1)	63.6	44.7	54.5	2.51/0.29	(0.00/0.98)
political leaders/party workers	40.6(90.9/14.3)	18.2	15.8	25.0	6.43/0.04	(14.54/0.00)
business leaders	34.4(63.6/19.0)	77.3	44.7	48.9	10.05/0.01	(4.54/0.03)
union leaders	18.8(36.4/9.5)	27.3	23.7	22.8	0.56/0.75	( )

APPENDIX II (cont'd.)
STATISTICAL SUMMARY OF DATA BY CENTRAL AGENCY (N=92)

Variable	Percentage Giving Each Response				Test Statistic for PMO/PCO/FPRO vs. Finance vs. TBS (PMO vs. PCO/FPRO in brackets)
	PMO/PCO/FPRO (PMO vs. PCO/FPRO in brackets) n=32 (11 vs. 21)	Finance n=22	TBS n=38	Total n=92	Chi-Square/Significance[1]
farm leaders	15.6(27.3/9.5)	31.8	7.9	16.3	5.86/0.05(°)
local govt. officials	28.1(45.5/19.0)	4.5	15.8	17.4	5.16/0.08(1.36/0.24)
provincial govt. officials	31.3(54.5/19.0)	68.2	44.7	45.7	7.19/0.03(2.74/0.10)
religious leaders	12.5(18.2/9.5)	18.2	0.0	8.7	6.70/0.04(°)
ethnic leaders	21.9(36.4/14.3)	4.5	2.6	9.8	8.19/0.02(°)
friends	46.9(63.6/38.1)	27.3	47.4	42.4	2.71/0.26(1.00/0.32)
citizen groups	21.9(36.4/14.3)	36.4	5.3	18.5	9.32/0.01(°)
polls	34.4(63.6/19.0)	13.6	15.8	21.7	4.64/0.10(4.54/0.03)
academics	12.5(9.1/14.3)	31.8	7.9	15.2	6.46/0.04(°)
consulting firms/research institutes/professional associations	3.1(0.0/4.8)	13.6	23.7	14.1	6.06/0.05( )
2. Finds Reliable media	12.5(18.2/9.5)	9.1	13.2	12.0	0.23/0.89(°)

political leaders/party workers	18.8(54.5/0.0)	0.0	0.0	6.5	12.03/0.00(°
business leaders	12.5(18.2/9.5)	31.8	10.5	16.3	5.15/0.08(°
local govt. officials	3.1(0.0/4.8)	0.0	2.6	2.2	0.66/0.72(°
prov. govt. officials	12.5(18.2/9.5)	22.7	15.8	16.3	1.01/0.60(°
friends	18.8(27.3/14.3)	4.5	5.3	9.8	4.48/0.11(°

3. Interest Groups

play a significant role	34.4(54.5/23.8)	68.2	42.1	45.7	6.33/0.04(1.81/0.18)
in touch frequently	31.3(63.6/14.3)	45.5	26.3	32.6	2.36/0.31(6.05/0.01)
share information	34.4(45.5/28.6)	54.5	42.1	42.4	2.17/0.34(0.32/0.57)
attempt to influence policy	40.6(63.6/28.6)	59.1	39.5	44.6	2.48/0.29(2.37/0.12)
contact is proper	34.4(54.5/23.8)	50.0	39.5	40.2	1.34/0.51(1.81/0.18)
proper, but seldom	12.5(18.2/9.5)	27.3	7.9	14.1	4.42/0.11(°
improper	12.5(9.1/14.3)	0.0	10.5	8.7	2.84/0.24(°
mentioned business groups	25.0(45.5/14.3)	40.9	23.7	28.3	2.30/0.32(2.26/0.13)
business influential	12.5^{m}(27.3/4.8)	27.3	13.2	16.3	2.55/0.28(°

[1] Chi-square serves as the basis of our test to see if the responses of officials in various central agencies differ significantly. The significance values are rounded to two decimal points. A significance value of 0.01 or less indicates very strong differences; a value of 0.05 or less suggests at least strong differences.

° The number of officials expected to have a particular response is so small that use of Chi-square might be misleading (i.e., if fewer than ten respondents in the contingency table gave the response in question even "corrected" Chi-squares have been omitted from this summary).

[+] In the case of interval variables, we employed F as the test statistic. See Hubert M. Blalock on analysis of variance in *Social Statistics* (New York: McGraw-Hill, 1972), pp. 318–29.

m mean

NA Not Applicable

Notes

Chapter 1

1. See, in particular, Bruce L. R. Smith, ed., *The New Political Economy: The Public Use of the Private Sector* (London: Macmillan, 1977), pp. 1–45; and also Thomas A. Hockin, *Government in Canada* (Toronto: McGraw-Hill Ryerson, 1976), pp. 64–97.
2. Alan A. Altshuler, "The Study of American Public Administration", in *The Politics of the Federal Bureaucracy*, Alan A. Altshuler, ed. (New York: Dodd, Mead, 1968), p. 56.
3. Ibid., p. 57.
4. Martin Landau, "The Concept of Decision-Making in the Field of Public Administration", in *Concepts and Issues in Administrative Behavior*, Sidney Mailick and Edward H. Van Ness, eds. (Englewood Cliffs, N.J.: Prentice-Hall, 1962), p. 10.
5. Matthew Holden, " 'Imperialism' in Bureaucracy", *American Political Science Review*, Vol. 60 (December 1966), p. 944.
6. Herbert Kaufman, "Administrative Decentralization and Political Power", *Public Administration Review*, Vol. 29 (January–February 1969), pp. 4–5.
7. Douglas G. Hartle, *The Objective of Government Objectives* (Ottawa: Treasury Board Secretariat, 1972), pp. 2–18.
8. Hugh Heclo and Aaron Wildavsky, *The Private Government of Public Money: Community and Policy Inside British Politics* (Berkeley: University of California Press, 1974), p. 3.
9. Richard Rose, *Managing Presidential Objectives* (New York: Free Press, 1976), p. 29.
10. A. W. Johnson, "The Treasury Board of Canada and the Machinery of Government of the 1970's", *Canadian Journal of Political Science*, Vol. 4 (September 1971), pp. 346–66.
11. Rose, *Managing Presidential Objectives*, pp. 47–54.
12. Heclo and Wildavsky, *Private Government of Public Money*, pp. 267, 274, 307.
13. Reante Mayntz and Fritz Sharpf, *Policy-Making in the German Federal Bureaucracy* (Amsterdam: Elsevier, 1975), pp. 3–6.
14. Mattei Dogan, "The Political Power of the Western Mandarins: Introduction", in *The Mandarins of Western Europe: The Political Role of Top Civil Servants* (New York: Wiley, 1975), p. 5.
15. William W. Kaufman, *The McNamara Strategy* (New York: Harper and Row, 1964); George J. Szablowski, "The Optimal Policy-Making System: Implications for the Canadian Political Process", in *Apex of Power*, 2nd ed., Thomas A. Hockin, ed. (Toronto: Prentice-Hall, 1977), pp. 197–211.
16. Aaron Wildavsky, *The Politics of the Budgetary Process*, 2nd ed. (Boston: Little, Brown, 1974).
17. Heclo and Wildavsky, *Private Government of Public Money*, pp. 368–88.
18. Charles J. Connaghan, *Partnership or Marriage of Convenience?* (Ottawa: Department of Labour, 1976), pp. 79–85.
19. Dogan, *Mandarins of Western Europe*, p. 19.
20. Ezra N. Suleiman, *Politics, Power, and Bureaucracy in France: The Administrative Elite* (Princeton, N.J.: Princeton University Press, 1974), p. 203.
21. Ibid., p. 146.

22. G. Bruce Doern and Peter Aucoin, eds., *The Structures of Policy-Making in Canada* (Toronto: Macmillan, 1971), and in particular G. Bruce Doern, "Recent Changes in the Philosophy of Policy-Making in Canada", *Canadian Journal of Political Science*, Vol. 4 (1971), pp. 243–64.

23. Aspects of these reforms were initially examined by G. J. Szablowski in "The Optimal Policy-Making System: Implications for the Canadian Political Process". See also his "The Prime Minister as Symbol", *Canadian Journal of Political Science*, Vol. 4 (1973), p. 517.

24. Alan C. Cairns, "The Governments and Societies of Canadian Federalism", an address delivered at the annual meeting of the Canadian Political Science Association, Fredericton, N.B., 1977 (mimeo.), p. 1.

25. For the origin of this conceptual framework see George J. Szablowski, "Decisional Technology and Political Process in Canada" (PhD thesis, McGill University, Montreal, 1978).

Chapter 2

1. For example, see Victor A. Thompson, *Organizations as Systems* (Morristown, N.J.: General Learning Press, 1973).

2. F. G. Bailey, *Stratagems and Spoils* (Oxford: Basil Blackwell, 1970), p. xii.

3. Letters Patent constituting the office of the Governor General, 1947. The Prime Minister, Mr. St. Laurent, described the effect of this delegation as follows: "... when the letters patent come into force, it will be legally possible for the Governor General, on the advice of the Canadian ministers, to exercise any of these powers and authorities of the Crown in respect of Canada, without the necessity of a submission being made to His Majesty....", *House of Commons Debates*, 1948, p. 1126.

4. *Treasury Board*, mimeo. (Ottawa: Treasury Board Secretariat, November 1975), p. 5.

5. For a good discussion of the royal prerogative, see S. A. de Smith, *Constitutional and Administrative Law* (Harmondsworth, Middlesex: Penguin Books, 1971), pp. 114–29.

6. *Organization of the Government of Canada* (Ottawa: Ministry of Supply and Services, 1976), p. 6001.

7. Sir W. I. Jennings, *The Law and the Constitution*, 3rd ed. (London: Cambridge University Press, 1943), p. 88.

8. An Act respecting the office of the Secretary to the Cabinet for Federal-Provincial Relations and respecting the Clerk of the Privy Council, 23 Elizabeth II, chapter 16. See also J. R. Mallory, "The Two Clerks: Parliamentary Discussion of the Role of the Privy Council Office", *Canadian Journal of Political Science*, Vol. 10 (March 1977), pp. 3–19.

9. Dr. A. A. Sterns, *History of the Department of Finance*, unpublished monograph (Ottawa: Department of Finance, May 1965), p. 4.

10. *Treasury Board Organization Manual*, mimeo. (Ottawa: Treasury Board, January 1967), p. 1.

11. Thomas d'Aquino, "The Prime Minister's Office: Catalyst or Cabal?" *Canadian Public Administration*, Vol. 17 (Spring 1974), p. 57.

12. Order-in-Council PC 1975–250.

13. Donald Gow, *The Progress of the Budgetary Process in the Government of Canada*, Special Study No. 17 (Ottawa: Economic Council of Canada, 1973).

14. S. A. de Smith, *Constitutional and Administrative Law* (Harmondsworth, Middlesex: Penguin Books, 1971), pp. 54–55.
15. Revised Statutes of Canada (RSC), 1970, chapter F–10.
16. Michael Pitfield, "The Shape of Government in the 1980s: Techniques and Instruments for Policy Formulation at the Federal Level", *Canadian Public Administration*, Vol. 19 (Spring 1976), p. 14.
17. RSC, 1970, chapter F–10.
18. This examination is partially based on information contained in a loose-leaf internal manual entitled *Functions and Responsibilities of the Treasury Board Secretariat* (Ottawa: Treasury Board, 1974, as amended).
19. Gordon F. Osbaldeston, "Implementation of Performance Measurement in the Federal Public Service: A Progress Report", *Optimum*, Vol. 7, no. iv (1976), p. 6.
20. Douglas G. Hartle, "Techniques and Processes of Administration", *Canadian Public Administration*, Vol. 19 (Spring 1976), p. 21.
21. A. W. Johnson, "The Treasury Board and the Machinery of Government", p. 346.
22. J. E. Hodgetts, *Canadian Public Service: A Physiology of Government, 1867–1970* (Toronto: University of Toronto Press, 1973), pp. 284–85.
23. Pitfield, "The Shape of Government", p. 15.
24. Lord Atkin in *Attorney General of Canada* v. *Attorney General of Ontario* (1937), Appeal Cases 327.

Chapter 3

1. See, for instance, several chapters in *Apex of Power: The Prime Minister and Political Leadership in Canada*, Thomas A. Hockin,

ed. (Toronto: Prentice-Hall, 1971).

Chapter 4

1. John Porter, *The Vertical Mosaic: An Analysis of Social Class and Power in Canada* (Toronto: University of Toronto Press, 1965); Robert Presthus, *Elite Accommodation in Canadian Politics* (Toronto: Macmillan, 1973); Wallace Clement, *The Canadian Corporate Elite: An Analysis of Economic Power* (Toronto: McClelland and Stewart, 1975).
2. Clement, *The Canadian Corporate Elite*, pp. 221, 259–65.
3. This general phenomenon is discussed briefly in Richard J. Van Loon and Michael S. Whittington, *The Canadian Political System: Environment, Structure and Process* (Toronto: McGraw-Hill Ryerson, 1976), pp. 326–29.
4. Porter, *The Vertical Mosaic*, pp. 433–44.
5. Robert Putnam, "The Political Attitudes of Senior Civil Servants in Western Europe: A Preliminary Report", *British Journal of Political Science*, Vol. 3 (July 1973), pp. 268–69.
6. Suleiman, *Politics, Power, and Bureaucracy*, pp. 64, 68.
7. Ibid., p. 44.
8. Ibid., p. 106.
9. David T. Stanley, Dean E. Mann, and Jameson W. Doig, *Men Who Govern* (Washington: Brookings Institution, 1967), pp. 78–84.
10. Joel D. Aberbach and Bert A. Rockman, "The Overlapping Worlds of American Federal Executives and Congressmen", *British Journal of Political Science*, Vol. 7 (January 1977), pp. 26–28.
11. Ibid., p. 31.
12. Ibid., p. 30.
13. P. J. Chartrand and K. L. Pond, *A Study of Executive Career Paths in the Public Service of Canada*

(Chicago: Public Personnel Association, 1970), pp. 32, 34.

14. This myth, which has considerable currency, is even supported somewhat by Porter. See his section titled "Dr. Clarke's Boys", in *The Vertical Mosaic*, pp. 425–28.

15. Robert Presthus and William Monopoli, "Bureaucracy in the United States and Canada: Social, Attitudinal, and Behavioural Variables", in *Cross-National Perspectives: United States and Canada*, Robert Presthus, ed. (Leiden: Brill, 1977), pp. 177–79.

16. Putnam, "Political Attitudes", p. 269.

17. Colin Campbell, *The Canadian Senate: A Lobby From Within* (Toronto: Macmillan, 1978), p. 52.

18. Ibid.

19. Aberbach and Rockman, "Overlapping Worlds", pp. 26–27; Presthus and Monopoli, "Bureaucracy in the United States and Canada", pp. 177–78.

20. Porter, *The Vertical Mosaic*, pp. 168–72.

Chapter 5

1. Max Weber, "Politics as a Vocation", in *From Max Weber: Essays in Sociology*, H. H. Gerth and C. Wright Mills, trans. (New York: Oxford University Press, 1958), pp. 90–91.

2. Putnam, "Political Attitudes", pp. 268, 279.

3. Suleiman, *Politics, Power, and Bureaucracy*, p. 117.

4. Ibid., p. 122.

5. Ibid., p. 143.

6. Ibid., p. 140.

7. Porter, *The Vertical Mosaic*, pp. 436–37.

8. Chartrand and Pond, *Executive Career Paths*, pp. 48–49.

9. Ibid., p. 70.

10. Weber, *From Max Weber*, pp. 87–88.

11. Ibid., p. 91.

12. Robert D. Putnam, "Elite Transformation in Advanced Industrial Societies: An Assessment of the Theory of Technocracy", *Comparative Political Studies*, Vol. 10 (October 1977), pp. 385, 390–92.

13. Ibid., pp. 385–86. Putnam cites F. F. Ridley, "French Technocracy and Comparative Government", *Political Studies*, Vol. 14 (February 1966), p. 43; S. Berger, "The French Political System", in *Patterns of Government: The Major Political Systems of Europe*, S. H. Beer *et al.*, eds. (New York: Random House, 1973), p. 426; J. Meynard, *Technocracy*, P. Barnes, trans. (New York: Free Press, 1969), p. 219; and J. D. Straussman, "Technocratic Counsel and Societal Guidance", in *Politics and the Future of Industrial Society* (New York: McKay, 1976), pp. 153–54, as the sources behind his hypothesis.

14. Putnam, "Elite Transformation", pp. 392–97.

15. P. M. Pitfield, "Business Administration and Public Administration", unpublished paper, The James Gillies Alumni Lecture Series (York University, Toronto, November 23, 1977), p. 12. Pitfield cites A. Paul Pross and J. Seymour Wilson, "Graduate Education in Canadian Public Administration: Antecedents, Present Trends and Portents", *Canadian Public Administration*, Vol. 19 (1976), pp. 515–41. A U.S. view of the same phenomenon is Michael Wilson, "What's Wrong With Political Science?", *The Washington Monthly* (September 1977), pp. 13–20.

16. Porter, *The Vertical Mosaic*, p. 437.

17. Campbell, *The Canadian Senate*, pp. 133–39.

18. Chartrand and Pond, *Executive Career Paths*, p. 24.

19. Putnam, "Political Attitudes",
    p. 266.
20. Matt. 17: 1–9.
21. For instance, Gordon Robertson
    argued in 1971 that no one should
    be able to make a career of a stint
    in the PCO. See "The Changing
    Role of the Privy Council Office",
    in *Politics: Canada*, Paul W. Fox,
    ed. (Toronto: McGraw-Hill,
    1977), p. 384. Many respondents
    in TBS's Program branch told us
    that a two-year term was thought
    to be the maximum that an indi-
    vidual should be expected to en-
    dure.

Chapter 6

1. Douglas G. Hartle, "Techniques
   and Processes of Administration",
   Canadian Public Administration,
   Vol. 19 (Spring 1976), p. 21.
2. Gordon Robertson, "The Changing Role of the Privy Council", p.
   381.
3. Presthus, *Elite Accommodation*.
4. Robert J. Jackson and Michael M.
   Atkinson, *The Canadian Legislative System* (Toronto: Macmillan,
   1974), pp. 19–21.
5. Campbell, *The Canadian Senate*,
   pp. 10–19.

Chapter 7

1. Pitfield, "The Shape of Government", p. 19.
2. Gordon Osbaldeston, *Notes for a
   speech by the Secretary of the
   Treasury Board to International
   Personnel Management Association, Ottawa, November 19,
   1976*, mimeo. (Ottawa: Treasury
   Board, 1976), p. 11.
3. Royal Commission on Financial
   Management and Accountability,
   press release (Ottawa: June 8,
   1977).
4. Allen T. Lambert, *Notes for remarks by Allen T. Lambert to the
   Financial Management Institute,
   Ottawa, September 20, 1977*
   mimeo. (Ottawa: 1977).
5. See, for example, Kenneth Kernaghan, "Responsible Public Bureaucracy: a Rationale and a
   Framework for Analysis", *Canadian Public Administration*, Vol.
   16 (Winter 1973), p. 572.
6. Thompson, *Organizations as Systems*.
7. Kernaghan, "Responsible Public
   Bureaucracy", pp. 598–99.
8. Suleiman, *Politics, Power, and
   Bureaucracy*, p. 13 and Chapter 8.
9. Ibid., pp. 222, 226, 231.
10. Ibid., p. 233.
11. Richard Rose, "The Variability of
    Party Government: A Theoretical
    and Empirical Critique", *Political
    Studies*, Vol. 17 (December
    1969), pp. 413–45.
12. Michael Gordon, "Civil Servants,
    Politicians, and Parties: Short-
    comings in the British Policy Pro-
    cess", *Comparative Politics*, Vol.
    4 (October 1971), pp. 29–58.
13. Putnam, "Political Attitudes",
    pp. 257–58.
14. Ibid., p. 277.
15. Aberbach and Rockman, "Over-
    lapping Worlds", pp. 23–47.
16. Ibid., p. 34.
17. Presthus, *Elite Accommodation*,
    pp. 60–63.
18. Presthus and Monopoli, "Bureau-
    cracy in the United States and
    Canada", pp. 184–87.
19. Lee Sigelman and William G.
    Vanderbok, "Legislators, Bureau-
    crats, and Canadian Democracy:
    The Long and the Short of It",
    *Canadian Journal of Political
    Science*, Vol. 10 (September
    1977), pp. 619–21.
20. George B. H. Cruickshank *et al.*,
    "The Tax Legislative Process", a
    report to the Hon. Jean Chrétien,
    Minister of Finance, from a com-
    mittee of the Canadian Tax Foun-
    dation, November 1977, pp. 2–4.
    The authors cite the *Report of*

the *Royal Commission on Taxation,* Vol. 5 (Ottawa: Queen's Printer, 1966), pp. 6–7; John Stewart, "The Tax Reform Bill in Parliament", *Canadian Tax Journal,* Vol. 19 (January–February 1971), p. 1; and M. A. Cohen, "Formulation, Enactment and Administration of Tax Changes", *Report of the Twenty-Fourth Tax Conference,* 1972, Canadian Tax Foundation, pp. 4–13, to support their characterization of the Finance department's role in the tax-policy process.

21. Putnam, "Political Attitudes", p. 277.

22. Suleiman, *Politics, Power, and Bureaucracy,* pp. 324, 327.

23. Ibid., p. 335.

24. Cruickshank, "The Tax Legislative Process", pp. 2–4.

25. Presthus, *Elite Accommodation,* pp. 211, 218.

26. *Report of the Royal Commission on Government Organization,* abridged ed., Vol. 1 (Ottawa: Queen's Printer, 1962), p. 33.

27. Ibid., pp. 51–52.

Chapter 8

1. Heclo and Wildavsky, *Private Government of Public Money,* p. 3.

2. Pitfield, "Business Administration and Public Administration", pp. 12, 13, 16.

3. Ibid., p. 18.

4. Hugh Heclo, *A Government of Strangers: Executive Politics in Washington* (Washington, D.C.: Brookings Institution, 1977), pp. 247–49.

5. A recent treatment of the role of No. 10 (the PMO) in the United Kingdom is G. W. Jones, "The Prime Minister's Men", *New Society,* Vol. 19 (January 1978), pp. 121–23.

6. Walter Stewart, *Shrug: Trudeau in Power* (Toronto: New Press, 1971).

7. Heclo and Wildavsky, *Private Government of Public Money,* p. 307.

8. Cruickshank, "The Tax Legislative Process".

Appendix I

1. Allan Kornberg and William Mishler, *Influence in Parliament: Canada* (Durham, N. C.: Duke University Press, 1976), pp. 342–64.

2. Robert Presthus, *Elites in the Policy Process* (Toronto: Cambridge University Press, 1974), pp. 481–511.

3. Suleiman, *Politics, Power, and Bureaucracy,* pp. 391–415.

Index

687262